JACOB
AND
JOSEPH

RITCHIE
CHARACTER
STUDY
SERIES

JACOB

J. HAY

JOSEPH

M. CAIN

JOHN RITCHIE LTD
CHRISTIAN PUBLICATIONS

40 Beansburn, Kilmarnock, Scotland

ISBN-13: 978 1 912522 82 8

Copyright © 2021 by John Ritchie Ltd.
40 Beansburn, Kilmarnock, Scotland

www.ritchiechristianmedia.co.uk

Typeset by John Ritchie Ltd., Kilmarnock
Printed by Bell & Bain Ltd., Glasgow.

Contents

JACOB

In these Character Studies, unless otherwise indicated, verses referred to are taken from the Book of Genesis.

CHAPTER 1

Background

O the depth of the riches both of the wisdom and knowledge of God! How unsearchable are his judgments, and his ways past finding out! For who hath known the mind of the Lord? Or who hath been his counsellor? Or who hath first given to him, and it shall be recompensed unto him again? For of him, and through him, and to him, are all things: to whom be glory for ever. Amen (Romans 11:33-36)

Jacob and the Plan of God

Jacob – patriarch, pilgrim, parent, Prince, and prophet: his life and history have been the theme of many sermons and books, his failures paraded before us as warnings of the "Jacob" in all of us. As we read his life we are reminded of the great principle of "sowing and reaping," the inviolable law of God. Thankfully, there is the occasional message we are privileged to hear which shows the development in the character of a child of God through patient moulding by God, and his eventual triumphant end. As we listen with amazement to God declaring Himself "The mighty God of Jacob" (Ps 132;5), we bow in wonder and worship before a God of such amazing grace.

The normal approach to the book of Genesis is either to consider the "*toldah*" (Strong 8435) structure, dividing the book by the expression, "the generations," or to consider it from the standpoint of the four great events (the formation of the earth, the fall, the flood, and the folly at Babel) and the four great men (Abraham, Isaac, Jacob, and Joseph). This latter approach assigns chapters 12 to 25 to the history of Abraham, chapters 21-27 to Isaac, chapters 25-36 to Jacob, and the remaining 14 chapters to the life of Joseph.

By this calculation, most view the story of Joseph as the dominant feature of Genesis. In reality, however, the life of Joseph is really intertwined with that of Jacob. We are not done with the history of Jacob until we arrive at chapter 50, the conclusion of the book. In many ways, Jacob is really the patriarch who receives the most attention from the Spirit of God and whose life is described in greater detail than those of the others. Abraham and his call are prominent; Isaac suffers the fate of having a famous father and son, thus receiving less attention from readers. But the story of Jacob attracts us all. We identify with this patriarch more than with Abraham, Isaac, or Joseph. Abraham, the great man of faith, awes us; Isaac on the altar humbles us as we consider our own resistance at times to God; Joseph seems light years removed by the beauty of his character. But Jacob and his life resonate with each of us. The biographies of the great men of Scripture have not, however, been provided either to intimidate us or to urge us to imitation. We are given these lives as instruction and inspiration. So there is something to be gained spiritually from a consideration of each of their experiences. It is, however, to Jacob that we turn in these pages.

Following the display of man's blindness displayed at the Tower of Babel, God, in infinite grace and wisdom, called out from the masses of men, a man, Abraham, through whom He would create a people whose purpose was to reveal Himself to the nations. But Abraham gave rise to other nations, some inveterately opposed to the purposes and people of God. The chosen line was to come through Isaac; but he also bore a son, Esau, who would oppose the chosen line. It was, however, through Jacob that the nation would develop. His twelve sons become the foundation for the nation of Israel. Thus, Jacob marks the goal toward which God has been advancing in Genesis. His twelve sons are the matrix from which a nation with eternal purposes would come. His blessing on Judah in Genesis 49 will further define the line of the coming Messiah.

The Jacob-Joseph history, therefore, brings into the foreground the very significant story of the prophetic Messianic line. The son who will become the chosen line through whom the Messiah will come is Judah. He moves from a self-serving callous man in Genesis 37, selling his brother, through the depths of moral failure as seen in chapter 38, and finally arriving at heights of sacrificial greatness in his moving speech in Genesis 44. All this occurs against the background of the story of Jacob and Joseph. This is capped by the prophetic pronouncement by Jacob that Judah would hold the sceptre (49:10). Jacob is the instrument of God for furthering His plan for the ages - the ultimate enthronement of His Son!

Jacob as a Preview of the Nation

Jacob's life also serves as a preview of the events which will befall the nation bearing his name.

Jacob and not Abraham was actually the founder of the nation. It was from his loins that the twelve sons and the twelve subsequent tribes sprang.

Jacob knew years of exile, away from the land. Abraham journeyed to the land; Isaac dwelled all his days in the land. In that exile Jacob knew years of toil and sorrow in Laban's home; his days ended, seventeen years of days, in Egypt. And yet his heart was always in the land. On his deathbed he gave instructions that Egypt was not to be his final resting place. "Bury me with my fathers ... in the cave that is in Machpelah ... in the land of Canaan" (49:29, 30). He longed to return to the land promised by God, prefiguring the centuries' long wish of the Jewish people.

Jacob was purified in the school of God by discipline and trial. Similarly, Israel will come under (and in many ways is under) the discipline of God. Jacob emerged as a man able to bless a Gentile king, Pharaoh, and a man able to bring blessing, through his son Joseph, to the nations. In this manner, the promise made to Abraham that in him all the nations would be blessed was fulfilled. Likewise, a restored Israel will bring blessing to the globe when it is linked with the antitype of Joseph, her Messiah.

Jacob as Picture of the Believer

One of the many reasons that Jacob appeals so much to believers is that we can identify with this man of flesh and blood. There are events in his life where he sinks to morally low levels of behaviour, only to soar to great heights of spiritual experiences. He prays and yet he schemes; he deceives and is deceived. We see his love for Rachel and trace something of the many sorrows he endured in his life. "Few and evil" (47:9) were his days, filled likely with regrets and some of the "if onlys" which mark the pathway of most believers.

We can identify with his ways, marked by failure and triumph. We can identify with his sorrows and grief. He knew the long years of heavy-hearted sorrow for a son presumed dead. He buried his "favourite" wife, a grief he recounted at the end of life. He knew what it was to be taken advantage of by a shrewd employer; to be manipulated and abused. He endured disappointment in his sons and strife in the family circle. He experienced virtually everything which it is possible for us to know.

In him, we see faith growing and moral stature increasing; we trace the hand of God and marvel at the ways and wisdom of God in his dealings with him. As we follow his life we learn how God deals with a believer, developing in him the fruit which brings delight to His heart. "The hound of heaven" relentlessly pursues him, transforming him from Jacob to Israel, a Prince with God.

Jacob and the Preparation of God

As we survey the life of Jacob in the chapters which lie before us, we will be privileged to watch God at work. How does God "make a man?" How does God take a Jacob and make him into Israel, a prince with God? Watch His methods; watch His ways!

With consummate skill linked with compassion, God moulded the man about whom Laban had to confess, that the Lord had blessed him since he had set foot in his home. Here is the pilgrim who, on being ushered into the court of the greatest king of his day, Pharaoh, is able to bless him! Here is a man at whom the world will wonder and from whom the world will receive blessing. The fullness of that blessing is still future and will one day fill a world with blessing and bounty.

Jacob and the Principles Unfolded

Central to our consideration will not only be a biographical history, but a culling of the many spiritual lessons which are apparent in Jacob's life. A few of these include:

- The principle of sowing and reaping
- The unconditional love of God
- The providential dealings of God
- The danger of self-designed stratagems
- The fruit of half-way obedience
- The prophetic nature of his death-bed utterances.

There are salient and vital lessons to be learned by all of us: parents, husbands, leaders, shepherds, servants, sorrowers, and saints. Few of the biographies penned by the Spirit of God afford such a wide-ranging ministry for our edification. It is my prayer that these lessons will be learned by the writer and faithfully conveyed to you, the reader.

When God Wants a Man

When God wants to drill a man and thrill a man and skill a man ...
When God wants to mold a man to play the noblest part;
When He yearns with all His heart to create so great and bold a man that all the world shall praise ...
Watch His methods;
Watch His ways!

How He ruthlessly perfects whom He royally elects ...
How He hammers him and hurts him,
And with mighty blows converts him
Into frail shapes of clay that only God understands.
How his tortured heart is crying and he lifts beseeching hands ...
How he bends but never breaks when His good he undertakes.
How He uses whom He chooses ... with every purpose fuses him;
By every art induces him to try His splendour out -
God knows what He's about!

When God wants to take a man and shake a man and wake a man ...
When God wants to make a man to do the future's will;
He tries with all His skill ...
When He yearns with all His soul to create him large and whole ...
With what cunning He prepares him ...
How He goads and never spares him! How He whets him and He
frets him and in poverty begets him ...
How often He disappoints whom He sacredly anoints!

When God wants to name a man and fame a man and tame a man ...
When God wants to shame a man to do His Heavenly best;
When He tries the highest test that His reckoning may bring ...
While He fires him and inspires him ...
Keeps him yearning, ever burning for that tantalizing goal.
Lures and lacerates his soul ...
Sets a challenge for his spirit;
Draws it highest then he's near it!
Makes a jungle that he clear it;
Makes a desert that he fear it ... and subdue it, if he can -
So doth God make a man!

                                                      (Anonymous)

CHAPTER 2

His Birth

What a piece of work is man, How noble in reason, how infinite in faculty, In form and moving how express and admirable, In action how like an Angel, In apprehension how like a god, The beauty of the world, The paragon of animals (Wm. Shakespeare)

His Parents

The story of Isaac and Rebekah is one of the best known in the Bible. The desire of the Master, the diligent servant, the direction of God, and the decision in the home, all capture the imagination of young and old alike. Here is a "heaven-made" marriage.

Isaac, we are told, "took Rebekah, and she became his wife; and he loved her: and Isaac was comforted after his mother's death" (24:67). Companionship, love, comfort – here are all the ingredients for a wonderful relationship. Here is a couple who seem to have been directed and blessed of God.

Isaac was last seen on the altar, submissive to the will of God. His history, while not as dramatic as that of his father Abraham, has shown all the hallmarks of a man called and blessed of God. But he has known sorrow as well, having buried his mother in Machpelah when he was 37 years old. Loneliness must have been very real until Rebekah came to him three years later.

Rebekah, in turn, was in a distant land living with her parents and her resourceful brother Laban. Was she an idol worshiper? Did she know anything through Terah's branch of the family of the true God? She was living in Mesopotamia, hundreds of miles removed from Abraham and his family. Yet God had a divine plan and purpose for this young woman. The direction of God brought Rebekah to Isaac, and at 40 years of age, Isaac took Rebekah to be his wife (25:20).

While courtships and marriages in the western world are not managed in quite the same manner as in Genesis 24, the underlying principles of the chapter still serve the purpose of teaching young believers important lessons. These lessons include the qualities to be sought in a spouse, the ability of God to direct, the limitation on choices, and the commitment so vital for a Christian marriage.

The Paradox

Isaac and Rebekah were God's vessels through whom His purpose for the nation, the earth, and His Son would be accomplished. Yet 20 years pass and Rebekah is without a son. Here is the only couple on earth to whom fertility has been assured; yet here is a couple struggling with infertility for all those years. Rebekah was barren! In her culture, barrenness would be viewed as a sign of divine disapproval. Reproach for barrenness is seen in several places in Scripture including Hannah and Elizabeth. To have obeyed God and left her father's house (Genesis 24), and now to be barren, would be both a reproach and a perplexity to Rebekah's mind. We think that obedience should immediately lead to blessing; such is often not the case.

Add to this the fact that Ishmael's line appears to have no problem with births and growth (25:12-17). Brother Ishmael without the covenant blessings and promises from God is prospering; Isaac with the divine promise is without a son.

God's timing is often a paradox to us. In many ways, Scripture is the story of the remarkable timing of God. He is never too early or too late. His actions literally define "timeliness." Joseph was left to languish two full years of days until the night of Pharaoh's double dream. Moses must know 40 years tending sheep, learning the desert landmarks and life-style, before God appears to him in the burning bush. David knew weary days and lonely nights waiting for God to fulfill His purpose and bring him to the throne.

The discipline of delay in the school of God is one of the most difficult courses through which we must matriculate. By its very nature, there are no shortcuts. Online courses are not available. Absences from class are forbidden. Attendance is mandatory. An elite few emerge with highest honours; most of us struggle through the course, passing by Job's "skin of my teeth" (Job 19:20).

Delay is difficult on the flesh; it is meant to be. We make our plans, plot out our schedules, and then expect God to work according to our timeline. We assist God by arranging all the times, places, dates, and events. If God would kindly oblige our schedules and plans, it will help the universe to run smoothly! Our folly is palpable and our carnality obvious.

In the delay which this couple knew, faith and confidence in God's word were being tested. To their mutual credit, they waited upon God and did not resort to any other expediency.

His Prayer

Isaac wisely did what should mark each of us when faced with a seeming paradox in the ways of God. He prayed. We are told that Isaac "intreated the LORD for his wife, because she was barren" (25:21). In this action, Isaac reveals sympathy and care for his wife. There is no blame-game, there is no complaint. He prays for his wife. We are not told the words he used; we are not privy to the arguments or promises he set before the Lord. It is enough to know that in his perplexity he prayed.

Unlike his father Abraham, Isaac did not resort to a concubine. He took the spiritual "high road" and set the matter before God in prayer. Unlike his son Jacob, he did not explode at his wife over her barrenness (30:1-2).

Prayer is vital amidst any trial; James reminds us to ask of God (James 1). We come to a God who gives wisdom liberally. As we confront the seeming inconsistencies of life and the events which defy our own wisdom, our only recourse is to God. Hannah knew this in her experience; Asaph was schooled in this as well (Ps 73).

Jewish tradition says that Isaac and Rebekah travelled to Mount Moriah to entreat the Lord. But the location is not as important as the fact that Isaac prayed. As will be seen, his prayer life set an example for his wife who, when confronted with a perplexing situation, resorted to prayer as well.

Isaac was marked by persistence in prayer. While not stated directly, there was a 20 year period of barrenness and Isaac may well have continued in prayer for his wife during all those years. "Men ought always to pray, and not to faint" (Luke 18:1) was certainly an axiom by which Isaac lived.

Their Progeny

We read that "the LORD was intreated of him (Isaac), and Rebekah ... conceived." Answered prayer is always a time of special encouragement and joy. No doubt the house was filled with thanksgiving and praise to the covenant-keeping God. But the answer to one perplexity only provides another. Within the womb of Rebekah a fierce struggle is ensuing. Wilson's *Old Testament Word Studies* suggests that the word for struggle is to "dash one another, to break." Perhaps Rebekah was concerned with her own life or the viability of the children in her womb. Was Esau seeking to slay Jacob in the womb? Was this another attempt of Satan to destroy the seed royal?

The struggle in the womb is often used as an analogy of the struggle which occurs in a newborn believer as he is confronted with the spiritual warfare of his flesh against his spiritual desires. The elder – our flesh – must be placed in subjection, mortified, put to death, so that the spiritual may prosper.

The problem drove Rebekah to prayer. A problem leads to a prophecy. The Lord revealed to her several things in His response:

- That the children will be born, for she is assured that the elder will serve the younger
- That two nations were in her womb

- That the twins would be as non-identical as possible – two manner of people will be separated from the womb
- That the elder would serve the younger.

Her problem and prayer led to a revelation from the Lord. It is encouraging for us to realize that the Lord allows "problems" in our lives with a view to revealing Himself in some new facet so that we might know Him better and trust Him more consistently.

When the time of birth came, she delivered the twin boys. Their names were linked with their appearance or actions. Esau came out red all over and was given the name, Esau. His colour and covering afforded him this name.

Jacob came out second, the younger of the twins. His hand took hold of Esau's heel (Hosea 12:3) and thus gained for him the name, Jacob – to take by the heel. The name in itself is neutral. It can mean someone who attains things by his efforts, or it can mean a supplanter. Jacob took a name which had a neutral connotation and gave it a bad one by his actions. The struggle in the womb and the grasping of the heel all pointed forward to a life of conflict and struggle. It will take many years, but God will take the man who took hold of his brother's heel in the womb and transform him into the man who had power over the angel (Hosea 12:4).

CHAPTER 3

The Birthright and the Blessing

Two roads
Two roads diverged in a yellow wood,
And sorry I could not travel both
And be one traveller, long I stood
And looked down one as far as I could
To where it bent in the undergrowth;

Then took the other, as just as fair,
And having perhaps the better claim,
Because it was grassy and wanted wear;
Though as for that the passing there
Had worn them really about the same.

I took the one less travelled by,
And that has made all the difference
(Robert Frost)

The Birthright (Ch 25)

The Differences in Twins

As the boys grow, character becomes evident. Esau is a cunning hunter. He is a man marked by skill and self reliance. We learn of his skill as a hunter; there is possibly something sinister in the use of "hunter" (cf. Nimrod, 10:9), and there is the sphere of his interest – the field, and not the tent. Jacob is described as a plain man, living in tents. Some have deduced from this that Jacob was somewhat of a weakling, or even an effeminate, soft type of person. Nothing could be further from the text. A brief reading further on in the book will show how that even in advanced years, Jacob could wrestle with an angel through the entire night. His physical prowess is shown in several places in his history.

The expression, "the boys grew" (25:27), is similar to the expression found elsewhere ("the child grew") of six individuals (Isaac, Moses, Samuel, Samson, John Baptist, and the Lord Jesus). It is difficult to know whether to make much of the lack of any additional description such as we have with Samuel ("Before the LORD") and with John ("in spirit").

The thought of dwelling in tents conveys a truth which is far from what some might imagine. Note that Hebrews 11:9 refers to Abraham dwelling in tents with Isaac and Jacob. Jacob preferred the company of Abraham in the tent. It was here that he heard of the ways and dealings of God and, perhaps, first began to wish that the birthright could be his. Esau apparently did not feel that he missed much by being in the field away from the tent.

A careful comparison of the years of Abraham, Isaac, and Jacob will support the fact that Abraham was 160 when Jacob was born (he was 100 when Isaac was born and Isaac was 60 when the twins were born). Since Abraham died at 175, he lived concurrently with Jacob for 15 years.

Allow one final word about the expression, "a plain man" (25:27). It really carries with it the thought of perfect or upright. It refers to Jacob morally. It is the same word used when God speaks of His servant Job (Job 1:8). We may wonder at its usage, especially in light of what we learn of Jacob later, but it is the word employed by the Spirit of God here. Nine times it is translated as "perfect," and on two occasions it is translated "undefiled."

The twins could not have been more different: appearance, aptitude, and aspirations set them apart for life and also for eternity. Contrasts, which began in the womb, became more apparent as time went on, and, like two diverging roads, they moved even farther apart throughout life.

The Divided Family

Isaac's love for Esau was based upon fleshly motives. Rebekah is mentioned as favouring Jacob. No reason is given for this. The seeds of future problems are shown to us here to prepare us for the next chapter.

There is no marriage in the entire Bible which is so clearly intended of God as that of Isaac and Rebekah. Add to that that the children were born into the world as a direct result of prayer. We would judge from this that we now have the ingredients for the perfect marriage and the perfect family. Indeed, the ingredients are all present, yet here is a family and marriage that knew strain and problems. The beginning may have been ordered of God, but along the way the flesh became very active.

Why he Desired it

Jacob coveted the birthright! No doubt Rachel had told him of the revelation from God, the message received at his birth that the elder, Esau, would serve the younger, Jacob. But there was something more that made deep impressions on Jacob as he grew up in his father's home.

We reviewed the ages of the patriarchs earlier. It indicated that for 15 years, Abraham, Isaac, and Jacob lived together. Now take this fact back to Genesis 25:27 where we are told that Jacob was "a plain man dwelling in tents." Esau was a man of the field, adventurous and "manly" in his ways. He was restless and was not interested in the company and truth which Grandfather Abraham could have imparted to him.

Jacob's desire was right but, as we shall see, he went about everything in a callous and unfeeling way. His bargain with Esau was the first of many such he would make in his life. Here again, God had to teach him the folly of scheming and depending upon his own negotiating skills.

We are reminded from his life that it is important not only to have right desires, but to act in a righteous manner in accomplishing those goals for the Lord. A right thing done in a wrong way can be detrimental to the work of God. Doing the right thing with the right motive, at the right moment, and in the right manner always marked the Perfect Servant of Jehovah. We should strive for likeness to Him in our lives.

The Details of the Birthright

In Deuteronomy 21:17 instructions were given as to the double portion to be given to the firstborn son in a family. There, the emphasis is on the material inheritance which passed from a father to his firstborn son. But, along with the double portion, there was a divine portion which was given first to Abraham and then was transmitted to Isaac and subsequently to Jacob. This "divine portion" involved the territory, the tribes, and, ultimately, the throne. The promise made to Abraham, as expanded in Galatians 3, related ultimately to the "Seed," the Lord Jesus Christ. Abraham was promised the land unconditionally. Ownership was assured; occupation would be based on obedience. The tribes were promised preservation and blessing in the land, conditional on their obedience. Through this Seed, all the world would be blessed. This was assured by divine promise, God pledging Himself unilaterally to the covenant with Abraham and with his seed (Genesis 15).

Thus, the birthright contained unspeakable spiritual blessings for those who received it. Esau despised it while Jacob was determined to obtain it!

The Decision

The story which follows (Genesis 25) is familiar to every Sunday School child. Esau comes from the field faint and hungry. He feels that he is at the point of death. The translation in some versions stresses the sense of urgency which marked Esau: "Quick, let me have some of that red stew! I'm famished!" (NIV). Whether real or imagined, it does not matter in the context of the ensuing events. Jacob is making a pottage of lentils. Esau's hunger becomes Jacob's opportunity. The Spirit of God does not put a moral commendation upon Jacob's action, but He does put a condemnation upon Esau's. Jacob is the opportunist; Esau is the "profane person" (Heb 12:16-17). Spiritual things in the future meant little to Esau.

Whether in a righteous or unrighteous manner, Jacob displays his priority. Esau, likewise, shows what is important to him: "What profit ... this birthright ... to me?"

"The words of Mark 8:36 virtually beg to be quoted here to Esau. He "despised" what God held valuable. Hebrews calls him "a profane person, a fornicator". He chooses the material instead of the spiritual, the momentary rather than the eternal.

The terms of the agreement are made and the deal is struck. Esau receives his bread and pottage - the most expensive meal ever eaten, and Jacob receives Esau's promise about the birthright.

The commentary of the Spirit of God is both stark and solemn: "he ... rose up and went his way: thus Esau despised his birthright." To his impiety and impatience is added insensitivity to his sin.

The Blessing (Ch 27)

Few chapters in our Bible record a family scene marked by such failure and unbecoming behaviour. In the chapter before us, each member of the family is seen in the worst light. It seems that each brings out the basest in the other. Modern psychologists have adopted the term "the dysfunctional family" to explain abnormal family dynamics and interaction. The term is appropriate for this family. Division, deceit, distrust, and disorder all mark and mar this home.

What adds to the gravity of the situation is that if there was one family on the face of the earth at the time which should have manifested righteousness, this was it. Consider as well that it was a family which had been brought together by God. The marriage of Isaac and Rebekah was certainly in the will of God (Genesis 24), and the birth of the two sons was the direct result of Isaac entreating the Lord for his barren wife (25:21). Finally, the blessing which set this family apart from the rest of the world becomes the very issue which wrecks the family.

It is not pleasant to realize that a good beginning in a marriage or family does not always guarantee that spiritual behaviour will continue. Here, carnality fuelled a story-line of falsehood and failure in which each member of the family played a significant role.

In the end, only Isaac appears to learn and grow from the events in the chapter. He is brought to a sudden, shocking repentance. The fact that the Spirit of God chooses the event in this chapter to be highlighted in Hebrews 11 is amazing and is an insight into the ways of God with His own

Isaac

It is frequently pointed out that Isaac moves on the basis of his five natural senses in this chapter, resulting in spiritual failure. His sense of sight (v 1), smell (v 27), taste (v 4), hearing (v 22), and touch (v 22) are all employed. Each disappoints him or deceives him. Moving on the basis of what his natural senses tell him, he falls short of the will of God.

Does this mean that our natural senses always deceive us? Does this mean that we cannot use "common sense" in the decisions of life and in spiritual matters? I think that we shall find that the basic problem was that Isaac was opposed to the will of God and thus doomed to failure. Having first rejected divine guidance, his own "natural ability" only facilitated his fall.

How delightful to think of the contrasts with Isaac. It was written of Moses at the end of his life that his "eye was not dim, nor his natural force abated" (Deut 34:7).

The first truth to note is that we have a man *opposed* to the will of God. God had clearly stated to Rebekah that "the elder shall serve the younger." The blessing belonged to Jacob. Yet Isaac, favouring Esau, desires to give the blessing to him. This is perhaps the crucial point of the chapter and a solemn lesson to fathers. If we are deliberately moving out of the will of God with our families, that disobedience and havoc can only have a "trickle down effect" to each family member.

A man who was moving in rebellion against God brought his family to the point of fratricide as well as deception and hatred. Leadership in a home carries with it the potential for incredible good and unimaginable evil. What brought Isaac to this point of carnality? In the previous chapter he was a man marked by greatness and prosperity. It may be that this was the basis for his altered behaviour. Certainly, the man of Genesis 27 does not resemble in the slightest the man who stepped to the altar on a mountain in Moriah. The fact that his blessing to Jacob begins and seems to be predominantly material rather than spiritual might suggest that his priorities had all been skewed by his prosperity.

Isaac is next seen as a man *occupied* with self-gratification. We are told that Isaac is old. Yet if Luther and others are correct, he is possibly 137 years of age at this point and was to live an additional 43 years. He, at least, lived through the entire time that Jacob was away in Laban's house. His eye is dim. At a time when God is, through natural limitations, teaching him dependence upon Himself, Isaac moves to satisfy his desires and enjoy a feast as a prelude to blessing Esau. His weakness for venison brought him under the influence of a man more carnal than he – Esau.

A few chapters earlier, Esau sold his birthright for a meal. Now, Isaac will dispense a blessing for a meal. There is a sobering moral correspondence between Isaac and Esau, Rebekah and Jacob. Genetics transmit to each of us a full propensity to evil. Environment (and example) frequently determines what specific evils will be developed.

Isaac *offers* to bless secretly. Some question if Isaac knew that he was moving outside the will of God. Perhaps Rebekah never recounted to her husband the declaration of God at the birth of their children. But Isaac's clandestine attempt to confer the blessing on Esau strongly suggests that he knows his dealings will cause a family uproar.

Isaac wills to give the blessing to Esau, who in turn hurries out to the field to secure it. But over this incident can be written the words of Romans 9:16: "So then it is not of him that willeth, nor of him that runneth, but of God." The sovereign purposes of God cannot be frustrated.

Rebekah

Into this scene of domestic "tranquility" comes Rebekah. Either through household servants who were in her confidence, or through her own suspicions, she becomes aware of the situation and sets about "stealing" the blessing for her favourite son, Jacob. Is Rebekah morally right? The blessing was for Jacob according to divine revelation. Is she not simply helping God in His work? Is it right to do evil that good may come? Does a "good" end justify an "evil" means? All these questions answer themselves.

Rebekah is equally culpable for her deceit, and, as we shall see at the end of the chapter, she will pay dearly. God's government is faithful and fair.

She calls Jacob and unfolds her plan to him. She calls upon him to obey her. Here, then, is an example of wrong filial obedience (Jacob may well have been about 77 years old). Isaac abused his authority to bless the firstborn by moving outside the will of God. Rebekah abused her authority as mother by insisting the Jacob obey her (vv 8, 13). Parents must use authority wisely and in keeping with Scripture.

Yet Jacob does not appear to be so concerned with the righteousness of his act, but with its risk. "I shall *seem* to him as a deceiver; and I shall bring a curse upon me." As noted earlier, Jacob is taking character from his mother, just as Esau is from Isaac.

The meat is found and prepared. Every potentiality is foreseen and every precaution is taken to prevent Isaac from discovering Jacob's identity: raiment and goats' skins are all employed to deepen the deception.

Of significance, when she speaks later to Jacob after the deception has been discovered, she appears to place all the blame on him: "Until … he (Esau) forget that which thou hast done to him" (v 45). She greatly miscalculated the future as she urged him to go away for a few days, a period of time that eventually stretched into 20 years.

The one redeeming feature in the chapter concerning Rebekah is that she does recognize Isaac's headship in the home by seeking his permission for Jacob to go to Laban. Even here, however, she manipulates him to get his permission (v 46).

Jacob

The depth of Jacob's deception is seen in this section. He is guilty of outright falsehood when he says, "I am Esau thy firstborn." The misgivings of Isaac are allayed when he again assures his father, "I am Esau" (v 24). Jacob freely and readily makes use of the name of God in his deceit when he says, in answer to his father's surprise that all has occurred so quickly, "The LORD thy God brought it to me." Jacob at this stage of his life thinks little of using God's name so easily.[1]

One deception, one lie, demands another to support it. Before Jacob is done he has lied on perhaps five points and added to that the use of the name of the Lord in vain.

On a practical level, Jacob caved in to temptation. Perhaps it was because it came from his mother. The source of temptation can make a huge difference in how we respond. Satan used the mouth of Peter in attempting to sway the Lord from His path of devotion. But the Lord Jesus recognized the source and did not succumb (Mark 8:33).

Jacob's deception is sealed by his kiss (v 27). The cunning Isaac thought to smell his son when he came near to assure himself that it was Esau. The equally cunning Jacob kisses his father with full assurances of his identity.

As will be seen in later chapters, every deception which Jacob employs will be reaped in his own life later. Deception by use of the garments, the falseness as to his identity, the claim of being the firstborn: these and others will all be tasted by Jacob himself, until he confesses to the angel at Jabbok, "I am Jacob" (32:27).

The deceitfulness of the flesh is evident in this section as well. Every natural sense deceives Isaac. He smells Esau when Jacob comes near. His touch tells him that it is Esau's hairy hands. His ears raise suspicions but are not sufficient to guide him. His taste cannot discern between goat's meat and venison. His eyes are too dim to discern whether it is Jacob or Esau. The natural man is shown to be utterly without ability before God.

The dispensing of the blessing follows in verses 28-29. It is comprised of (1) Prosperity in material things: the dew and fatness of the land are to be his; (2) Preeminence over his fellow man, including Esau; (3) Possessor and Provision of blessing to the world. God will have an even greater blessing for Isaac in the next chapter.

Esau

Jacob is scarcely gone from his father's presence when Esau comes to Isaac. *The arrival of Esau* is dramatic and shocking to Isaac. What bewilderment on Isaac's part must have been attended by the words of Esau, "Let my father arise, and eat of his son's venison, that thy soul might bless me"?

The awakening of Isaac is equally dramatic. He "trembled very exceedingly." Is it possible that in a moment's time Isaac suddenly realized how close he had come to opposing God's will? Did he realize that in his favouritism he was not only damaging family relationships, but seeking to alter divine purposes?

In his response, "... and he shall be blessed," there is the suggestion that he is brought to repentance. Recognizing the error he had made, and understanding that God has overruled him in His sovereignty, he bows to the will of God and owns what God has done.

The anguish of Esau follows. He cries with a "great and exceeding bitter cry". He longs for the blessing. Hebrews 12 reminds us that though he wanted the blessing, he "found no place of repentance, though he sought it (the blessing) carefully with tears." There is much remorse in Esau's cry, but no repentance. The statement, " ... he found no place of repentance" could mean one of two things: it could mean that Esau did not repent; or it may mean that he could not get Isaac to repent and change his mind and confer the blessing on him.

His cry is followed by his charge. Notice how he accuses Jacob of taking away the birthright (v 36), as though Jacob had stolen it. There is no suggestion that Esau recognizes his sin in selling it to Jacob. The sorrow of the world is not godly repentance (2 Cor 7).

He receives a small compensation from his father. Esau's tears and remorse extract from Isaac an *alternative and lesser blessing*. The blessing of which Esau is to learn is a poor consolation prize in light of what he lost. He remains forever a man who missed God's best for his life. The promise of liberty from the yoke of his brother was fulfilled in 2 Chronicles 21:8.

His comfort is seen in the resolve to kill his brother. The thought in his mind may have been that, in killing him, he would prevent Jacob from acquiring the blessing and it would then fall to him. Or it may be that his anger was so great that only vengeance would slake it.

Family

Esau's response to Jacob

Esau is marked by resolve and revenge. He envisions two burials. Once Isaac has died, he intends to kill Jacob. The works of the flesh are evident throughout his life. Hatred and wrath are carefully nursed here, awaiting an opportunity to be satisfied.

Rebekah's response to Esau

Rebekah learns of Esau's anger (what did she expect?) and fears for Jacob's life. Instead of prayer, she resorts once again to plotting. Sin is added to sin, deceit breeds deceit. The plot must deepen and become more involved. Once again she appeals to Jacob to "obey" her voice. She gives instructions to him to flee to Laban, until she is able to fetch him home again.

It is significant that she uses the exact same word for "fetching" the goats (v 9), as she does for "fetching" Jacob home again. When we resort to plotting, people become mere objects, pawns in our plans. There is no mention of the sin and deceit in securing the blessing. Rebekah tells Jacob to flee, until Esau forgets "that which thou hast done to him." There is no mention here of her involvement. She treats the entire matter as one requiring cunning and not confession.

Yet, tragically, while her plan worked in part, she was ignorant of two great truths: she little knew what Jacob would endure from her brother Laban, and she did not know she would never see him again. Her great fear was that she would be deprived of both of them. Her own plotting left her separated from Jacob for the remainder of her days.

Rebekah's response to Isaac

In order to facilitate Jacob's escape without loss of face, Rebekah resorts to manipulating her husband. She feigns a deep spiritual concern for Jacob's marriage and prevails upon Isaac to send him away to secure a wife from amongst the family of her brother Laban. Even here, manipulation and deceit are evident between Rebekah and Isaac. Openness and communication are essential for any marriage, but imperative in a Christian marriage. The amazing aspect of all this is how the Lord overruled and did provide not only the needed discipline in Jacob's life, but the very wife (wives) which would build up the nation of Israel (Ruth 4:11).

Isaac's response to Jacob

The next chapter shows Isaac sending Jacob away. How different from the manner in which Isaac secured a bride!

Us - What it has Cost Us

What if Jacob (and Rebekah) had not stooped to the deception which marked them in obtaining the birthright? God's eternal purpose was that it should be Jacob's: "The elder shall serve the younger" was God's inviolable decree. How would God have over-ruled the impulsive carnal act of Isaac and assured that the birthright would come to Jacob?

The sad reality is that Rebekah's ruse has denied us the privilege of seeing God at work frustrating Isaac's plan and preserving the birthright for Jacob. While we do not know how God would have done it, we can be assured that had Jacob and Rebekah left all in the hands of a sovereign God, He would have been competent to carry out His purposes. Human ingenuity has prevented us from seeing God's superintendence of His eternal plans.

God allowed and used the devices of Rebekah and Jacob, but He did not need them. Similarly, the Lord frequently is hindered from revealing to us His ability to work on our behalf due to our own impulsive tendencies to arrange things on His behalf.

[1]It is interesting that Jacob never refers to God as his God until the end of his life - Genesis 49:24: "The mighty God of Jacob."

CHAPTER 4

Bethel

God is looking for broken men who have judged themselves in light of the cross of Christ. When He wants anything done, He takes up men who have come to the end of themselves, whose confidence is not in themselves but in God (Henry A. Ironside)

Bethel (Ch 28)

Jacob's life differs markedly from that of his father Isaac and his grandfather Abraham. Cunning, intrigue, struggle, failure, and growth distinguish him. There is not the quiet contentment of life as seen in Isaac. Nor is there the ideal life of faith as seen in Abraham. As a result, we tend to identify more with Jacob than with the others because we see ourselves here in clearer, more life-like colours. Yet the truth is that we are only little Jacobs. In many ways, Jacob grows into a spiritual giant.

Eight or nine chapters are devoted in their entirety to this man, and the closing chapters dealing with Joseph's life are inextricably linked with Jacob as well. He occupies at least as prominent a place, space-wise, as any other man in Genesis.

His life is instructive and can be viewed in at least three ways:

Dispensationally

Elected by God

Look at Genesis 25:22-6 and Romans 9. He is a picture of Israel as elect by God.

Exiled at Padan-aram

Amidst disciplinary toil and sorrow, he is in bondage and at the mercy of man. His sin and failure have brought him into his suffering. Yet, he is preserved and made prosperous by God. He is a picture of Israel through the ages.

Enabled by divine power

God takes him into His power, a power that appeared on the surface to cripple, but in reality was his enabling. He changed him from Jacob to Israel.

Discipline in the School of God

Jacob is a picture of every believer who reaps what he sows. Every scheme and device which Jacob used for his own benefit is seen to be an act sown which he must eventually reap. Consider the following deceptions and their return upon Jacob:

The Firstborn	Genesis 29:26
Deception of Father in the dark	Genesis 29:23
Deception with the Coat and a Goat	Genesis 37:31-33
Impatience	Genesis 31:37-41
Falseness as to Identity	Genesis 32:27
Favouritism	Genesis 29:31
Self-Will in Acquiring Blessing	Genesis 30:2.

The thoughtful reader will no doubt add others to this list. It serves, however, to emphasize the truth that the government of God is inescapable. The principle of sowing and reaping is inviolable. Thankfully, the grace of God can, at times, mitigate the full consequences as in Numbers 16:46 and 2 Samuel 24:16.

Development of a Child of God

Jacob is a picture of the Spirit's work in us. In Abraham we see the heart of the Father displayed in Genesis 22. In Isaac we have a picture of Sonship. But in Jacob the emphasis is on the transforming power of the Spirit in the life of a child of God.

Jacob can be appreciated personally in a number of ways. He is the Worm (Isa 41:13-15), the Wanderer (Gen 28:1-3), the Wrestler (Gen 32:21-31), the Weeper (Hosea 12:3-5), and the Worshiper (Heb 11:21). An overview of his life as seen in chapters 28-35 shows further aspects:

Genesis 28	Removal from Canaan	The Sojourner
Genesis 29-31	Reaping in Laban's House	The Servant
Genesis 32	Reality and Revelation	The Supplicant
Genesis 33	Reconciliation with Esau	The Servile
Genesis 34	Ruin of Testimony	The Shamed
Genesis 35	Restoration	The Sorrower.

Genesis 20 is one of the better known chapters in the life of Jacob. The tragic behaviour of chapter 27 is now history and the patriarch is about to set off on a journey which will shape his life and that of the nation of Israel. As we embark on a consideration of the chapter, notice:

The Guile of Rebekah and Jacob's Departure

The previous chapter closes with Rebekah scheming to enable Jacob's escape from Esau. Her professed spiritual concern actually hides a deep natural fear. Isaac, either knowingly or ignorantly, complies with her request. Jacob is sent to seek a wife amongst Rebekah's family in Padan-aram.

The fruit of Isaac's experience in the previous chapter is seen in the character of the blessing which he now confers upon his son. It is far more spiritual and lofty than the blessing which Jacob "stole" from him in chapter 27: "God Almighty bless thee." "El Shaddai" or God all-sufficient becomes Jacob's portion. Little does he realize how completely he will need such a God. The journey, the years of toil, the fear of Esau, and the circumstances through which he is to pass, will all cast him more and more upon the all-sufficient God.

The blessing is not merely the dew of heaven and the fatness of the earth, the servitude of men and the homage from others; the blessing now reaches out to embrace "the blessing of Abraham" and the promise of the land. Isaac has risen to greater spiritual heights in his blessing here. This is the fruit of his repentance and restoration.

With the blessing of Isaac ringing in his soul, Jacob takes leave from his father's house. Little does he know or have any idea of how many years will elapse before he returns. Rebekah does not know that she is bidding him farewell, never to see him again. Isaac sends him away to procure a wife, not knowing that he will return with two wives, two handmaids, and twelve sons. Yet for all this, there is the consciousness that there is an "all-sufficient God."

Isaac is sending him away as a result of being manipulated by his wife; yet underlying this entire chapter is the sovereignty of God who will use the failure of men and women, even at their worst, to accomplish His pleasure and purpose. It also underscores the marvel of the grace of God.

The Groping of Esau and his Desperation

Esau's spiritual blindness is obvious in his response to his father's expressed wish for Jacob. Perhaps he thought that he could impress his parents and return to favour and prominence if he likewise married "in the family." How poorly he understands divine purposes! Esau links himself with the family of Ishmael by marrying his daughter. He attempts to impress Isaac by marrying someone in Abraham's lineage. He failed to realize that he had lost the blessing because of his choice and God's choice. We see his continued lack of repentance.

The Grace of God and Jacob's Dream [1]

If Jacob gloated in the blessing which he had extracted from his father by deception, and if he was pleasantly surprised by the blessing which his father had given him at his departure, he is about to be overwhelmed by the grandeur of what God is going to give by grace. Jacob is going to learn of blessing for which he does not have to connive or steal; he will receive it while asleep. "He gives to His beloved in sleep."

Was this his conversion? This is likely the first encounter with God in his life although his desire for the birthright might indicate his faith in the promises.

The fugitive makes his way toward Padan-aram. He stops to spend the night in Bethel. (Did he purposely avoid the city, or was he lost and too far away to make it there?). He comes to a certain place and takes of the stones of that place for a pillow. Sleep comes easily and readily to the weary wanderer.

Jacob's dream is punctuated by three "beholds." "Behold a ladder," "behold the angels of God ascending and descending," and "behold the LORD stood above it." We have the ladder, the link, and the Lord. Putting aside, for a moment, the unfolding which is given to us in John 1, what did God wish to communicate to Jacob here?

Is there not in picture language the truth of the *Interest of Heaven in a Man on Earth*? There is a *"sullam"* or way or staircase set up on earth whose top reaches unto heaven. There is an intimate link between heaven and earth, because angels are ascending from Jacob to God and descending from God to Jacob. At the top of the ladder, there is the Lord Himself. Some versions suggest that the Lord stood beside the ladder on earth.

The idea of a ladder whose "top" or *"rosh"* reaches to heaven actually goes back to Genesis 11:4 and the tower of Babel. What men who were opposed to God sought to obtain in their rebellion against God, Jacob obtains by grace. Consider also that men desired to make a name for themselves; in contrast, Abraham was given a name. Men tried to avoid being scattered; Isaac knew contentment in the land. Men wanted a tower whose top reached unto heaven; Jacob saw a way cast up and the top reached to heaven. Those called and blessed by God received, by grace, what men instinctively knew they needed but refused from God.

In the promises which God makes to Jacob, we see the *Intention of God for a Man on Earth*. God gives the Promise of the Land, the Prosperity of his Lineage, and a Pledge of His Loyalty. He will not leave Jacob until He has finished all that He has promised. But there is also a glimpse into the *Intimacy of Heaven with a Man on Earth*. Notice the language which must have thrilled Jacob's heart: "with thee ... keep thee ... bring thee ... not leave thee." The angels, ascending before descending suggest that the angels have been with Jacob all along. The presence of God was with him, even though he was unaware of it. God's presence is promised to Jacob, regardless of where he moves. The presence of God transcends national and geographic boundaries[2].

In His revelation to Jacob, God addresses every need which Jacob has. His revelation always fits the spiritual experience of His saints. This is the first of eight revelations made to Jacob. Profit can be had by noting the others: 31:3, 11-13; 32:1-2, 24-30; 35:1, 9-13; 46:1-4.

Gratitude and Dedication

Jacob awakens from his dream to the awareness that God has spoken to him. "Surely the LORD is in this place; and I knew it not." His fear is not so much that of terror, but of reverence. "How dreadful" means how awe inspiring or reverent is this place.

"House of God" and "gate of heaven" are important terms. This is the first mention in the Scriptures of "House of God" and, true to the "Principle of First Mention," it is replete with instruction. Without digressing too far from the chapter, it can be noted that it is a place of revelation, angelic interest, reverence, testimony (the pillar), consecration, and government.

The mention by Paul in 1 Timothy 3 of the House of God, "the pillar and ground of the truth," has many links with the first mention here in

Genesis 28. Not the least of those connections is the thought of "how one ought to behave."

This last characteristic, government, is what is suggested in the expression "gate of heaven." It is not the idea of the entrance into heaven. The gate, in the Old Testament, was the place of administration. See, for example, Genesis 19:1; Ruth 4:1; Psalm 69:12. Jacob owns that he is under the administration of God. The presence of God will not only protect him, but it will control his behaviour.

The awareness of the divine presence leads to the memorial to a divine encounter. "Bethel" will become a significant place in Jacob's life. (Note its mention in 31:13, 35:1, and 48:3.) The encounter with God in Genesis 28 has life-long consequences on Jacob. Every revelation of God to our souls should have life-long effects. Bethel is first noted in connection with Abraham in Genesis 12. The place of Abraham's altar becomes the place of grace for Jacob.

The stone which had been his pillow now becomes a pillar. The stone would be forever linked in Jacob's memory with a night of sleep and a night of revelation. Every believer's life should have pillars which mark out where God has been revealed in a special way to the soul.

The chapter concludes with Jacob uttering his sacred vow. It has been interpreted in various ways. Some see in it the same bargaining tendency which Jacob displayed with Esau when he obtained the birthright. Others see it as a vow of consecration. Some deprecate Jacob for only giving back one tenth of all that God gives him. Some argue that the "If" of verse 20 should be understood in the sense of "Since." In whatever way we are to understand it, we must keep several things before us. Jacob's promise predates the law and the need to tithe. Only Abraham before this expressed a similar spiritual insight in Genesis 14. The pouring of oil on the pillar is actually a drink offering. It expresses Jacob's joy and commitment to God.

It is perhaps best to view this incident in Jacob's life as a point on the spectrum of his growth and development. There is no need to pigeonhole this into a category of "very spiritual" or "very carnal." At this stage of spiritual development he is responding to the revelation of God to his soul in an appropriate manner. We should learn always to respond to divine revelation in a similar way.

Since this is the first mention of "House of God" in Scripture, it is worthwhile gathering together a number of truths linked with this event; these are principles which will be true wherever we find "House of God," be it in relation to the Tabernacle, Temple, or local assembly.

Residency and Reverence

When Jacob awoke from his dream and became conscious of the presence of God, his immediate response was that it was a place demanding reverence, an "awe-full" place, or a place filed with awe. When the presence of God filled the Tabernacle, Moses was not able to enter; when the glory of God filled the Temple, the priests were not able to enter. While the presence of God inhabiting a local company of believers should not hinder us from entering, it does demand reverence in our attitude in His presence. Any thought of a casual attitude professedly due to intimacy and familiarity with our Father belies a lack of appreciation for His glory and greatness.

If an assembly is functioning as prescribed by the Scriptures, the resultant effect of those who are "unlearned" visitors will be the awe which marked Jacob (1 Cor 14:24-25).

Administration and Authority

As intimated earlier, the "gate of heaven" is not denoting a means of entrance but a place of administration and authority. We are now under the authority of the Word of God. Administration suggests divine order. Paul's letter to the Corinthians and his pastoral epistles stress the need for divine order in the House of God. Order must never degenerate into ritual; neither must it give way to confusion. The book of Judges ends with the four-fold refrain: "There was no king ... every man did that which was right in his own eyes". An assembly must never become an arena for opinions, majority decisions, convenience, or compromise. It must always retain the character of the "gate of heaven" as seen in Matthew 18:16-20.

Along with giving us a process for handling difficulties between brethren, the truth of Matthew 18 is that there is no higher court of appeal for assembly matters than the local assembly. While overseers may seek the advice and counsel of other overseers or godly men, the ultimate decision and responsibility is upon the leadership in that local assembly. Elders from other assemblies and workers are not in a position to override local leadership.

Commitment and Consecration

It is the writer's thinking that Jacob's vow to give God the tithe was not a bargain but carries the thought of the fact that "since" God had promised, Jacob was going to consecrate his life and material prosperity to Him. Paul takes up the challenge and applies it to Timothy in 1 Timothy 4. Having stressed how one ought to behave in the house of God in 1 Timothy 3:15, he urged a similar consecration to Timothy in chapter 4:13-16. There is no thought that Timothy was not a committed and consecrated servant prior to this; Paul's ministry was reinforcing as well as corrective.

The "House of God" today will only be able to prosper if the believers in the company are marked by devotedness to the person of Christ.

Angelic Interest and Attendance

It is significant that at this very first mention of the "House of God," angels are in attendance. An "angel of the LORD," possibly an appearance of the pre-incarnate Christ, had met Hagar in Genesis 16. Two angels had hastened Lot and family out of Sodom in Genesis 19. Now, however, it is a host of angels who are in attendance at Bethel. Angelic forms adorned the tabernacle and Temple. Angels gaze down upon sisters who have a sign of authority on their heads (1 Cor 11:10). They were present when another host of angels refused the place which God had given them and rebelled (Jude v 6; 2 Peter 2:4, 5). Now they must gaze in silent wonder on sisters who intelligently and willingly take the place God has given them in both the creatorial and redemptive spheres, symbolically declaring this by their long hair and head covering.

Paul also, in one of his most solemn charges, reminded Timothy that angels were viewing the righteous decision-making of an assembly in its various functions (1 Tim 5:21). They had viewed the righteous character of God as angels that rebelled were cast out of heaven. Now, they are watching to see that the character of God is being reflected in the righteous decisions of leaders and saints in an assembly.

Although Paul's description of the revelation of God's wisdom to those in the heavens is linked with the Church, the Body, it is nonetheless begin expressed in a local company, as well (Eph 3:10).

Revelation and Responsibility

Bethel was a place where God communicated with Jacob. This first revelation of God to Jacob's soul had an influence on his entire life. The content of the revelation provided Jacob with all he needed for "life and godliness." Likewise, an assembly should be a place where the mind of God is communicated to the believers through the Word of God.

But revelation brings responsibility. The response of Jacob is seen in his vow at the pillar. In contrast to Jacob, we have been blessed with a far greater breadth of revelation than he was. How much more responsible we are in light of this!

Wonder and Worship

Bethel was a scene of awe-inspiring wonder and worship. Every House of God ought to be a place where the marvel of the grace of God is celebrated at every gathering of the saints. That wonder should lead to worship. Jacob wondered that the God of his father Abraham and his father Isaac would have a interest in him. The revelation at Bethel came when he, perhaps, was conscious of what his sin and deceit had cost him. Aware of his own unworthiness, he marvelled at the grace which met him as he escaped from the wrath of his brother.

The Pillar and the Pouring Out

Jacob is the man of the pillar, erecting five during the course of his life. Some were linked with significant events; some were to mark places of deep sorrow. It is of interest to note that in the same context that Paul speaks of the assembly as having "House of God" character, he speaks of it as being "pillar and ground of truth" (1 Tim 3:15). As the pillar we proclaim truth; as the bulwark or fortress, we protect truth. And the two are inseparable. As we publish and proclaim truth, we protect it and maintain its purity.

Presence and Purity

Although not present in Genesis 28, the next time Jacob went up to Bethel, he was conscious that the presence of God demanded purity in the lives of all who were there. His command in Genesis 35 was marked by three things:

- Put away the strange gods
- Be clean
- Change your garments.

Affections, attire, and activities all had to be in keeping with the character of the place. Character (garments) and conduct (be clean) must be consistent with the claims of God (put away strange gods) upon the devotion of His people.

[1] Note how often the word "place" occurs in this section: vv 11, 11, 11, 16, 17, 19.

[2] This is the first occurrence of this wondrous promise which will reappear throughout Scripture at critical moments: "I am with thee and will keep thee and will not leave thee." Note its use in Deuteronomy 31:6; Joshua 1:5; 1 Chronicles 28:20; Hebrews 13:5.

CHAPTER 5

Bartering

Ill that God blesses is our good,
And unblessed good is ill;
And all is right that seems most wrong,
If it be His sweet will

(Frederick Faber)

The Circumstances which God Granted Him (29:1-14)

The Well - The Right Place (vv 1-8)

Having met God at Bethel, Jacob continues on his journey. The margin of many Bibles will read that "Jacob lifted up his feet and came ..." almost suggesting a sense of fresh strength and encouragement after Bethel. But he is little aware of the school he is about to enter. At Bethel he learned the character of God; in Haran he will learn the corruption of man. At the House of God he received a divine promise; in the house of Laban he was a mere pawn in the hand of a master manipulator.

Perhaps he takes the road with the thrill of the romantic adventurer. Or perhaps his heart is filled with nostalgic sentiment, as he thinks of the family history and the childhood home of his beloved mother. But he is about to register in a school which will remove all romantic ideas and nostalgia from his thinking.

God first brings Jacob to the right place. He was instructed by his father to go to Padan-aram and the house of Bethuel. His journey leads to a well in that country. Just as a servant years earlier could say,

"I being in the way, the LORD led me" (24:27), so Jacob learns that God has brought him to the well at the right time. Divine providence is in the timing and events.

Jacob's greeting to the men at the well is answered by the knowledge that he has come to Laban's country. It is difficult to know whether the response of the shepherds, "We know him (Laban)", is a statement which is tantamount to our "Boy, do we ever know him!" or is simply a statement of fact. But to Jacob, it at least conveyed the truth that he was in the right place.

Jacob's shepherd instincts are aroused as he sees the flocks gathered at the well awaiting the removal of the stone. The attitude of the shepherds contrasts starkly with the industry and energy of Jacob the shepherd as revealed later in chapter 31:38-41. It appears that the shepherds were preparing for the night, gathering the sheep together. Jacob's practical experience as a shepherd suggested to him that they should be watered and allowed to return to grazing in the pasture.

The Woman - The Right Person (vv 9-12)

Jacob's inquiries lead to his being introduced to Rachel. Did his mind race back to the story (doubtless often repeated by the fire side at night) of how the servant met Rebekah at the well? Did God graciously frame the circumstances for the comfort of His servant? Was all to remind him of a sovereign God who could control circumstances though he, Jacob, was hundreds of miles from home? If so, it was exceedingly kind of God to fortify and brace Jacob for what lay ahead by this token of His power and sovereign control.

God mercifully strengthens His servants for trials which loom on the horizon. Abraham was met by Melchizedek; David was strengthened by Jonathan; Paul had his coterie of companions, several of whom endured his imprisonments as well as his shipwrecks. In contrast, those whom the Lord Jesus took with Him into the garden were overcome by sleep as He faced the dark tomorrow alone.

It is interesting to note that Eliezer, Moses (Ex 2), and here Jacob all had significant meetings at a well. When we come to the New Testament we find the Lord Jesus at a well with a woman, but He established entirely new relationships for her after the six sinful ones she had known (John 4).

Rachel is a shepherdess. She is caring for the flocks of her father, Laban. In a similar vein to Rebekah, she is not averse to hard work and responsibility. As she arrives at the well she confronts Jacob who, in turn, waters the flocks and then weeps as an outlet for the tension and anxiety of his journey. He has arrived at the right place and found the right person. Notice the three fold mention of "mother" in verse 10. This is to emphasize that Jacob had been guided by God to the right family.

The Welcome - The Right People (vv 13-14)

Tidings reach "Uncle Laban" that a visitor from his sister's country has arrived. Rachel dutifully reports everything to the head of the home. Is it the memory of the servant's wealth in Genesis 24 that causes Laban to run to greet Jacob? It certainly is not a warm hospitable spirit. Laban's mind is already calculating how he can make use of Jacob and gain from him. Subsequent chapters will show us that Laban had not been a very successful shepherd prior to Jacob's arrival. He likely was quite poor (30:30). Whatever wealth the servant had conferred upon him in Genesis 24 had been squandered. When the sisters are seen conferring in the field at a later time (31:14-16), there is the suggestion that money had been wasted by Laban. Perhaps Laban sees in Jacob an opportunity to increase his own wealth.

The Man Through whom God Governed Him (Ch 29:15-30)

The Deal - Governed by Laban's Lust (vv 15-20)

Recall the words of God to Rebekah, "The elder shall serve the younger" (25:23), and the words of Isaac to his son, "Let people serve thee ..." (27:29). Now bring those prophecies alongside Jacob in Laban's house. Listen to the offer of Laban to Jacob: "tell me, what shall thy wages be?" Centuries later, God commented upon it by saying, "Israel served for a wife, and for a wife he kept sheep" (Hosea 12:12). The man who was to be served, now must serve in the house of Laban. His own sin and deviousness had brought Jacob to a low point in his career.

Laban's offer to reimburse Jacob is met by Jacob's counter offer to serve seven years for Rachel. Laban's somewhat uncomplimentary reply, "It is better that I give her to thee than that I should give her to another man," would do little to boost Jacob's ego. But such was his love for Rachel that he overlooked his treatment by Laban and the toil of the years. The seven years of hard work were probably meant to serve as a dowry for his bride.

The stage for future conflict is set in these verses by the contrast in the description between Leah and Rachel. Rachel, we are told, was beautiful. Leah was "tender eyed." Several different suggestions have been made as to the meaning of this term. They extend from being cross-eyed to being very plain and lacking in physical beauty. It nowhere tells us of jealousy or friction between the sisters, but Rachel knew that Leah would need to be married first; so her expectations of marriage were being hindered by the lack of interest some might show in a "tender-eyed" sister.

If there was no conflict prior to Jacob's arrival on the scene, his presence and offer of marriage certainly would create one, a conflict which was virtually life-long.

The Deceiver Deceived - Learning Lessons from God (vv 21-27)

The seven years pass and seem to Jacob as only a few days. With a heart filled with joy and a deep sense of relief that his toil is over, Jacob asks for his bride. The story of the deceit of Laban is well known. Allow me simply to point out that God in His sovereignty allows the wickedness of Laban to teach Jacob the lesson of sowing and reaping. The rights of the firstborn and deceit must have come home with thundering force upon Jacob's conscience.

Did Jacob's own conscience bother him? Did he suddenly see something of the justice of God played out in Laban's deceitful act toward him? Divine reaping is evident. Isaac was blind and Jacob could not see his bride in the darkness of the eastern night. Isaac mistook Jacob for Esau and now Jacob mistakes Leah for Rachel.

Sowing and reaping are part of the moral universe of God. David learned it to his great grief. The ten brothers of Joseph all had to own that God had found out their sin. Adoni-bezek (Judges 1:7), a heathen Canaanite king, had to confess the inescapable truth as he endured the judgment of God.

Laban's excuses for his behaviour (vv 26-27) are all very poor and self-serving. He places the practice of the culture over the integrity of his word. "It must not be so done in our country," becomes his justification for lying and deceit. Nothing must ever be allowed to compromise a believer's word or to cancel the Word of God. Cultural practices, if not contrary to Scripture, can be observed; but when culture is at cross purposes to the Word of God then Scripture must be obeyed and culture altered. The norms of society must never become the standard for a believer. One of the vital threads running through the Epistle to Titus is that the grace of God transforms men and allows them to rise about cultural norms and characteristics.

Laban posits the propriety of his action, as well as his justification. Why didn't he inform Jacob of the custom of the land? Why did he not forewarn him prior to the wedding night? It is obvious everything was intended to serve Laban's ends. Truth, integrity, and honour did not enter into his dealings with others.

The Desire Realized - Overshadowed by Love (vv 28-30)

Seven more years are demanded of Jacob for Rachel. What can Jacob do? When a man's heart is captivated, he will entertain no options. He fulfills Leah's week, and then is given Rachel. Jacob's testimony was such that Laban could trust him to keep his word as to the remainder of the seven years he owed his father-in-law. Whatever else we may say about Jacob, he maintained a pure testimony in Laban's home both here and as evidenced in his words to Laban in chapter 31:21-42.

The tone of the next 13 years is established by the statement that Jacob loved Rachel more than Leah. Rivalry, resentment, and ruse will all come into Jacob's house just as it had existed in his heart toward Esau.

In a sense, no one was to blame for the situation except Laban. Jacob had not asked for Leah. Leah, while probably aware of what her father intended and perhaps thankful for the opportunity of marriage, could not make Jacob love her. Rachel loved Jacob. Jacob had "Uncle Laban" to thank. But behind it all is the disciplining hand of the God of Abraham, Isaac, and Jacob.

CHAPTER 6

The Boys

Genesis 29:31 to 30:24

The importance of this section is impossible to over-emphasize. The birth of the twelve sons of Jacob (Benjamin, the 12th, will be in Genesis 35) is monumental in its significance. There will follow, perhaps, twenty occasions when the twelve tribes, as a group, will be mentioned by name in the remainder of the Old Testament. Here are the founding members of the twelve tribes; here are the progenitors of a long line of people, a race which will number more than the sands of the sea. In Ezekiel 48 their names will adorn the partitioning of the land of Israel. Their names will be upon the twelve gates of the city, the New Jerusalem (Rev 21:12). Their names will be eternally honoured and remembered. And it all begins here, in these chapters, marked by carnality, envy, and human manipulation. Grace has marked every step of the divine history and will continue to do so.

The grace of God worked with some fairly unusual clay in carrying out His purposes. We would be surprised by it except that we have known in our own experience something very similar in God's dealings with each of us!

The Triangle

Many times well-meaning believers as well as critics comment on the silence of God concerning the evil of polygamy. While God never verbally confronted any of the godly men who engaged in the practice, wherever it was entered into it was accompanied by sorrow and problems: Abraham with Sarah and Hagar, David with his several wives, Solomon with his harem, and Jacob with Leah and

Rachel. The triangle was fraught with problems from the very first day.

The Divine Designer instituted marriage in Genesis 2. His expressed will was for one man and one woman to enjoy the blessing of an intimate life-long relationship. Any deviation from His pattern will inevitably result in a loss of the fullness God intends for a marriage, and will encounter problems resulting from its departure from the ideal.

The Tension

As you read the story of Jacob and his wives, you cannot but be struck with the fact that the home must have been filled with tension. Rivalry, envy, and jealousy appear in virtually every interaction. The sisters vie for place in Jacob's affections and he almost becomes a pawn in their struggle with each other. Manipulation, mandrakes, and malice are all part of the struggle between the girls. In turn, their handmaidens become pawns in their hands in the attempt to outdo each other.

Something of the built-up tension in Rachel and Jacob is seen in the emotional outburst which begins chapter 30. Similarly, the quiet desperation of Leah was revealed in the naming of her sons. All in all, it was not a happy household. Rachel felt the reproach of barrenness; Leah felt the shame of being second-rate; Jacob had to endure the strained atmosphere which filled the tents.

In Leah's naming of her sons, insight is afforded as to the longing of every human heart. It was not enough that Leah had a husband, albeit one she shared with her sister. It was not enough to enjoy physical intimacy and the bearing of sons. What she longed for was love and the security which that love would provide. All the things which accompany marriage were of little value in her eyes without the undivided love of her husband.

The human heart longs for love and security. In our state of innocence in the Garden we had the security and love issuing from our relationship with our Creator-God. When sin entered by the fall, man lost his significance – he was only dust and would return to dust; woman lost her security – she would henceforth struggle to regain it (3:16). Sin brought in its wake immeasurable consequences at every level of our being. So distraught was Leah, that she referred to her marriage as "my affliction" (29:32).

This constant struggle to regain our significance and security fuels many of our efforts. For some, materialism provides the needed sense of security. Others find significance in the size of a home, the vacations and experiences of which they speak, and the "toys" accumulated throughout life. While none of these things are wrong in themselves, if we seek our significance and security in them we will find disappointment. Grace has provided for security and significance in our relationship with a Redeemer.

The Testing

As we read the story and as it unfolds, multiple questions present themselves to us. Why did God work as he did? Why was Rachel barren while Leah was fertile? While ultimate answers are not in our province to provide, a few suggestions as to the lessons being taught may suffice.

The first and most obvious of lessons is the *Providence of God*. Despite the preference of Rachel and the likely desire on Jacob's part for her to bear his firstborn, God intervenes and Leah is the first to give Jacob a son. The sovereign control of God over life's events is a salutary lesson which we learn and relearn throughout our pilgrim journey. Our plans and devising, our aspirations and dreams, all are subject to His sovereign control. He, at times, shatters our dreams. He wants us to find ultimate satisfaction in Him.

We must always distinguish between responsibility and control. I am responsible for my life, its choices and actions; I am not, however, in control of my life. Ultimate control is in the hands of Another who is far wiser and more skillful in His ways.

In the events in Jacob's home we see the *Pitying eye of God*. The divine record hints at not only the controlling hand of God, but His compensation: "When the LORD saw that Leah was hated, he opened her womb" (29:31). As often noted, the word "hatred" is a relative term, contrasting Jacob's feelings for her with his more intense and genuine love for Rachel. God looked on and saw the grief and sorrow of Leah's heart and in sympathy opened her womb and gave her fruit. But in the circumstances of the home, the *Purposes of God* for Rachel were also being worked out. God was testing and teaching Rachel; she was a slow learner as most of us are, as well. Why didn't she reflect on the folly of Sarah in her impatience (Genesis 16)? Why didn't she follow the wise course of Rebekah who waited twenty years for a child even though God had made a promise to her (25:19-22)? Though favoured with beauty, she appears to lack the spiritual character of her sister, and her progress in God's school is painfully slow.

The Tantrum

Genesis 30:1-2 is the record of a frustrated woman, filled with envy and bitterness, who speaks rashly, to her own loss. We have the recounting of her demand: "Give me children, or else I die." Her statement not only revealed a lack of spirituality, it also revealed the bitterness and resentment of her heart. Perhaps at home she had always had all her wishes fulfilled by her father. Physical beauty can open many doors and can be employed to manipulate and cajole. She acted like a spoiled child in her demand from Jacob.

Her resentment led to a rebuke from her husband: "Am I in God's stead?" Jacob freely owns that only God can meet the need. Rachel no doubt felt some pressure from the success of her sister in bearing children for Jacob and knew that public opinion would be that she was barren as a result of some secret sin. The reproach of her barren state was eating away at her.

Sadly, she will reap the harvest of her ill-advised tantrum. When she ceased to bear any more children, she died (Genesis 35). She died when there was but a little way to go Ephrath; Jacob had to bury her on the way at Bethlehem. Hasty vows and ultimatums are heard by the God of Heaven and He may take us at our word.

The sorrow of the way was never forgotten by Jacob. He recounted it in his old age; his words still evoking a sense of grief and loss.

The Tactics

In the battle with her sister for recognition and honour, Rachel resorts to birth by proxy. Her handmaid, Bilhah, is required to act as a surrogate mother. Jacob acquiesces and the fruit of their union is Dan. In Eastern cultures, this was not a rare recourse, although not Scriptural. Her attempt to "save face" is successful on the surface, but does not really satisfy her heart's longing. She has what Leah wants – Jacob's love; and Leah has what Rachel wants – sons for her husband.

Later in the story Leah offers her handmaiden, Zilpah, as the race intensifies. A certain kind of madness seems to be driving the sisters in their rivalry.

Finally, we come to the strange incident with the mandrakes. Reuben gathered "love apples" and brought them to his mother. Rachel, hoping that they would cure her infertility, bargains with Leah to have the love-apples. Rachel's ability to manipulate Jacob and make him spend a night with Leah reflects something of the "control" which Rachel wielded over him. But the ruse backfires, as do most ruses, and Leah conceives and Rachel is left without a son. Leah's response to Rachel's request, "Thou hast taken my husband" (v 15), shows the depths of her own sorrow and loneliness in her marriage. Despite children and being the mother of the firstborn, Leah's heart was not satisfied. She was deprived of her greatest longing in life.

The Tribes

Both the order of their birth and the names given to Jacob's sons are suggestive. The experience of every soul in conversion and its consequent spiritual progress is mirrored in such names as Reuben -

"behold a son", Simeon - "hearing", Levi - "joined", and Judah - "praise", as well as the names which follow. The names of Jacob's sons also can be traced in the experience of the child of God as developed in Romans 8: Reuben – vv 1-14, Simeon - v 14, Levi - v 16, etc.

The experience of the children of Israel is also mirrored in the names. Even a superficial perusal of Exodus 3:7 suggests this. But our approach will be simply to look at the historical facts and their immediate spiritual import upon Jacob and his family. This does not deny their pictorial or prophetic value.

The prophetic aspect of their names will be more apparent when we come to Genesis 49 and the blessing of Jacob on his sons. Their names will be linked with the division of the land in the book of Ezekiel (Ezek 48), and their names will adorn the gates of the holy Jerusalem in a future day (Rev 21:12). The Lord Jesus also revealed to His twelve that they would sit on thrones "judging the twelve tribes of Israel" (Luke 22:30). Thus the twelve tribes are not only seen in history but in prophecy. These names will be preserved eternally.

Their names and order of their birth also give us a history of the nation. In the first four sons, it has been suggested that there is a preview of their history in Egypt. "A son" reminds us that God saw the affliction of His people in Egypt. But He also heard their groaning, a reminder of Simeon or "hearing". Levi means "joined" and in Jeremiah, God spoke of how He was a husband to them (Jer 31:32). Judah, or "praise", marked them on their deliverance as they sang to God on the banks of the Red Sea on the day of their deliverance.

Israel's time in the wilderness is pictured in Dan and Naphtali. In the former, there is prefigured the ten judgments for murmuring; in Naphtali, the conflicts with Amalek and others.

The experience of Israel in the land is seen in the next four sons: Gad and Asher remind us of the "good fortune" which accompanied Israel as they took possession; Asher, of their happiness and joy in entering into their possession. Issachar, or "hire" and Zebulun, "God hath endued me with a good dowry," certainly speak of God's faithfulness in bringing them into a land of "milk and honey."

But what of the last two sons, Joseph and Benjamin? Is there perhaps a picture of Israel in the land under David who took away the reproach of the Philistine oppression? Benjamin, "the son of my right hand," is a link with Solomon, the King who sat at the pinnacle of the glory of Israel as a kingdom.

Leah's Sons

"When the LORD saw that Leah was hated, he opened her womb." God is once again using family life to teach Jacob important lessons. Favouritism was operative back in Isaac's home. Rebekah and her favourite, Jacob, had outwitted Isaac and his favourite, Esau. But Jacob must learn that this will not be the spiritual way to bear fruit.

Leah's response to her sons is worthy of note. In the naming of her sons ("*She* called his name ..."), her heart is revealed in a unique way. In three of the first four, she employs the name "Jehovah" in her expressions of joy. Raised in the idolater's home, she must have come to embrace the Lord of Israel.

But her sense of rejection, her deep desire for love from Jacob, and eventually, her spiritual development is reflected in these names as well. She moves from the deep desire to win Jacob's love, to the deeper and more spiritual plane expressed in her naming of Judah: "Now will I praise the LORD." She progresses from the satisfaction of having bested her sister, to an appreciation and praise of God. In some ways, the implication is that Leah is the more spiritual of the two sisters.

Years later, there is the suggestion that Jacob came to understand how Leah felt. When he confronted Laban (31:36-41), he did not complain about the ruse which led to his marriage to Leah instead of Rachel. He never humiliated Leah in front of others.

The fruitfulness of Leah has a message of tremendous encouragement to every sister who remains in a difficult marriage out of faithfulness to the Lord. Notice that Leah bore children when Rachel could not. She had the privilege, as well, of bearing Levi and Judah, the two tribes which would supply the priestly and the kingly lines. Finally, she had the blessing of being the mother of Judah from which tribe the Lord sprang. God honoured her and has put her name into the genealogy of His Son.

God honoured her and will honour her eternally in this manner. God may not compensate every sister in the same way, but He will be faithful and recompense any who endure the heartache and grief which only a poor marriage can cause, for the sake of the Lord's honour. Do you think that Leah will feel slighted in eternity?

Bilhah

The rivalry in the home leads to a sense of reproach in Rachel. Her feelings give vent to an ultimatum which must have been especially frustrating to the man who was always able to get what he wanted by one means or another. Suddenly, he is confronted with a bitter and barren wife for whom he can do nothing. God is again teaching Jacob valuable lessons.

The cry, "Give me children, or else I die", has already been noted. To add to the previous comment, it is sad to see that Rachel little realizes how prophetic her words were. She will die in the act of childbirth. But so great is her envy and bitterness that she feels life is not worth living. Jacob retorts, "Am I in God's stead?" He is learning that fruitfulness comes from God alone.

It is of interest that the first mentions of "reproach" in both the Old and New Testaments are linked with barren women who are under the suspicion of divine disapproval. In the Old Testament, it is Rachel. In the New, it is Elizabeth in Luke 1:25.

Rachel offers her handmaiden, Bilhah, to Jacob. It is almost a repeat of the Sarah - Hagar scenario, and should have been rejected by Jacob. But, in his frustration to satisfy his wife, he consents to the "child by proxy" scheme. Dan and Naphtali are born. The first tribe became the door through which idolatry would enter the nation centuries later. "Naphtali," or wrestling, shows us Rachel's view of the current rivalry with her sister.

Rachel named the child Dan, suggesting that she thought God was "judging" or vindicating her in her action. There is here the solemn reminder of how we can be guilty of self-deception when we are driven by our own carnal natures. She had a false concept of God and of His purposes. She had manipulated the event and forced the circumstances. In naming Naphtali, there is again the mistaken concept that she had somehow "won" in the struggle with her sister.

Zilpah

The competition intensifies and Leah offers Zilpah to Jacob. The loan of Zilpah for the purpose of exactly two births suggests that Leah was trying to duplicate Rachel's children through Bilhah. The result of Zilpah is first Gad, and then Asher. The name of Gad can be translated to mean, "What good fortune", and the name of Asher means "happy." And yet, Leah's naming of these two sons belies the true grief in her heart because of the lack of Jacob's attentive love. She is also guilty of self-deception.

Leah

We are not to take from the episode of the mandrakes, or "love apples", that there was anything other than the belief of the people of that day. Every culture at almost every period of time has had its "aphrodisiacs" and folk remedies for infertility. What we can learn from the episode is the intensity of the rivalry between the sisters and the longing of Leah's heart to be Jacob's closest wife.

Reuben's discovery is of such interest to Rachel that she is willing to part with Jacob for the night so that she might acquire the love apples. As a result, Leah conceives and bares Issachar. Leah conceives a second time and bares her sixth son, Zebulun, amidst the fervent hope that now Jacob will dwell with her and not Rachel.

Nazareth, the place of the Saviour's home, would be in the land given to Zebulun, although He Himself would be of the tribe of Judah. Leah also gives birth to Dinah (v 21). The cursory manner in which heɪ birth is mentioned may be attributable to several factors: the birth of a girl would not weigh heavily in this rivalry between sisters. It was the number of sons which could be provided for Jacob that was important. A girl was not a very potent weapon in this battle. Sadly, it may reflect the relative value placed on women as compared to men in ancient society. It was Christianity which conferred dignity and worth upon womanhood although the Old Testament did honour women and note their role in the plan of God.

Rachel

"And God remembered Rachel." God's time has arrived. Jacob has made remarkable progress in the school of God. He is about to be transferred back to the land of Canaan. The great impetus for his own desire to return is the birth of Joseph. It is perhaps here that Rachel rises to her highest spiritual experience. We have 1) Answered Prayer - "God hearkened to her." 2) Awareness of Ultimate Sources - "God hath taken away my reproach." 3) The Anticipation of Faith - "The LORD shall add to me another son."

Kell suggests that the name "Joseph" has two meanings: "taking away" and "adding." The first meaning is a look back at the past reproach, now banished and gone. The second meaning, "He will add," is a look to the future, and the desire for God to add another son.

The Turning Point

In some way, the birth of Joseph becomes a turning point for Jacob. It may be that Joseph was born at the close of the contracted fourteen years of service. Or it may be simply that Joseph's birth turned his thoughts to home and family.

Laban, always ready for a one-sided bargain, is hesitant to allow Jacob to leave. He has learned by experience or divination (linked with his idols) that since Jacob came, the Lord had blessed him. This strange connecting together of his own gods and the Lord is reminiscent of what we will read of centuries later when, at the removal of the ten tribes from the land, the displaced Samaritans fear the Lord and worship their own gods.

Jacob is able to say without inviting contradiction that he had worked for fourteen years, and that during those years Laban had prospered. Jacob himself had nothing but his two wives and his eleven sons as the payment for his labour. He was anxious to provide for his own family.

In Jacob's expressed wish to care for his own, Laban sees another opening for a one-sided bargain and seizes upon the opportunity.

The Terms of the Agreement

It is Jacob who suggests the terms of the next six years of labour for Laban. He agrees to work for part of the herd. Even as Jacob is speaking, Laban is thinking how he can outwit and deceive him. Jacob in turn agrees that the speckled and spotted cattle and the brown sheep will be his.

The Treachery of Laban

Laban then separates the spotted and speckled from the rest of the herd, putting three days journey between them and the rest of the herd under Jacob's care. It may be that this was part of the agreement, but it is more likely that Laban was trying to make it harder for Jacob to start up his own herd. It is Laban's own insurance policy against Jacob's prosperity.

Tactics which Jacob Employed

Much has been written to explain Jacob's breeding techniques. Certainly, we should not fail to give Jacob credit for being a skillful shepherd. It may be that some of the genetic principles later discovered by Gregor Mendel were known in a rudimentary form to men who bred animals centuries before Mendel. However, genetics and breeding had nothing to do with Jacob's success.

But, perhaps the simplest way of dealing with Jacob's tactics is to stop where Jacob stops: "God hath taken away the cattle of your father, and given them to me" (31:9). God blesses Jacob and causes his flock to grow and prosper. Jacob may employ breeding techniques which seem almost superstitious to us today, but God overrules and his flock grows.

CHAPTER 7

The Breach

We all want progress, but if you're on the wrong road, progress means doing an about-turn and walking back to the right road; in that case, the man who turns back soonest is the most progressive (C. S. Lewis)

The Manner in which God Guided him

The Circumstances which Awakened him

How do we discern the will of God? Before embarking on the principles seen in the incident before us, it should be plainly stated that 95% of the will of God is clearly revealed to us in His Word. I do not have to agonize over whether I should be baptized. There is no need for an all-night prayer vigil to determine whether I should date or marry an unsaved person. These and a myriad of other practical day-to-day issues are all answered in non-negotiable ways between the covers of the book we hold in our hands, God's infallible Word. What limits our discernment is our lack of knowledge of His Word.

Having established the clarity with which Scripture directs us for the decisions of life, we must add that there are times when we do need guidance as to a choice or direction. There are times when any of several choices are within the province of Scripture and we must choose one of them. Are there guidelines for such occasions? Are there principles to show us the way?

Numerous writers point to the manner in which God guides Jacob as a pattern for His guidance of believers. First of all, there was the personal exercise which began with the birth of Joseph (30:25). Something about the birth of Joseph awakened in Jacob a desire to "go home."

To this is added the change in circumstances unfolding in our chapter. The relationship between Jacob and his brothers-in-law and father-in-law altered. The atmosphere chilled and the smiles were exchanged for looks of suspicion and disfavour. As Jacob surveyed the panorama of Laban's home, he knew that change was in the air.

Finally, there is a direct word from God (31:3). There may have been 20 long years of silence; we are not told of any communications from God to Jacob during that time. But now the voice of God came with commanding clarity. Personal exercise, compelling circumstances, and the Word of God: these three elements give confidence to the child of God that he or she is in the mind of God. Jacob experienced all three.

Look first at the circumstances. The complaint of the sons of Laban is matched by the changed countenance of Laban. God's prosperity did not bring admiration but an evil eye. Perhaps the sons, now enjoying some measure of prosperity after years of difficulty, were concerned that their future inheritance was being appropriated by Jacob.

Laban no longer can look upon Jacob as a useful tool. Jacob had been a blessing to Laban as God had promised Jacob (28:14). But now he has become a formidable rival. Laban had been able to outmanoeuvre Jacob, but he could not outmanoeuvre God. He was no longer self-satisfied at taking advantage of Jacob, but fearful that soon all would be Jacob's. Circumstances had suddenly reversed and further prompted Jacob to consider leaving Laban's service.

Situations, as the sole means for guidance, may not be a safe barometer by which you can chart a course. God can use events in one of two ways: when His Word is clear, He may allow conditions to point in a different direction as a test of obedience. Jonah had a clear command from God to travel to Nineveh and to preach to it. Yet every circumstance was so favourable for a trip over to Joppa: the boat was there; he had the fare; they were willing to take him; and it was going in the opposite direction, away from the very place to which he did not wish to travel.

On other occasions, when there is no clear principle or precept in Scripture to guide your choice, the Lord may well employ circumstances such as open doors, to guide the believer in decision making. In some measure, the Lord used circumstances to guide the apostles in their movements in Acts 16.

A believer is also guided by his own desire to please God and by the integrity of his character. "The integrity of the upright shall guide them: but the perverseness of transgressors shall destroy them" (Prov 11:3).

The Counsel from God which Advised him

In tender mercy, God added one final element to the instruments employed in guiding Jacob. Suddenly, into apparent years of silence, bursts the voice of God. This is the first word from God to Jacob recorded in Haran. "Return unto the land of thy fathers, and to thy kindred; and I will be with thee" (31:3).

There is clear and obvious direction as well as the reminder, however subtle, of the promise of 28:15. God graciously has made the decision clear for Jacob. With such a call, Jacob can only obey.

The Confidence in God which Assured him

Rather than risk a discussion which Laban's sons might overhear, Jacob calls for his wives and holds a conference in the field. His words reveal a deep consciousness that he has been under the disciplining hand of God. In what he says, we see:

The presence of God owned (vv 4-5)

Whatever may be the attitude of Laban, Jacob recognized that God had been with him. Jacob may not be in favour with the master of the house, but he was in favour with the Master of All.

The protection of God owned (v 7)

Something of the frustration and heartache of the twenty years is revealed in Jacob's words, "... your father hath deceived me and changed my wages ten times." Whether this is an idiomatic expression or to be taken literally, at the least it conveys to us the truth that no fair labour laws existed in Laban's employment. Yet despite this, Jacob recognized that, "God suffered him not to hurt me." It was not Jacob's power, wisdom, or skill which had kept Laban at arm's length, but God.

The prosperity of God owned (vv 8-9)

To reinforce to his wives the hand of God in it all, he says, "Thus God hath taken away the cattle of your father, and given them to me." It is not his superior shepherding skill or insight into breeding techniques; nor is it his wisdom or energy to which he points. He owns that all has been of God.

In owning these three mercies from God - His Presence, Protection, and Prosperity - Jacob is going back to his vow in Genesis 28:20: "If God will be with me (His presence) and will keep me (His protection) in this way that I go, and will give me bread to eat (His prosperity) ... come again to my father's house in peace." God had fulfilled his request at Bethel. In this character, God reminds him of returning to his home.

The pathway of God owned (vv 10-13)

Possibly this goes back to a time prior to Jacob's prosperity and explains the source of his plan. Did God direct him concerning the mating? Is this the direct manner in which God increased his flock? If that is the case, then verse 12 to verse 13 with its six-year interval is merged as one.

The Cooperation of the Family which Agreed with him

The testimony of Laban's daughters

"Is there yet any portion or inheritance for us in our father's house?" There is, perhaps for the first time, no rivalry or contention. Both are in agreement. Their future is with Jacob. Laban must have been a cold and calculating father. The girls had been used by him as pawns in his chess-match with Jacob. They had experienced all they wanted to of their father's callous manner.

The treatment they had received

The words of Leah and Rachel give us insight into Laban and his treatment of his own daughters: "Counted as strangers" and "sold us", and again, "devoured also our money". Laban was cold and calculating as a parent as well as a business man. Warmth, love and sentiment are missing. Homesickness is not a disease endemic to Laban's country. Their father had failed to be a father to them, treating them as pawns in his business dealings.

The treasures they owned

They recognize that God had taken riches from Laban and transferred them to Jacob's bank account. This is remarkable testimony from two girls who had been raised in idolatry. To Jacob's credit, he had managed to reveal the true God to his family in a pagan world. Owning that the future is with Jacob in Canaan and not with Laban in Padan-aram, they encourage Jacob to obey God. Every hindrance to moving is now removed. Those he loves are willing to move with him. Jacob is ready to return to his own country.

Jacob displays the character of a husband-leader, and his wives willingly and readily submit to his leadership. He is transparent, honest, gracious, and patient in his communication with them. His manner serves as a model for how a husband should communicate with his wife.

The Providence through which God Guarded Him

Liberation

The verses before us detail the secret flight of Jacob and his family, and the swift pursuit by Laban and his friends. Jacob marks his time well and steals away while Laban is off shearing his sheep. The drama is enhanced by the statement that Rachel steals her father's idols. Perhaps she thinks that it will hinder his being able to "discern" where Jacob has gone. Later, Laban's search for his idols suggests that he was looking for them to help "divine" Jacob's whereabouts.

Laban is told about the escape and quickly mobilizes his family and friends for the chase. He travels approximately 300 miles in about seven days. What is more remarkable, and perhaps an insight into Jacob's sense of danger and fear, is that with women, children, and flocks, Jacob had traveled the same three hundred miles in ten days.

On the seventh day of Laban's pursuit, he spies the fleeing Jacob in the area of Mount Gilead. One can easily imagine the smug, seething anger of Laban as he looked at his son-in-law in the distance. He will deal with him in the morning. Likely, Laban was boasting to his army about how he would teach Jacob a few lessons about running off and about stealing his idols. For the present, Laban will allow himself one last good night's sleep before settling his score with Jacob.

Intervention

But that very night, God comes to Laban "the Syrian" in a dream with a firm warning. It is significant that it is "God" in His sovereignty who appears to Laban. Equally important is the inspired writer's description of Laban as "the Syrian." God is sovereign and able to deal with and speak to Laban, even though he is an idolater. Laban is an outsider, a Syrian, who cannot touch God's anointed.

God could easily have prevented Laban from leaving Haran; or He could have hindered his pursuit. The intervention, however, was left to the very last night. All this was to strengthen Jacob's faith. It was not merely inconvenience or circumstances which hindered Laban. Nothing and no one other than God could have stopped the intentions of this hostile man. God was reminding Jacob of the promise at Bethel: "I am with thee, and will keep thee in all places wither thou goest, and will bring thee again into this land" (28:15). God was proving to Jacob His faithfulness.

In a similar manner, the Lord may allow a trial in a believer's life to be prolonged. His arm is able to intervene at any moment, but He chooses to allow the trial to continue. His goal is to preclude every other possible form of deliverance so that the believer will learn to trust Him more fully in the trial.

Confrontation

In these verses we see Laban's insincerity, intention, and inability. He claims that he would have sent Jacob's people away with feasting had he only known. His words, obviously, did not make an impression on Jacob or even his daughters.

"It is in the power of my hand to do you hurt," was the true intention of his heart. What he is actually saying here is, "My hand serves me as god" (Hab 1:11; Job 12:6). Hatred and revenge filled him when he left in pursuit of Jacob. What is restraining him? It is the limiting hand of God which hinders Laban.

Accusation

"Wherefore hast thou stolen my gods?" It is amazing that after Laban has been confronted by the true God, and has had to own his own inability to go beyond the permissive will of God, that he still is crying over the loss of his own "gods"! How tragic and blind the grip of idolatry upon the souls of men! He has to look for lost idols, idols that can be sat upon and hidden.

Jacob's words reveal the fear with which he lived and which motivated his secret flight. In his anger, however, he rashly proclaims that Laban may put to death whoever has stolen his gods. Laban's search is nearing completion when he ventures into Rachel's tent. She is seated upon a heap of furniture under which the "gods" are hidden. Her excuse is accepted and Laban departs. Laban's deceitfulness must have been contagious for his younger daughter had a bit of Laban in her.

Vindication

Laban's search being fruitless, Jacob is finally emboldened to speak his mind before his father-in-law. Jacob confronts Laban with three stinging rhetorical questions and a final challenge. But beyond simply proclaiming his innocence, Jacob now points to his years of faithful service. In the verses and expressions which follow, we gain an insight into a true shepherd[1]: faithfulness (twenty years), compassion (ewes and lambs), selflessness (rams not eaten), personal loss (I bare the loss), hardship (drought and frost), self-sacrifice (loss of sleep). While we may profitably spiritualize these to the responsibility of shepherds today, the testimony to Jacob's years of physical work should not be dismissed.

Laban did not appreciate Jacob's service. But Jacob is conscious that God had His eye upon him and owned his service: "Except the God of my father ... God hath seen my affliction and the labour of my hands, and rebuked thee yesternight." Shepherds serve for the pleasure and approval of God alone. Every true shepherd of God, serving in local assembly capacity, should take great encouragement from the assurance that all that has been sacrificed for the flock has been noted by the Chief Shepherd. The Labans of the world (and of the assembly) cannot appreciate the service and sacrifice which has been rendered to God.

Negotiation

Laban's Plight

What transpires is the final contact between the Patriarchs and their relatives in Mesopotamia. Laban, recognizing that he is helpless before the power of God, seeks for a way to save face before all who are with him. In what he hopes will seem a magnanimous gesture, he offers to make a covenant with Jacob.

The Pillar of Separation

Jacob erects a pillar and a heap of stones to be a "heap of witness."

Galeed or Mizpah becomes its name. It is not that each was wishing the other well, or invoking the watchful care of God over the other in his absence. It is rather the concept that each did not trust the other and was calling upon God to judge between them while they were apart.

The Place of Sacrifice

Jacob, rising to his patriarchal character and dignity, assumes the priestly role which is his and offers sacrifice. Interestingly, this is the first recorded sacrifice by Jacob. Having known the hand of God with him and sensing the place he occupies in the divine economy, he rises morally to his calling as God's representative to the nations.

The Point of Sundering

The next morning finds Laban rising early, kissing farewell to each of his family, and departing. The road he walked took him back to his land and his gods. He is never heard from again in the Genesis story.

---

[1] Jacob the shepherd became aware of circumstances which snuff out the life of sheep:

Wild beasts which slay the sheep

Thieves who steal the sheep

Drought that starves the sheep

Frost that shrivels the sheep

Losses which stagger the shepherd.

CHAPTER 8

Jacob: The Brook, the Battles, and the Blessing

When God wants to drill a man and thrill a man and skill a man ...
When God wants to mold a man to play the noblest part;
When He yearns with all His heart to create so great and bold a man
that all the world shall praise ...
Watch His methods;
Watch His ways!

(Anon)

These words were quoted at the beginning of this study on Jacob. They seem particularly apposite to this section:

Verses 1-2   The Sign to Assure Jacob
Verses 3-8   The Scouts to Assess
Verses 9-12   The Supplication to Appeal
Verses 13-24   The Strategy to Appease
Verses 25-32   The Struggle with the Assailant.

Confirmation of a Divine Escort (32:1-2)

It is January, 1885 and British Army hero, General Charles Gordon, is in charge of Khartoum, in the Sudan. Around him, closing in relentlessly, is a vast horde of fanatical followers of the self-proclaimed prophet Muhammad al-Mahdi. Britain has been reluctant to send reinforcements. Desertion is rivalled only by starvation. Imminent defeat and death face Gordon and his small group of Egyptian soldiers. Gordon takes his pen and in his last message back to Britain writes,

"The angels of God are with me - Mahanaim." One cannot help but wonder how many present-day generals would even know what "Mahanaim" means.

Jacob had escaped the danger of Laban behind him only to be faced with the danger of Esau in front of him. God is squeezing him between the two foes. He cannot go back – chapter 31:45-53 has shown us that. To go forward is to face danger. Yet God's word has commanded him to return to the land even if he has to confront his brother.

A man walking in the will of God will receive confirmation of that step. It is so with Jacob here. He approaches the land and is met by a host of angels. Perhaps his mind sped back over twenty years when he left the land and had a vision of angels. Perhaps he simply takes heart to realize that God is with him and able to protect him. At the very least, he appreciates that he is not alone. He calls the name of the place "Mahanaim," or "Two Hosts." Once again God's timing is impeccable. Just when needed, Jacob's eyes are opened to see the provision of God for his crisis. Foes may be encountered in the pathway of obedience, but God will provide "angels" for the escort.

Before he sees the hosts of Esau, he sees the host of the Lord. What he does not know is that before he would see the face of Esau whom he feared, he must see the face of God. Commentators are divided about the reason for this designation. It appears that the naming is linked with the addition of God's angelic host to his family. No longer would he be advancing alone. His host and God's host would be two hosts. This angelic escort would be a Reminder of Divine Faithfulness and a Reassurance of Divine Protection.

Resolution born of Natural Expediency (32:3-8)

In verses 3-5 we have *The Scouts and their Message*. Undoubtedly, these men were sent with the dual purpose of assessing Esau's intentions and of allaying Esau's anger. Some have seen a difficulty in verse 3 where Esau is alleged to be in the land of Seir, the country of Edom, while chapter 36:6, four chapters later, states that Esau took his family and departed from Canaan. There is no real conflict here.

Two possible explanations are suggested. Chapter 36 could well be a summary chapter which looks back and brings together all the details of Esau and his family. In this literary way, the Spirit of God "closes" the book on Esau before introducing us to Joseph. Another explanation is that Esau departed further still from Jacob in chapter 36.

The language of Jacob in verses 3-5 would serve two purposes: It is fawning and flattering - "my lord Esau" and "Thy servant Jacob," and it is full of reassurance that Jacob is wealthy in his own right. He is not coming to challenge Esau or to demand the material benefits of the birthright from his father Isaac.

In verse 6 we have *The Sobering News and its Menace*. The scouts probably never even approached to speak with Esau. The sight of 400 battle hardened men riding across the land to meet Jacob is enough to cause them to turn and report back to Jacob. How Esau knew of Jacob's return is not explained.

In verses 7-8 we see *Jacob's Strategy and its Motivation*. Despite the recent visit by the angelic host, Jacob is filled with dread at the meeting with Esau: "conscience does make cowards of us all." Before we all rise in condemnation of Jacob, remember that there is a little of Jacob in each of us. His fear leads him to divide the company into "two hosts" (Mahanaim, again) with the hope that at least one would be able to escape and not all would be lost. Undoubtedly, Jacob plans to be amongst the host which escapes.

Supplication marked by Spiritual Earnestness (32:9-12)

We need to pause at these verses for several reasons. This is actually the first recorded prayer as such in our Bibles. No doubt someone will object and ask about Genesis 18. That remarkable occasion is really a conversation between God and Abraham. Here, then, is the first recorded prayer, which contains valuable and weighty lessons. This inaugural prayer of Jacob is actually a pattern prayer.

Another reason for drawing attention to these verses is the strange combination (not so strange in reality to our experience) of human planning and prayer. We must be gracious to Jacob. He is taking what he views as prudent measures in his dealings with Esau. We must credit him with a high level of spiritual appreciation and apprehension when we examine his prayer. To his credit we have to own that at least he prayed!

There are seven elements to his prayer which are worthy of consideration:

The Perception he has

"O God of my father Abraham, and God of my father Isaac, the LORD ...". Here Jacob reminds God of a relationship which had been established. He intelligently uses the names of God: He is the God of Abraham and Isaac, but He is the Lord who called and commanded Jacob. As God, Elohim, He is mighty and able; as Jehovah, He is faithful and true.

This centuries old prayer teaches us the need for intelligent uses of divine names in our prayer life. Names are not meaningless terms to be used interchangeably for variety. They are vital to addressing God.

The Promise he enjoys

"The LORD which saidst unto me, Return unto thy country and to thy kindred, and I will deal well with thee." Jacob moved in obedience to God. In the path he is free to call upon God in this way. One of the greatest blessings in our Christian life is to be able to call upon God in our distresses, reminding Him that we are where we are in obedience to His Word. When we are out of His mind in deliberate disobedience we may pray, but we cannot do it with this boldness and confidence.

It is noted that he prays back to God the promise which God made to him. He reminds God of His word, not because God is forgetful, but to "hold" God to His promise.

The Personal Unworthiness he confesses

"I am not worthy of the least ...". Jacob is not impressing heaven with his humility. Confession should always accompany our petitions (Daniel 9, Ezra 9, etc). Jacob here rises to a spiritual mountain peak in his own life. Few statements made by the patriarch are as noteworthy.

The Prosperity he experiences

There is a deeper and additional element here. Jacob tells the Lord that he was never worthy of anything which God chose to give him. He had crossed over Jordan, a fugitive from home, with only a staff. God had graciously appeared to him and blessed him. Blessings had continued in the house of Laban. Now here is Jacob with all the children which God had given him.

When we think of the stewardship of truth which God has committed to us and the burden of testimony, we should emulate Jacob and remind God that we were never worthy of such mercies. Only His hand can enable us to preserve truth and testimony for coming generations and for His glory.

The Problem he faces

"Deliver me, I pray thee from the hand of my brother, from the hand of Esau." Jacob's prayer is brief, pointed, and spiritual. He brings his problem before God. His words are simple and earnest, consistent with the dangerous situation in which he finds himself. He has seen God miraculously restrain a Laban only a little earlier. Now, faced with an Esau, he looks again to God.

The Peril he fears

"I fear him, lest he will come and smite me, and the mother with the children." Jacob's responsibility as leader of his people moves him to pray as he did. As he thinks of women and children, he calls upon God.

The Promise he claims

"And thou saidst, I will surely do thee good, and make thy seed ...".
Jacob comes now to the critical point: God had promised seed "... as
the sand of the sea." That very promise was in jeopardy. So he rises
above the danger to his own life and that of his family to the danger of
God's word being violated. Jacob reminds God of His word. He is not
simply filling blanks in his prayer or "dressing it up" to sound lofty. He
applies the word of God, which his own soul had depended upon, to
the current crisis. If we are able to speak to God on terms such as this,
we are praying spiritually.

Preparation based on Human Experience (32:13-23)

"And he lodged *there* that same night; and took of that which came
to his hand a present." The very same night and the very same place
in which he prays and speaks as though all depended upon God, finds
him calculating and plotting as though all depends upon his cunning.
Jacob sends a gift offering, or *min-chah*, to Esau. This is the word
used in Genesis 4:3 for Abel's "offering". It is the word for the "meal
offering" in Leviticus 2. The purpose behind it is in Jacob's words: "I
will appease ..." (*kah-phar* or atonement).

In verses 3-5 we saw verbal expressions of humility; but now we
see visible expressions of homage. A total of 550 animals are culled
from Jacob's wealth and sent out to meet Esau in at least five droves.
The animals were sent in waves, possibly with the hope of gradually
abating Esau's anger and determination. This amount, the selection
of animals, and the manner of approach are all calculated to impress
and soften Esau for the inevitable meeting. Jacob's great concern is
to try and appease Esau so that he will "accept of me" or "accept my
face". All of this is setting the stage for Penuel - "I have seen God face
to face." But, as is usually the case, the best of human preparations
gives no peace in a trial and Jacob is left to a sleepless night. He arises
and takes his wives, children, and women servants and crosses over
the brook at the ford Jabbok. All that Jacob loved, possessed, and held
dear is now separated from him, and he is alone.

A valuable and helpful line of ministry can be followed by considering the different brooks of Scripture:

BROOK	CHARACTER REVEALED	LESSON	REFERENCE
Elah	The Fearless Shepherd	Redemption	1 Sam 17
Kidron	The Forsaken Sovereign	Rejection	2 Sam 15
Eshcol	The Fruitful Salvation	Riches	Num 13:23
Cherith	The Faithful Supplier	Resources	1 Kings 17
Zered	The Faithless Sinner	Reaping	Deut 2:13,14
Kishon	The Fearless Servant	Repentance	1 Kings 18:40
Jabbok	The Faltering Supplanter	Restoration	Gen 32
Besor	The Fainting Soldiers	Reward	1 Sam 30:9.

Subjugation of Fleshly Energy (32:24-32)

The next verses are critical to a right understanding of Jacob and God's dealings with him. The great lesson which God taught Jacob here stands as a sentinel to guide us in our spiritual relationship with the Lord. This experience has been subjected to an amazing variety of interpretations and applications by various writers. We are assured by most that this could not have been a real physical struggle with the angel. This is just an internal mental and spiritual struggle. Besides, what value would there be for Jacob actually to have a wrestling match with God?

While all this has a veneer of plausibility about it, it is difficult to understand how writers then explain the weakness and the withering of the flesh which marked Jacob the rest of his life. No, this is a real encounter with God. It is physical, but not merely physical. In the realm of the physical, God is teaching Jacob critical spiritual lessons. Everything in life, the physical, material, and temporal, all subserve the purposes of God in the spiritual realm.

The second difficulty which we must face directly is the application of the struggle which is often made. We are told that we have a picture of a man wrestling in prayer with God. The sentiment and the phraseology sound fine, but it does not fit the context. Let us move then to the passage itself and see what it teaches. We must avoid the temptation of bringing our sermons into the passage and making the passage conform to our interpretation.

The thought of verse 24 is *Wrestling*. It is critical to see that the text states, "There wrestled a man with him." In other words, the wrestling is initiated by the man and not by Jacob. Who is the man? Our text simply calls him a man. Hosea 12 tells us that it is the angel of the Lord. Jacob's own testimony is that he had seen God.

Allow a little imagination for just a moment. Jacob must have been as tense as a man could be. Pacing back and forth in the dark of the night, he is prepared for anything. Every sense is on alert. Every muscle is tense and awaiting a call to service. Apprehension and uncertainty fill his mind. Suddenly, silently, from out of the dark, an unknown assailant leaps upon him and commences wrestling with him.

Can you sense the questions running through our patriarch's mind? His body is struggling to survive and his mind is questioning: "Is this Esau?" "Is this a messenger of Esau?" "With whom am I fighting?"

The struggle continues through the night until the breaking of the day. An interesting consideration here is that, while it is difficult to give Jacob's age with exactness, he must be between 90 and 100 years old at this point in time. Yet he is able to wrestle all night with his assailant!

In verse 25 the thought is *Weakness*. When the man sees that Jacob will not give up, He touches the hollow of Jacob's thigh and puts it out of joint. All hope on Jacob's part of continuing the struggle is lost. A wrestler with a weakened leg cannot wrestle. All Jacob can do is to cling. God was testing Jacob to see if he would long for the blessing which He alone could provide.

Jacob began his life with a struggle. Back in chapter 25:22 he struggled in the womb with his brother. His entire life has been characterized by struggling and supplanting. These two issues must be confronted and judged before the fullness of blessing which God has for him can be known. This then is the lesson of Penuel: God subdued a man and caused his flesh to wither. God attacked a man at his strongest natural point to teach him that weakness is the way to strength.

Some may question how God could so richly bless Jacob in Laban's employ when, in truth, Jacob had not been fully restored to God. We have to remember that many times the goodness of God leads to repentance (Rom 2:4). Also, when evil men attack the people of God or abuse them, God takes up the cause of His own. Israel was guilty of carrying the idols of the heathen gods with them through the wilderness, yet when Balaam sought to curse them, God blessed (Num 23, 24).

As we continue down the chapter the thought of verses 26-27 is *Witnessing to Truth*. God has addressed Jacob's self-reliance and dealt him a crushing blow. God still has another issue to bring up. In his weakness, Jacob must have begun to appreciate the real identity of his assailant. Jacob thought that he had been fighting against Laban for twenty years and that now he must confront Esau. Jacob had to learn that it is really God whom he had been resisting for so long.

In his weakness, Jacob can only cling. Realizing the identity of his assailant, he cleaves and cries for a blessing. To this request, he hears a strange but familiar question: "What is thy name?" Once before he had been asked a similar question. But in his desire to obtain the blessing, he had answered, "I am Esau thy firstborn" (27.19). Now he will have to own that he is only Jacob - the supplanter. He owns his past and his character. It must be brought out into the presence of God and judged. God not only touched Jacob's thigh but touched his conscience as well.

In verses 28-30 the thought is the *Wealth of Blessing* which the broken man receives. The Lord gives him a new name - Israel. Definitions differ here: some suggest "God fights"; others, "God rules or orders"; a number of margins still give "A prince with God". It would appear that "God fights" is the closest to the meaning of his name. He is no longer a supplanter but a man whose name would carry with it the reminder of Penuel. To generations to come, who would take the name of the patriarch as the name of the nation, it would be a cogent reminder of God's ability to withstand every foe. That night, Jacob lost a wrestling match but won a great blessing as a result.

Paul expressed similar truth in 2 Corinthians 12:9 when he spoke of his weakness and the power of God: "Most gladly therefore will I rather glory in my infirmities, that the power of Christ may rest upon me ... when I am weak, then am I strong." Gideon learned it by the threshing floor. Saints of every age since then have tasted their own helplessness and frailty that they might know God's power.

Jacob, in turn, asks the Angel of the Lord His name. However, Jacob, while advancing in the school of God, is not yet morally fit to receive such a disclosure. He must return to Bethel and purge the idols and the uncleanness before God can give him this revelation.

Jacob's blessing was at least two-fold that night. He received a new name, Israel; he also received a revelation of God. Throughout the book of Genesis (and, it can be argued, throughout Scripture) the concept of blessing is linked with revelations of God to the soul. At times it is in salvation while at other times it is in spiritual growth and maturity. Jacob's blessings are intended to prepare him for the encounter with Esau. Our knowledge of God is not merely for the sake of data collection but for the purpose of spiritual strengthening amidst the trials of life.

To Jacob, Penuel is a turning point, a crisis in his life. He commemorates the place and the event with a name: Peniel, stating, "I have seen God face to face, and my life is preserved." It is absolutely essential, dear young believer, to have experiences with God. Without them, there is no true usefulness. Without them, there is no growth. They are painful and costly at times. Witness our patriarch in his experience here. There are no shortcuts or exemptions in this school.

In verses 31-32 we have the Withering of the Flesh. One of the great results of being in the presence of God is that the flesh withers.

Jacob learns that here. From this day forward he bears the marks of his experience with God. His thigh, the place of natural energy and fruitfulness, becomes marked by death. He halts for the remainder of his days. As he leaves Penuel, he is less fit naturally now to face Esau; but he is more fit spiritually.

Jacob spent the night at Jabbok and wrestled with the man. The words of verse 31 are delightful: "the sun rose upon him." A new day has begun for Jacob, a day in which he is marked by Israel character rather than that of Jacob. The night of self-will and self-reliance has past and he moves in dependence upon God.

It is thrilling to consider the last reference in our Bibles to someone's "thigh." Here in Genesis 32, it marked a man in his weakness and failure. When we turn to Revelation 19:11-16, we see the Lord Jesus coming forth from heaven. Upon *His thigh* will be a name: "KING OF KINGS AND LORD OF LORDS." No mark of weakness in Him. No need to halt. He will *tread* the winepress of the wrath of God. No confession of "Jacob." Rather, His name shall be called "The Word of God." The contrasts are marked and delightful.

The Final Encounter with Esau (33:1-20)

The Peril which God Removed (vv 1-7)

The preparation for the meeting (vv 1-3)

With a few brush strokes of his pen, the writer of Genesis paints the tension and drama of the moment. "And Jacob lifted up his eyes , and looked, and, behold, Esau came, and with him four hundred men." Imagine the thoughts racing through Jacob's mind. "Why such a large army?" "Will he have pity on the women and children?" "He must be beyond negotiating since he has refused the presents." These and a multitude of other thoughts fight for space in Jacob's mind.

Hastily he makes preparation for the meeting. The family is strategically placed with special care for Rachel and Joseph. Then, perhaps to everyone's surprise, Jacob moves to the front. The time and usefulness of hiding and cringing is over. There is no hope for Jacob. He cannot run or fight such a company.

As Jacob approaches his brother, he bows seven times as a token of humility and honour. Some may see in this a sign of mock humility or hypocrisy, but doesn't Jacob owe at least this to Esau after his treatment of his brother? This is not to excuse the carnal choices of Esau. But Jacob had not acted righteously to his brother when at home.

The peaceful encounter (vv 4-5)

Suddenly, Esau breaks into a run. Then, to the amazement of Jacob and others, his arms are around Jacob's neck and tears are flowing from his eyes. God, the God who could subdue a Laban and hold in check his evil propensity, is able to control and to change an Esau. God answered Jacob's prayer of chapter 32. We learn that when God directs and we obey He is able to handle the circumstances. At Jabbok, Jacob found a struggle which he did not expect; here, at the meeting with Esau, he expected a struggle but did not have to encounter it.

Jacob has learned that sin brings Wasted Years (in Laban's house), Needless Tears (at Peniel), and Groundless Fears (in meeting Esau). God is sufficient for all of these.

The presentation of the family (vv 6-7)

One by one the family is presented to Esau. They are, "The children which God hath graciously given thy servant." With what amazement Esau looks on. Perhaps the very size of the family and the riches of Jacob are a silent testimony to the fact that God has indeed blessed Jacob and preserved him.

The Present which Jacob Bestowed (vv 8-11)

Failure in testimony

It is difficult to be sure if Jacob's language is simply a courteous eastern style of speech or if it is tinged with his old tendency to employ a bit of guile. Certainly, some of his expressions reveal the latter.

He speaks of Esau as "my lord." The man who had just seen God "face to face" at Peniel now tells Esau, "I have seen thy face, as though I had seen the face of God."

Faithfulness in testimony

But Jacob also rises to great heights in the same encounter. We should not think this strange. Who amongst us has not been marked by moments of both spiritual victory and folly almost simultaneously?

Jacob owns that all he now possesses is from God: "God hath dealt graciously with me." There is also an interesting contrast between the words which Jacob and Esau employ: Esau says, "I have much ... keep that thou hast." In turn, Jacob replies, "God hath dealt graciously with me ... I have ALL."

The word employed in verse 9 is a gift offering; but in verses 10-11, Jacob presses Esau to receive his "barak" or blessing.

The Parting which Guile Effected (vv 12-15)

The proposal (v 12)

Esau offers to accompany his brother and his family in their return journey. Undoubtedly, the dangers of the way and the relative vulnerability of a man traveling with his children and family prompt Esau.

The pretence (vv 13-14)

However, Jacob, secretly, has no intention of returning to live side by side with Esau. In this, Jacob is probably very wise. Reconciliation over the past does not guarantee a future free of strife. A bit of distance is probably prudent. Jacob, however, in true Jacob fashion, will get to his end in a less than straight manner. While fellowship with a "profane person" was not possible, Jacob could have been more open and transparent.

His reasoning is excellent. His argument would appeal to an outdoorsman such as Esau. The hard and fast pace of Esau and his army would not suit the flocks and the children. Jacob does not wish to be a hindrance to Esau. He will come as the flocks are able to be moved. Perhaps, Jacob's shepherd heart is seen here and his concern for the flocks and sheep is genuine, but he may be employing it for his own ends.

The protection declined (v 15)

A final offer of protection is made by Esau, and this again is refused by Jacob, with the assurance that he will follow behind and arrive at Seir to be with Esau. Centuries later Ezra would also refuse protection, this time from a king, for the sake of the testimony (Ezra 7).

The Pilgrim who lost his Way (vv 16-20)

Succoth - the builder (vv 16-17)

Little is said about Jacob's sojourn in Succoth. He builds a house and makes booths for his cattle. The last house builder in Genesis, Lot, ended in tragedy. Jacob's building career seems to be at odds with his calling: a pilgrim dwelling in tents (Heb 11:9). It is, perhaps, for this reason that the Spirit of God passes over the period with no mention of spiritual growth or profit.

The time spent here must have been a few years, since by chapter 34 Dinah is a mature woman. But time outside the will of God is a blank in our lives.

Shechem - the business man (vv 18-19)

From Succoth, east of Jordan, Jacob travels to Shechem and returns to the land of Canaan. Though in the land, he is probably not where

God intends him to be. When God speaks to him in chapter 35, he is directed to Bethel. The call of God in chapter 31:13, "I am the God of Bethel ... get thee out from this land, and return unto the land of thy kindred," strongly argues that God's intention for Jacob was Bethel and not Shechem. Spiritual compromise will carry a heavy price, as Jacob will discover. The ominous expression given by the Spirit that he "pitched his tent before the city" is an echo of the choice which Lot made years earlier.

All this is of immense importance. For if Jacob is in the wrong place, then an altar (v 20) cannot preserve him. A man in the wrong place, outside of the will of God, is not only losing time, but courting disaster.

Jacob now purchases ground. God had promised him the land free of charge. Abraham, it is true, had an emergency need for a burial place and had to purchase land; but Jacob did not need to be in the land-speculating business. The fact that he buys land and erects an altar suggests that he intended to settle down in this area, without returning to his kindred as instructed in chapter 31:13. Incomplete obedience is really disobedience.

Some seventeen centuries later, another figure is seen sitting at a well, on this parcel of ground which Jacob had given to his son Joseph at some time. His arrival and visit bring blessing to the people of the area and especially to a woman of questionable character (John 4). How different His conduct and ways from those of Dinah and Jacob's sons (Genesis 34)!

The altar - the believer (v 20)

To Jacob's credit, he seeks to establish testimony for God in an idolatrous land. But, as we shall see, an altar in the wrong place cannot preserve Jacob from sorrow and loss. Disobedience cannot be ameliorated by an altar of worship.

CHAPTER 9

The Blight

Genesis 34

The only real spiritual disease is to think that one is perfectly well
(G. K. Chesterton)

The divinely inspired portrait artist has reserved some of his darkest hues for the chapter before us. No bright colours suggesting hope are placed on the canvas. No vibrant hues depicting the dynamic, Spirit-directed life of Jacob grace the scene. All the dark somber tones reserved for tragedy, despair, and defeat are present.

Commentators are quick to point out, and rightly so, that the faithful presentation of character weaknesses and failure is an indirect evidence of the inspiration of Scriptures. Biographers, as a rule, unless interested in appealing to lust and base desires, do not frequently portray the sordid details of their "heroes". God does not delight in revealing the failure of His saints. In fact, in the New Testament God is silent about the failures of His Old Testament saints.

Cynics are likewise quick to point to Genesis 34 as an example of what they call the sordid sections of the Scripture in an attempt to discredit its value. Amazingly, while ignorant of so much of Scripture, they are well acquainted with a few sections in which human behaviour is revealed in its depravity.

But God has something even greater for us in this chapter concerning Jacob's life. All the Old Testament was written for our learning and presents lessons of rich and valuable spiritual significance. What lessons are here for us?

In Genesis 34 we see:

- the Danger of Incomplete Obedience
- the Disaster of Inconsistent Associations
- the Disorder from Inadequate Headship
- the Disgrace from Intense Anger.

This is sobering; for while most of us reading this chapter would view the events at a distance, who among us has not been guilty of incomplete obedience? Or who does not look back on occasions marked by failure in our role of headship in the family or of inconsistency in our associations? Has anger never welled up so rapidly and forcibly that potential harm to your testimony may have resulted had God not intervened? So this chapter is not a distant, irrelevant episode. It is "for our learning."

The Fault within the Family

As noted in the previous chapter, Jacob has been guilty of incomplete obedience. As a result, when danger arose, he forgot the promises of God and these past experiences of God's deliverance. He had been miraculously preserved from Laban's anger and Esau's revenge. Now he fears for his life once again. The disciples in the boat forgot the past deliverance they had known (Mark 4 and then Mark 6). They failed to remember that the One who fed 5,000 could just as easily feed 4,000 (Mark 6 and Mark 8). Jacob forgot the angelic host which met him in chapter 32 and the divine wrestler who blessed him there as well. Solomon, likewise, forgot his past experiences with God and turned to idolatry in his old age. Sadly, we also forget His past mercies when faced with new challenges. Thus Peter, guided by the wisdom of the Spirit of God, wrote to "stir up" the believers and to put them in "remembrance" (2 Peter 1:12; 3:1).

Dinah was likely a teenager at this point in her life. What may have begun as innocent curiosity soon devolved into a tragic situation and defilement.

It must be stressed here that not every family disaster results from disobedience by parents. Many godly parents have wept tears of bitter remorse over choices that their children have made. Family failure must never be viewed as a proof of parental failure. What Genesis 34 teaches us is the tremendous danger of coming short of the will of God and the door that it opens for additional problems. In contrast, the father of the prodigal (Luke 15) was not the one who needed to repent; it was the errant son who had to change.

The Failure of World Bordering

Shechem! What thoughts link themselves with this place! What stark contrasts can be found here! Allow your mind to move centuries from the scene about to unfold in Jacob's life. Come to a well in Shechem and watch as a lone traveller, dressed in obvious Judean garb, sits to rest at a well. Shortly, a Samaritan woman comes to draw water: perfect purity meeting fallen, immoral humanity. What follows bows us in worship as we trace the grace, tenderness, and faithfulness of the Lord Jesus at the well. The Man of Sychar's well is "altogether lovely."

The scene at Shechem in Genesis 34 stands, tragically, in bold contrast. A pure and undefiled woman meets a man and sin and defilement result. How tragic! How did all this come about? Can we discover the initial acts which opened the way for this calamity? We noted at the close of chapter 33 that Jacob appears to have come short of God's intention for him. Rather than at Bethel, he settles in Succoth and then, crossing into the land, he comes to Shechem. Despite the tent and the altar, he is short of God's place for him. A man in the wrong place is a man in danger. Perhaps one of the most remarkable features of Genesis 34 is that God's name is not mentioned. The next chapter will begin abruptly with, "And God said unto Jacob ...", but God is absent from the chapter here.

With the family settled in Shechem, Dinah, perhaps drawn by curiosity at first, goes out to "see the daughters of the land." Whether her curiosity arose from the protective life of Jacob's family, or from a wish to be "culturally broadened," she is soon found in the company of the daughters of the land and then in the company of Shechem. Defilement follows and then an offer of marriage.

It is helpful to notice that two different words in the original are both translated "defiled" in the chapter. In verse 2, the word carries the thought of taking captive or oppressing. This suggests that it was a forcible act against Dinah. The word employed in verses 5, 13, 27 simply means to render "unclean."

The danger of being in the wrong place cannot be over emphasized. Two elements are required for a fall: opportunity and desire. Any experienced believer can look back to occasions when, through spiritual weakness or weariness, desire raised its grasping hand. God in His mercy did not allow opportunity to come. But then on other occasions, opportunity did present itself. However, through the faithful ministry of our High Priest we were prepared and spiritually strong to stand. To intentionally move outside the will of God and place ourselves in a vulnerable position is to expose ourselves to opportunity when in the weakest of spiritual conditions. Only disaster can follow.

The Fierceness of Carnal Anger

When the deed was done and known, it is striking that Jacob is silent. He does not speak until verses 30-31 when it is too late. There is an abdication of leadership and headship in the entire encounter. The vacuum in leadership is quickly filled by the sons of Jacob. As in every occasion when leadership is abandoned, failure ensues. When leadership fails to lead, then others will come to the fore and move according to their own will.

Genesis is the sad record of surrendered leadership: Adam followed the lead of Eve; Abram followed the lead and suggestion of Sarai; Rebekah attempted to wrest leadership from Isaac; and now it is Jacob and his sons.

When Hamor arrives to speak with Jacob, it is Jacob's sons who take over and "negotiate." In verse 7, the sons of Jacob "were very wroth."

The sin committed against God, Dinah, and Jacob's family is great. Yet, from among these righteously indignant sons, two would themselves later commit moral evil: Judah with his daughter-in-law, and Reuben with his father's concubine, Bilhah.

In all the dealings of Hamor and Shechem, there is no sense of guilt or shame. There is no confession of wrong done or of sin committed. The offer of marriage is in a measure honourable, yet it does not excuse the sin committed. We may try to acquit them on the basis of the normal practices in their culture, but in the eyes of God it was still sin and defilement.

The sons of Jacob engage in a game of mental gymnastics. The sin of Shechem is countered by the rationalizing and sin of the sons. They answer deceitfully (v 13) and excuse it by telling themselves, "because he had defiled Dinah." The expression "deceitfully," means "with guile." The genetic pool appears to be running uninhibited in the family. These are true "sons" of Jacob. One of life's most frightening and sobering lessons is to see our own weaknesses and failures reproduced in our children.

The negotiations are complete. The stipulation is that the men of the city must all submit to circumcision before Dinah can be married to Shechem. The sons apparently feel no hesitation in employing the sign of their covenant with God as a tool of deceit in their dealings with men. To Jacob's credit, the ultimate intention of Levi and Simeon is not known to him at this point in time. In Genesis 49:6 he speaks of their "secret conference," of their anger, and of self-will. His mention of it upon his deathbed is a poignant reminder that Jacob never forgot the blot on his testimony.

Hamor and Shechem hurry back to the city to persuade all the men of the city about the wisdom of the terms made with Jacob's sons. In their argument we learn what is important to men. Hamor and Shechem tell the men of the financial advantages which will accrue to them by this step. It is this consideration which appears to sway the men of the city to comply with the terms of the agreement. The combining of religion and financial gain has longed plagued the testimony of God; here it was used to persuade men to embrace a sign of the covenant without the reality of the covenant in their souls.

On the third day, when the men of the city are all disabled due to the surgical operation which they had undergone, Simeon and Levi arise and slay all the men of the city. Hamor and Shechem are mentioned as particular targets of their anger. Dinah is "rescued" from the home of her fiancé and returns to the family. Simeon and Levi, sons of Leah, thought that they had to avenge the dishonour done to their sister, a daughter of Leah. Was their lack of consideration for their father the fruit of the obvious preference Jacob had for Rachel and Joseph? Did they feel they had to take measures into their own hands? Add to that the observation that when Jacob rebuked them there was no sense of remorse or apology given to their father. They were acting in a rebellious and defiant manner, disregarding their father's name.

There is little question that Shechem had sinned against God and against Dinah. He was worthy of punishment. But the sons of Jacob were guilty of doing a right thing in a wrong way and with a wrong motive. Sadly, discipline in God's assembly can also, at times, be carried out in a wrong way and with wrong motives. We should never discipline to get rid of someone. Nor should discipline go beyond the boundary of Scripture. Cruelty marked the actions of Levi and Simeon. Secret counsels bred the plot of brutality and harshness. Discipline should always be with a view to the honour of the name of the Lord being upheld, and for the restoration of the offender. Yet the fruit of their act was to make Jacob's name to be dishonoured among the heathen. When discipline is carried out in personal (not righteous) anger, we add carnality to carnality; the results are rarely for God's glory.

The sons of Jacob then arise and sack the city. Possessions are appropriated; women and children are taken captive. The city is razed, and vengeance is taken upon it and its men. The sword has answered for Simeon and Levi against the men of Shechem. As a result of their use of the sword, Simeon and Levi will know the displeasure of their father and loss at his parting benediction. But in one of the most amazing instances of God turning circumstances to good (i.e. their scattering in

Israel, 49:7), God will use the scattering of Levi to be a blessing to the nation. It is, once again, their use of the sword (Exodus 32) which brings upon them an eternal blessing. In this instance the sword is used to honour God and perform His will.

The Flight of a Disgraced Man

The deed perpetrated, Jacob realizes the need to escape. It appears from his words to Simeon and Levi that he is more concerned with his reputation and safety than with his testimony: "Ye have troubled *me* to make *me* to stink ... gather themselves together against *me,* and slay *me.*"

Flight has not been foreign to Jacob's experience. He had to flee from Esau due to his (Jacob's) deceitfulness. He had to flee from Laban due to Laban's deceitfulness. Now he must take to his heels once more due to the deceitfulness of his sons. God was teaching Jacob the evil of deceit. From this moment on, Jacob appears to have learned his lesson and to abandon deceit from his list of coping mechanisms.

This is the last mention of Dinah's name other than in Genesis 46:15 in Jacob's genealogy. Her desire led to defilement (vv 5, 13, 27) and the blight on the family. The danger of social relationships with the unconverted is very real and palpable. She fades from the page of sacred history, a defiled and tragic figure.

The Faithfulness of God

Far more was at stake here than Jacob or any of his family realized. The offer by Hamor that the Israelites settle down and live together with them would have meant several things: it would have hindered the progress of Jacob back to Bethel and the blessing he was to receive there. But, more importantly, it would have meant the mingling of the holy seed with the Gentiles of the land. This would have led to the seed of Judah not being kept pure and would have had implications for the coming of the Messiah. Thus we see that behind this event was far more than the failure of Dinah and the lust of Shechem; at the root of this was the strategy of Satan to impede the coming of the Messiah. Invariably, deeds of devotion and deeds marked by dereliction have consequences far beyond what we can measure or conceive.

What of the failure on Jacob's part? What recourse is before a parent who recognizes failure? Is it proper to give up responsibility and to abdicate further the divine role of headship and its obligations? The only course is to return to Bethel and to assume the place as head of the family which is Jacob's by divine appointment. The remedy every believer has when faced with failure is first to confess that failure to God and enjoy the forgiveness offered. Then, the choice must be made to learn from the past or to live under the past. This is the truth of the next chapter.

CHAPTER 10

Back to Bethel

Failures, repeated failures, are finger posts on the road to achievement. One fails forward toward success (C. S. Lewis)

The theme of chapter 35 is "The Restoration of a Believer". It would be wrong to think that the work of restoration in Jacob's soul had not begun before this. Events as far back as Laban's house had started this great work in the soul of the Patriarch. But the chapter before us will see this work brought to fruition. Jacob returns home.

A number of interesting lines of thought are presented here. Once we realize that the Spirit of God has brought the death of Isaac into this chapter, years before its actual occurrence (Isaac died when Joseph was 29 years old, at which time Joseph would have been in Egypt for 12 years), we sense that we are being taught moral and not chronological lessons.

One of the lessons is "The Burials which Accompany Restoration." There are perhaps five burials in Genesis 35: the strange gods were buried (v 4), Deborah was buried beneath an oak (v 8), Jacob's name is buried and he is again addressed as Israel (v 10), Rachel is buried on the way to Bethlehem (v 19), and the burial of Isaac serves as a fitting conclusion to the chapter (v 29). The spiritual significance of this will be touched upon later.

Restoration is not, however, simply a negative issue. Along with the burials, the chapter will detail "The Building which Follows Restoration," and then, "The Blessing which Results from Restoration."

In terms of the spiritual development which Genesis opens up, there is a principle contained in chapters 35-37: in Chapter 35 we have burials, in chapter 36 we have the end of Edom, and in chapter 37 we have the introduction of Joseph, the son of his father's love. In chapter 35 we have links with an old life which are severed. In chapter 36, the profane man and his line are traced and set aside. Then, in chapter 37, we have a man introduced who displays Christ-like features. There is a moral progression and development seen in these chapters.

Consider, then, the chapter as it unfolds.

The Command to Arise - the Voice of God (v 1)

In our previous chapter we had the voice of Jacob - "And Jacob said ..." (34:30), and the voices of Simeon and Levi - "And they said ..." (34:31). Now we have the voice of God - "And God said ..." (35:1). Into the darkness and distress of man's sin and failure, the voice of God resounds with clarity and instruction: "Arise, go up to Bethel, and dwell there ... God, that appeared unto thee." All genuine restoration begins with the voice of God being heard in the believer's soul.

Jacob is reminded of a place to dwell - Bethel, of a position to resume - a worshipper at the altar, and of a promise kept - God that appeared when he fled from Esau. The voice that spoke in rebuke and direction must also have given Jacob some degree of comfort, knowing that God had not abandoned him. Jacob certainly had grounds for concern: he had stopped short of the will of God and had spent wasted years in Shechem, leaving in such disgrace that the name of Jehovah was linked with the most heinous of deeds. Yet, despite Jacob's disobedience and failure, God did not forsake him. One of the most encouraging lessons from Jacob's life is that "failure is not final" with God. Restoration rests on the mercy and grace of God just as much as does salvation.

Jacob's partial obedience was costly. He had been told to return not only to his country, but also to his kindred (31:3). He stopped short and paid a huge price for his failure. Further, he had made a promise back in Genesis 28 that if God would be with him and bring him again to his father's house in peace that he would return to Bethel. His direction was "up" geographically, morally, and spiritually.

The Charge to Adjust - the Vital Steps (vv 2-5)

God does not command the events which follow in verses 2-5. It is spiritual intelligence which marks Jacob here. There are things which are not consistent with Bethel and its altar. Behaviour and character must be adjusted. Jacob, to his commendation, now takes the place of leader. His failure in leadership was patent, but his change is also clearly seen. His word is clear and unambiguous: "Put away ... be clean ... change your garments ... arise, and go up." Consecration led to cleansing and to changes in their lives. Peter in his epistle follows the same sequence of events in a believer's life: we are to gird up the loins of our minds, to be holy, and to pass the time of our sojourning here in fear (1 Peter 1:13-17).

Jacob gives direction and focus to his family. Much has come into his life. Laban's house and idolatry have taken their toll of Jacob's family. Were these the idols stolen from Laban? Were they idols that had infiltrated the family during its many years in Shechem? Were they part of the spoil of Shechem? Bethel demands reality. A hasty but thorough collection of idols and earrings is taken. A fit burial is given them under the oak in Shechem. What was linked with Shechem must be left in Shechem!

The idols suggest that which is inconsistent Godward; the need to be clean reminds us of inward adjustment; the change of garments points to what the world sees. Many claim that only the inward and Godward are important in spiritual things. The great difficulty with that way of thinking is that the world cannot see my heart. They can only see my "garments," my outward testimony. I am responsible to be sure that the outward is consistent with the inward. It is vital to see, however, that the first area of change is a relationship toward God – the idols need to be put away. A mere outward change of garments without an inward change in God-fearingness will not avail. All restoration must begin in the heart and with my attitude and relationship with God.

As Jacob journeys, the fear of God restrains the cities round about so that no one thinks of retaliation. God in His sovereignty moves to Jacob's defense. There is no need to justify God. He is sovereign and does according to His own counsels. Jacob is a marked man, except for the hand of God upon the cities. God had intervened in protecting him from Laban and Esau; now His hand is evident protecting him from the cities around him on his journey. Someone has well-noted the parallel with, and yet the difference from, the mark placed upon Cain which afforded him "protection."

In submission to the divine edict, Jacob enjoyed divine security. For the child of God the pathway of submission and obedience, while it may entail sorrow and trial, is always a pathway which enjoys both His presence and His protection.

The Construction of the Altar - the Visible Sign (vv 6-8)

Jacob and all who are with him arrive at Bethel. No one is exempt from the return. On his arrival, he rebuilds the altar and names it El Bethel, or "The God of the House of God." Only a brief time before he built an altar and called it El-elohe-Israel, "God the God of Israel." But now he shows spiritual maturity. He has progressed to appreciate not only the House of God, but the God of the House of God. This is the spiritual height seen in 1 Timothy.

Others have pointed out the parallel with Psalm 43. There, the longing of the Psalmist is not merely to arrive at the holy hill and the house of God, but to "God my exceeding joy" (v 4). Beyond the visible and tangible, which marked the worship and ritual of Israel, the devout Israelite saw the invisible God and found everything in Him.

Sadly, the departure from Bethel and his long absence led to the altar being in disrepair. While there was an altar in Shalem, and he was technically in the land, the lack of any mention of worship at the altar must have some significance. Having come short of total obedience to God's command, genuine worship does not mark him as it will in Bethel.

In the pathway of restoration, there are sorrows - the next event in the chapter is the death and burial of Deborah. This fills Jacob with great sadness as he names the place, Allon-bachuth, the "Oak of Weeping." Deborah was his mother Rebekah's nurse. It may be that she sent her to Jacob when he was in Laban's house; or it may be that upon the (unmentioned) death of Rebekah, Deborah asked and received permission to go to her mistress' favourite son. In whatever way we understand it, she was Jacob's tie with an old life. Progress to Hebron will mean that not only the things of the old life must be buried, but the ties that bound us to it must be buried as well.

She must have had some special bond with Jacob as servants were rarely given burials marked by memorials and weeping. His deep affection must have been linked to happy memories in the home of his mother under the tutelage of Deborah as his nurse.

The Confirming Appearance - the Visitation of the Sovereign (vv 9-15)

In verse 9 we learn of the divine *Estimation* of Jacob's time in Padan-Aram: "God appeared unto Jacob again, when he came out of Padan-Aram." There was no appearing in the far-off land. Now that Jacob has made the move, God appears to him. In the reckoning of God, years which do not contain fellowship with God are not of value. The Scripture does not mention Shechem but Padan-Aram. The years of partial obedience appear almost as a blank, an empty page in Jacob's life. It is reminiscent of Hebrews 11:29, 30 where 40 years of wandering and failure are deleted and only the two triumphs of faith – the Red Sea crossing and the fall of Jericho – are recorded. None of this gives us licence for straying or self will; in contrast it magnifies the grace of God in our lives.

How thankful we can be for the small word "again" which appears in verse 9. It reminds us of the mercy and grace of God. He did not forsake His servant. In a similar manner, God spoke to Jonah "the second time" (Jonah 3:1); He tenderly dealt with Elijah in a similar manner, and in wondrous grace He called Samuel three times. How great are His mercies!

We are introduced to the divine *Transformation* in verse 10: "Thy name shall not be called any more Jacob, but Israel." He had been given the name "Israel" at Peniel but had not lived a life consistent with it. In the land, restored, with an altar, Jacob should now feel morally the obligation to live the "Israel" life.

To the restored patriarch is given a fresh *Revelation* of his God. "I am El Shaddai" (v 11). Abraham had learned this name in chapter 17:1; Isaac came into the good of it in chapter 28:3. One of the blessings of restoration to Jacob, however, is this fresh revelation of the character and sufficiency of his God.

In obedience to God, moving in the pathway of God, and returning to the House of God, Jacob enjoyed a fresh revelation of the character of God. Gaining the knowledge of God is the most precious pursuit of life.

God reveals His name at Bethel. Jacob asked for this at Peniel but did not get it. He receives it by grace at Bethel, even without asking. This is the last revelation of God in Genesis. From this point on, God will appear and reveal his purposes in dreams.

A renewed *Confirmation* of the covenant is given to Jacob. It is of importance to note that every mention of the covenant blessings to the patriarchs, with the exception of the initial appearing to Abram in Ur, is made in the land. God does not appear and promise blessing even to His chosen patriarchs when out of the land. The practical implications are tremendous. Our enjoyment of the purposes and blessings of God are known only in the path of His will.

"And Jacob set up a pillar ... and he poured a drink offering thereon, and he poured oil thereon." Jacob's act reveals that he now enjoys a renewed *Appreciation* of God and the blessings which are his in the covenant. This is the first drink offering in Scripture. In Genesis 28, it is only oil on the pillar; here it is oil and wine. The joy, of which the drink offering speaks, is known by the man of God when he is in the right place. Every drink offering in the Old Testament is in the land.

The Cloud of Adversity - the Vale of Sorrow (vv 16-20)

Immediately after the scene of joy in verses 9-15, we are introduced to a scene of sorrow. The natural mind is stunned to think that amidst the many blessings of restoration there is this dark cloud. The cynical mind goes much further and mocks the idea of restoration and devotion to a God who brings only sorrow.

But there is a dimension which is often overlooked. How would Jacob have reacted to Rachel's death had it occurred in Padan-aram or on the way to meet Esau? Would he have resolutely and courageously challenged the one and met the other? Is it possible that restoration strengthened him for this singular overwhelming experience? Restoration fortified him for trial. He may never have risen to the heights he did (v 19) had he been away from God.

But tragedy is followed by triumph. Grief and sorrow name the child Ben-oni. Faith calls the child Benjamin - son of my right hand. It has been pointed out by others that this dichotomy of meaning - "son of my sorrow" and "son of my right hand" - can be traced in each reference in the New Testament which brings together the Lord Jesus and His mother Mary. She expressed sorrow in her encounters with Him, culminating at the cross (John 19:25-27). Yet, on each of these occasions, He was the Son of His Father's right hand, accomplishing His will and bringing delight to His heart.

Rachel dies when there is only a little way to go to Bethlehem. Something of Jacob's sorrow can be seen from his account of it in chapter 48:7. He is no indifferent, callous husband. In his sorrow he erects a testimony to her memory. The pillar-builder has this one final pillar to build - the ultimate of life's sorrows. She is not buried in the cave at Machpelah. It is significant that this is the one pillar which Jacob does not name. Restoration involved the loss of his dearest affection. There must be significance to the words of Scripture that Jacob buried Rachel, but it was "Israel (that) journeyed". The ways of God are a seeming paradox at times. It is in John's Gospel that the incredible statement is made that the Lord Jesus calls us His friends (John 15:14). Yet it is in John's Gospel that two specific men are referred to as His friends: John the Baptist (3:29) and Lazarus (11:11). In the former case, John was allowed to languish and ultimately die in prison without even a visit, as far as we know, from the Lord. Lazarus, whom He loved, is allowed to die and then is brought back to life. Our conventional concept of "friendship" would demand that He extricate both with the minimum of suffering, yet in His wisdom He acts differently.

An additional and sobering lesson relates to Rachel's rash and unwise demand on Jacob earlier in chapter 30:1, "Give me children, or else I die!" It was the fruit of envy, impatience, and being discontented with the will of God. Poignantly, it was in childbirth that she did die. Fortunately, God is merciful to us in many of our moments of rash speech; but we cannot presume upon Him.

The Committing of Adultery - the Vile Deed of Sin (vv 21-22)

In verses 21-22 the name, "Israel", is employed three times. In stark contrast to the "Prince with God" is the behaviour of Reuben. Immorality, incest, and shame are the result of his relationship with Bilhah, his father's wife. It may be that he was trying to establish his place as firstborn and heir by claiming the handmaidens of his father. But, along with his immorality, he was premature in his actions. Bilhah had been Rachel's handmaiden and it may have been the death of Rachel which precipitated the sin of Reuben.

Was his sinful deed done on the heels of Rachel's death? Did he add family problems to the personal loss which Jacob mourned? Jacob may have seemed silent at that time of the incident, but he recalled it in later years to Reuben's great shame and loss.

Sin always reaps unforeseen consequences. Through his act, Reuben lost the birthright - the priesthood going to Levi and the birthright to Joseph. Thus, when Jacob gave the coat of many colours to Joseph, bypassing Reuben, Simeon, Levi, and Judah, he was acting righteously and not showing favouritism. All of the first four had disqualified themselves by their actions.

The chapter closes with a listing of Jacob's family - "These are the sons which were born to him in Padan-aram." This much has been salvaged for God from those years - sons who have potential, by the grace of God, to be of use for, and to represent God, in Canaan.

The final return to Isaac must have been an emotional reunion. Had his father forgiven him, having recognized the overruling hand of God? Did Isaac express satisfaction at having seen him again prior to death? Did he recount the details of the death of Rebekah?

But the years of Isaac draw to a close and the chapter is marked at its completion by one final funeral. Isaac, 180 years old, dies. Jacob and Esau unite to honour their father in burial. While the death is not in its chronological order, it is in the right place both morally and structurally. The structure of Genesis is such that it deals with "generations", and we are about to come to the close of Isaac and move on to the generations of Esau (36:1). Morally, it marks the severance of all ties which Jacob has had with the past, and the last phase of his life which he is about to enter.

CHAPTER 11

The Burdens

The Lord will perfect that which doth concern me,
Will do it in so many different ways;
By loss or gain, by high success or failure,
By steady course or unexpected phase
(Winifred Iverson)

The chapters which follow Jacob's return to Bethel would, at first perusal, appear to be related primarily to others. Chapter 36 details the "generations of Esau" (v 1). Chapter 37 onwards relates the beautiful and familiar story of Joseph. There is, however, an unmistakable intertwining of the life of Jacob with the life of Joseph; still evident is the disciplining hand of God and the development of the Israel with whom God has been working for many years. The best of Jacob's life, despite the obvious sorrows, is yet to be.

While the lesson is superficial it is nonetheless salutary: when the spotlight of God's activity appears to turn from one to another believer, it does not mean He has concluded His work with others. He is working in each life simultaneously and allowing His dealings with one believer to have an influence on other believers. The Jacob to which we are introduced in the earlier chapters bears only a faint resemblance to the man we will consider in Genesis 49. God was doing His own unique work with him even while attention is focused on Joseph. A valid argument could be made that the story of Joseph is really the continuing saga of the life of Jacob.

The intervening chapters, Genesis 37-49, detail a number of burdens and sorrows which Jacob would experience. There is the loss of Joseph, the disappointment in Judah's moral behaviour, the famine in Canaan, the loss of Simeon, and the departure of Benjamin with its attendant anxiety. Little wonder that Jacob could exclaim, "... all these things are against me" (42:36). What he did not realize was that God was behind the scenes, working all things after the counsel of His own will for Jacob's spiritual growth and blessing.

Many believers are overwhelmed by the problems of life. Disappointments in the family are among the most bitter. Children are raised, prayed for, taught the Scriptures, and faithfully brought to gospel meetings. Parents look forward to the day when, as a family, they will be together, around the table, remembering the Lord. Yet, the dream is shattered and rebellion and disappointment are known.

Health problems which invade the "golden years" are another source of burden for many. While the time for various looked-for activities such as travel is now available, the frailty of the human vessel imposes limitations. Travel is now limited to a visit to the doctor's surgery!

Difficulties in the workplace, in finances, and in the fellowship can all descend upon a believer and become almost intolerable burdens to bear. As in Jacob's case, these burdens frequently descend in later years. Abraham knew his sorest trial (Genesis 22) near the end of life. The same can be said for Moses, David (the Absalom rebellion), Jeremiah, and others. Perhaps one reason that some trials are left for the end of life is that we have needed the maturing effect of many years to enable us to bear these burdens.

Hostility in the Home

The home to which we are introduced in Genesis 37 is far from the Edenic family scene for which Jacob must have longed. There were sons who were not behaving in a manner that was commendable. Joseph brought unto his father "their evil report" (37:2). His sons had brought his name into dishonour in Shechem; the same was occurring in the land of Canaan. We are not privy to what the "evil report" consisted of, but it grieved the sensitive soul of Joseph to the point that he brought the news to his father. Some might fault Joseph and view him as a spoiled child; but his father's honour motivated him, not selfish interests.

Many godly parents have known similar grief from the choices their adult children have made. Along with rejecting the gospel and the God whom their parents love, unsaved children have lived lives which shocked and saddened their parents. While parents are not responsible for the choices of their adult family, every parent feels an enduring sense of involvement in the lives of his or her children. It seems at times that the godliest of parents have known the greatest sorrows in this regard.

Here, along with the evil report, was the envious rivalry that stamped its character on the house. Reuben, Simeon, and Levi each behaved in a manner which disqualified them for leadership. Judah's actions detailed in chapter 38 may well have occurred at the same time as the events in chapter 37, showing his unfitness (a valuable study is to trace the transformation in Judah up to chapter 44). The first four sons of Leah being set aside, the place of honour would pass to the firstborn of Rachel which was Joseph. The very atmosphere of the house must have been charged with tension and hatred.

His faithful recounting of the dreams to his brothers and his father led to the intensifying of his siblings' hatred for Joseph, to the point that they "could not speak peaceably unto him." Lest any should fault Joseph for relating his dreams, it must be emphasized that this was a communication from God to him, the word of the Lord to Joseph, and fidelity demanded that it be revealed.

The coat of many colours, the communication from God, and the choice by his father, all conspired to make Joseph the object of envy and hatred. The atmosphere in Jacob's home was far from congenial.

Many believers who wear a smile when present at assembly meetings go home to conditions which are unknown to others. There are those with unsaved spouses; there are parents whose teenage and adult children make life in the house very difficult. Sadly, every Christian home is not a paradise. If and when we become aware of these needs, these believers need our support and encouragement.

Lamentation over his Loss

As chapter 37 unfolds, and while our attention is rightly on Joseph, it is Jacob who is seen weeping out his heart at the close of the chapter. Humanly speaking, it seems so unfair that the closing years of his life should be marked by a trial as grave as the one to which he has been called to endure. The "golden years" are, in the estimation of many, a time for enjoying the fruits of a life well lived. Yet for many believers, the fiercest trials are left for the latter years of life. It was so in the case of Abraham as he was called to take Isaac to a mountain in Moriah. Moses underwent this experience as he dealt with the rebellion at the rock. David passed this way in the numbering of the people near the end of his reign. And many believers could add their own personal testimonies here as well.

There is something so pathetic as well as cruel as Jacob is seen weeping over the loss of Joseph, surrounded by sons who could have assuaged his grief in a moment's time. Yet none of them dared relate the truth to their father. A broken heart and broken hopes all combined like a deluge to overwhelm the spirit of the patriarch. All he sees before him in his closing days is the prospect of going down to his grave in sorrow.

It brings God no pleasure to see His children weeping out their days over the folly of family members. Isaiah 1:2-8, however, reminds us that God has known sorrow over incorrigible children. The tears of the godly Jeremiah were but a reflection of the tears of God for His people. Any believer grieving over the actions of a child can find some comfort in the fact that God knows the feelings of your heart!

The loss of a child is one of life's greatest griefs. For a parent to have to bury a child seems so incongruous. Yet there are many who have known this tragedy and sorrow. Added to this is the strain that the death of a small child can have upon a marriage. Since each individual grieves in a different manner, the one who wishes to talk about it may assume that the "quiet" griever does not care as much about what has happened. A distance can begin in the grieving process which may have lethal affects upon the relationship. Each must recognize the individual nature of that process and be supportive of each other.

Distress over Disgrace

We are not told of Jacob's reaction to Judah's behaviour in chapter 38. There can be little doubt, however, that it did not bring him any joy. One son, deprived of all fellowship and family, will stand against temptation in Egypt (ch 39); another son, surrounded by all that could have strengthened him morally, falters miserably in his testimony.

Judah's behaviour carries very little if anything commendable. And yet, even here there may be a glimmer of hope.

The Judah encountered in Genesis 37 at the sale of Joseph is not the Judah who pleads so eloquently for his father in Genesis 44. It is possible that the sad incident with Tamar actually marked a turning point in his life. His confession, "She hath been more righteous than I" (v 26), may signify a repentance and awareness of his own sinfulness. When next encountered in chapter 43, he rises above the suggestion of Reuben (42:37) by offering to be the personal guarantee for Benjamin. He is willing to give his life for another out of an awareness of the grief his father's heart would experience in the event of the loss of Benjamin.

Whether the incident in chapter 38 was a turning point or not, one comforting fact does emerge - the failures of the past do not have to define our lives and limit us. The Judah of Genesis 37 and 38 develops under the disciplining hand of God into the Judah of Genesis 44. His blessing in chapter 49 is commensurate with the change in character which occurred in him.

God is the God of recovery. His disciplining hand, while righteous, is always in mercy. Some of the adjectives and other descriptive phrases used to describe God's mercy are worthy of study and meditation: greatness of (Num 14:19), great (1 Kings 3:6), multitude of (Ps 69:13), plenteous (Ps 86:5, 15), everlasting (Ps 100:5), delight in (Micah 7:18), and abundant (1 Peter 1:3). Couple with this the fact that the most oft repeated sentence in Scripture is, "His mercy endureth forever," and we begin to appreciate something of the wonder of His mercy.

At any time in our experience, we can turn to Him for restoration. While the choices and their consequences of the past cannot be undone, we always have a choice as to the future. Although we dare not presume upon God, part of the wonder of His ways is that He can use even our mistakes to further His purposes and our blessing. The revelation of His character vouchsafed to Moses on the mount is our ultimate security: "The LORD God, merciful and gracious, longsuffering, and abundant in goodness and truth, Keeping mercy for thousands, forgiving iniquity and transgression and sin" (Ex 34:6-7).

Facing Famine

While in Canaan, Jacob and his family knew famine conditions. God "called for a famine" (Ps 105:16). We read that the famine was "sore" in the land. The ten different famines of Scripture may have been allowed for different reasons, but this famine came for a very specific propose. Famine may test commitment as it did with Boaz; famine may, as well, be sent to touch our consciences as it did with David (2 Sam 21). At the onset of this famine, it does not appear that there was any stirring of conscience within the hearts of the ten guilty brothers. They are sent to Egypt to purchase bread. It is interesting that during a period of famine for bread, they did have balm, honey, spices, myrrh, nuts, and almonds (43:11); but they did not have bread.

If we were to think of this in a gospel context, it reminds us that many have an abundance of what can temporarily satisfy, but they still lack the essential bread of life. If applied to the life of a believer, the same reality can be seen. We can go through personal periods of famine condition, filling the void with lots of nice smelling and nice tasting substitutes. But what we vitally need is the Bread of Life. Getting back to the Bread of Life will entail movement, tears, confession, and the restoring kiss and intimacy which marked Joseph as he restored his brothers.

We can know famine in our assembly testimony. Sadly, famine conditions exist in many places. The Word of God is not prominent in many assembly meetings. Opinions and anecdotes are supplied during Bible study instead of the wholesome food of the Word of God.

Believers come and go from assembly meetings with little of the "fine wheat" which the Scriptures contain.

Famine always entails the risk of departure to "greener pastures." It was so with Abraham and Elimelech. It has been true of many others through the centuries. It is not easy to stay by the field of the assembly during days of famine. Moab is very near at hand and accessible. The fields and prospects always seem so much brighter and hopeful. Egypt is beckoning as it did with Abraham, and so convenient. Yet faithfulness does have its rewards. Boaz exited the famine "a mighty man of wealth" (Ruth 2.1).

The Binding of another Brother

It was with heavy hearts that nine brothers returned to their father Jacob in the land of Canaan. They had corn in abundance; the silver they had brought to purchase corn had miraculously returned to their sacks. What they did not have was Simeon. Ten brothers had gone down into Egypt, but only nine came back.

In his wisdom and plan for their restoration and blessing, Joseph had kept Simeon as a pledge of their return and of doing so with Benjamin.

The grief and heartache expressed in Jacob's words are palpable to all: "Me have ye bereaved of my children: Joseph is not, and Simeon is not, and ye will take Benjamin away." Grief has been added to grief, and linked with it is the prospect of Benjamin having to go into Egypt. It almost seems as though Jacob is willing to sacrifice both Simeon and corn to protect Benjamin.

Grief piled on grief has assailed many believers. It was Shakespeare who said that "when sorrows come, they come not as single spies but as battalions" (*Hamlet*, Act 4; scene 5). Wave after wave of calamity engulfed Job, threatening to drown him in sorrow. David knew betrayal, rebellion, and humiliation at the rebellion of Absalom. Mary and Martha had to endure not only the sickness of their brother, but the inexplicable delay of the Saviour and then Lazarus' death. Paul was under house arrest and confined, but then was made aware of brethren preaching out of contention (Phil 1).

Only divine grace can enable a believer to remain steadfast and unmovable amidst the trials of life. Jacob's analysis was that "all these things are against me" (42:36). In reality, God was working to bring him the greatest joy he had ever known.

The Fear for his Favourite

The corn brought out of Egypt did not last forever. A decision must be made about a return trip to Egypt. Simeon has remained there, captive until his brothers' return. The price for a return visit is Benjamin accompanying his nine brothers.

Initially, Jacob is adamant that Benjamin is not to go into Egypt. Judah's promise and guarantee finally move the heart of Jacob, albeit with great reluctance: "If it must be so ... Take also your brother, and arise, go again unto the man. And God Almighty give you mercy before the man ... If I be bereaved of my children, I am bereaved" (43:13-14).

We are not privy to Jacob's anxiety during the time the brothers made their journey down and back to Egypt. There is little doubt that his heart was heavy, with fear and uncertainty rising up to confront him each morning. His experience mirrored that of his grandfather Abraham who was called upon to part with the dearest object of his heart. As with Abraham, however, it would lead to the greatest blessing of his soul. Little did Jacob know what God was about to do in his life. Letting go of what was precious (Benjamin) led to the embracing of what was even more precious (Joseph).

In Christian experience, many have known their own Gethsemane when they have bowed to the will of God, relinquishing their grasp on what was the dearest wish, the closest person, the most cherished of hopes; in so doing, they have discovered a God who blessed beyond their greatest expectation.

The Destiny of Descendants

Jacob joins an elite group of grandparents in Scripture who had an influence on their grandchildren. As noted earlier, Abraham, Isaac, and Jacob lived together in tents (Heb 11:9) for fifteen years, prior to Abraham's death. Those years left indelible impressions on Jacob, very likely whetting his appetite for the birthright.

Genesis ends with the touching reference to Joseph and his great-grandchildren (50:22-23). The place of importance he held in Egypt and the busyness of life did not hinder him from setting time aside for grandchildren. Few grandparents need to be reminded to spend time with their grandchildren, however.

The book of Ruth which begins with burials ends with a birth. Linked with that birth is the mention of a grandmother, Naomi, who nurtured a new life for God. In that babe, Naomi saw not only the resurrection of all her hopes, but the promise for the future. Little did she know that the future would include the Davidic line which would bring blessing to the world. While her vision was circumscribed by the limitations imposed by time, her love and care were not. She nourished a new generation with an eye to the future. Would that all grandparents had a similar exercise!

In the New Testament, Lois stands out as a woman of faith who had an influence on her grandson Timothy (2 Tim 1:5). The Bema of Christ will reveal the value of that impact for God. It certainly involved the teaching of the Temple Scriptures (2 Tim 3:14-17). It transformed a "child" (v 15) into a "man of God" (v 17).

In Exodus 10:2 the people of God were to relate to future generations their experiences with God. Deuteronomy 6:2 speaks of "thy son's son." Psalm 103:17 and 128:6 are also worthy of consideration. Solomon in his proverbs is not silent on the matter, even though he appears to have failed in influencing his own grandsons (Prov 13:22; 17:6).

In the case of Jacob, he claimed a generation for God. The dramatic scene is related in Genesis 48. The aged patriarch is sick. Perhaps Joseph feared that his father's death was near. But the place of weakness, Jacob's bed, became a place of blessing for others. As Joseph brought his two sons, Ephraim and Manasseh to Jacob, the words of the patriarch must have rang out with all the pathos and authority the ancient voice could muster: "they are mine" (v 5, Newberry margin). Jacob would not allow Egypt to have them. Great potential lay before them as sons of the governor of the land. Their prospects were bright. Jacob was saying, in effect, that prospects with God are brighter than those of Egypt. It may well be that Jacob knew the prophecy given to Abraham (Genesis 15) that the Israelites would be slaves in the land, but far better to be a slave and know God than to be a prince and live in darkness.

As grandparents, we should boldly claim our grandchildren for God. We cannot save them, but we can covet them for God, pray for them, and live before them. Our lives should be of such a character that it only adds to their desire to know Christ as Saviour and God as their Father. While it is admirable and legitimate to leave a material inheritance to our grandchildren, what they will value the most is the spiritual heritage which we have bequeathed to them.

Jacob, while enjoying the comforts and blessings of Egypt, saw beyond it all. He had his priorities right. The wealth and splendour of Egypt did not blind him. It was by faith that he blessed the sons of Joseph (Heb 11:21), a faith that saw beyond Egypt, piercing the unseen and viewing eternity.

Each burden he carried eventuated in blessing for Jacob and his family. There is little doubt that as he was experiencing each sorrow, he would have wished life to have been otherwise. But in the end, looking back on his life, he, like all of us, worshipped the God who wrote the script for his life.

CHAPTER 12

The Bedside and the Blessings

When Jacob neared the end of his earthly sojourn, he called his sons together to tell them what should befall them at the end of the days. Here we have recorded, through the lips of Jacob and by the pen of Moses, God's own unfolding, by the Spirit, of the sad history of Israel. Sad history indeed, yet it concludes with blessing from the Lord Himself   (William Reid)

Jacob is presented in many different ways: a patriarch of a family; a pilgrim in a foreign land; a poet in his blessings to his sons; and practically as a son under the disciplining hand of God. But in the chapter before us, we see him as a prophet who, by the Spirit of God, shows keen insight into the character of each of his sons, recognizes their potential and their weaknesses, and affords us a panoramic view of the future of the nation.

Before venturing into chapter 49, allow me to draw together a few strands which will bring us to the bedside scenes of the patriarch.

The Message of a Living Son

Evidence in Genesis

A sense of hopeless despair filled Jacob's heart as expressed in his words in Genesis 42:36: "Me have ye bereaved of my children: Joseph is not, and Simeon is not, and ye will take Benjamin away: all these things are against me." From the ashes of a ruined life, Jacob is roused to fresh hope and joy by the sight of the wagons (45:27). Throughout the book of Genesis and particularly in the life of Jacob, physical tokens of evidence have played a strong role. Isaac was deceived by false evidence; Jacob was deceived by supposed evidence of Joseph's death. Potiphar's wife had "evidence" of Joseph's attempted seduction to show her husband. The tokens which Judah gave to Tamar served as evidence against him. Here the wagons are visible evidence of a living son who was in power and glory in a distant land. These and other tokens of evidence can all be traced through the book.

The wagons and the rich provision sent from Egypt were enough to cause Jacob's heart to "revive" or be rekindled. "It is enough" were the words of Jacob. Proof of a living son had been furnished and he could rest in the assurance that he would see him. It was not Joseph's glory that occupied him; it was his son, Joseph.

The descent of the Spirit and the spiritual blessings made good to each believer are the tokens of a living Saviour at God's right hand. Like Jacob, we can say, "It is enough!"

The Movement into Egypt

The message of a living son and the sight of the wagons caused Jacob to arise from Hebron and begin his journey to Egypt. He travelled perhaps 25 miles and came to Beersheba. Now about to leave the land of Canaan, he stopped and paused before continuing his journey. Did he recall the result of Abraham's sojourn in Egypt during a time of famine? Did he suddenly remember that he had not consulted God about the move? Whatever the reason, he stopped and offered sacrifices, calling on the name of the God of his father, Isaac. Once again it is noted that he does not refer to God as his God until later.

In response to his sacrifices, God graciously answered and confirmed his desire to move into Egypt. God gave him a four-fold assurance. He guaranteed His Presence with Jacob, His Purposes for Jacob and the nation, His Protecting Hand, and His Prosperity.

Every new avenue opened to a believer should have these assurances from God; honest confession, however, demands that we acknowledge that they are often best seen in hindsight rather than when the initial steps are taken.

The expression concerning Joseph putting his hands upon the eyes of Jacob (46:4) may indicate that Jacob would die in Egypt and that Joseph would be the last sight he would see. Joseph would have the honour of closing his father's eyes at his death. It had been 22 years since his eyes had last beheld his son, but now he had the assurance of seeing him and not being separated until death visited him.

(The double call, "Jacob, Jacob," is a reminder of the double calls of Scripture: Genesis 22:11; Exodus 3:4; 1 Samuel 3:10; Luke 10:41; 22:31; Acts 9:4. Each occurred at a very crucial juncture in history.)

Having considered some of these events in Jacob's life, we can now move to the final scenes which mark him in chapters 48-50.

The Meetings

Jacob and Joseph

As Jacob approached the land, he sent Judah ahead to arrange the meeting. It is significant that it was Judah who was sent as he was the mediator who pleaded to spare his father grief over the loss of Benjamin. Judah has risen from the sad profile painted in Genesis 38, to become a leader and dependable man. His life is an encouragement to all who may have started off poorly; each has the opportunity of ending well. Recall the long list of sins for which Solomon made intercession in 2 Chronicles 6. Yet in God's answer in chapter 7 His grace makes clear that whatever the past, "If my people, which are called by my name, shall humble themselves, and pray, and seek my face, and turn from their wicked ways, then will I hear from heaven, and will forgive their sin, and will heal their land" (v 14). Failure is never final; recovery is always possible with God. The remarkable transformation of Judah stands as eloquent testimony to the transforming and restoring grace of God.

The touching reunion of father and son is described in only a few words: "... he fell on his neck, and wept on his neck a good while" (46:29). Joseph shed many tears. To his credit, none were shed for sins of his own (in contrast to David). Such is the joy of Jacob's heart that he can ask no more of life. He is now content to die.

While not wishing to spiritualize too fancifully, one can only ponder the welcome that another Son received from His Father when He ascended back to heaven after 33 years, stepped into the throne room, and sat Himself down at His Father's right hand. There were no tears, but there was a fullness of joy which is unique to the divine presence (Ps 16:11) that was enjoyed on that occasion.

In passing, it is helpful to notice, from a very practical standpoint, two important lessons from Joseph and his dealings with his brothers. He was careful to maintain separation between his family and Egypt; and the usefulness and blessing of the brothers depended on their obedience to Joseph (46:31-34).

Jacob and Pharaoh

Jacob's meeting with Pharaoh is one of the highlights of Genesis. Here, finally, after a chequered past, Jacob becomes what God intended him to be from the very outset – a blessing to the Gentile nations. Lest we be harsh in our judgment, how many of us can attest that we have reached the goal God had for us in our lives? Even though Jacob arrived at it late in life, he did reach it.

The scene is lovely to behold; the aged patriarch coming before the grandeur of Pharaoh the mighty ruler of the day. Twice over we read that Jacob blessed Pharaoh. God's gentleman was superior in moral dignity and spiritual power than was even a Pharaoh. The less was indeed blessed by the greater.

In the presence of this august king, Jacob gave honour to God by owning that he was a pilgrim in a strange land. Egypt was not his home.

Jacob is now a changed man through the discipline of God. He does not ask for anything from Pharaoh; he has come to give. Jacob is able to bless Pharaoh; later he will bless two grandsons; then twelve sons; then twelve tribes; ultimately, through Judah he will bring blessing to the world.

Jacob and Joseph's Sons

In Genesis 48, word is sent to Joseph that his father's time is quickly drawing to a close. Joseph hastened to his bedside with his sons, Ephraim and Manasseh. Manasseh may have been about 22 and Ephraim about 20. The inspired writer paints a scene of pathos and promise, of the touching final moments of a man's life and the bright prospects for the future. What is of import for us to note is that a death bed became a place of blessing. Here was a man able to dispense blessing at the close of his life. Let any believer who is confined to a bed or wheelchair take heart: you can still be a tremendous blessing to the people of God. Avoid self-pity and despondency; feed on Christ and speak of Him to all.

Natural sight may have failed (v 10) to the point that Jacob could not recognize Joseph's sons, but spiritual vision was more acute than ever.

His mind went back to the Bethel appearings and the promises of God. At the close of life, he was resting on God's word, a good practice for every believer. The promises were not dimmed because he had not personally received them (Heb 11:13-16). He died in faith, looking for a city.

In a bold and calculated manner, Jacob claimed Joseph's two sons. Here is one of the many examples of Scripture of a grandfather influencing his grandchildren. Jacob full-well knew the prospects for Joseph's sons in Egypt: sons of the second ruler of the kingdom would have unlimited privileges and opportunities. Yet, in claiming them he was witnessing that the prospects with God were greater than those which Egypt could offer. He very probably knew of the prophecy to Abraham that the people would be oppressed in Egypt (Genesis 15). Yet he still testified to the value of being among the slaves who knew God rather than the great of Egypt who worshipped the sun god.

It should be the burden of every grandparent to claim their grandchildren for God. The prospects of advancement and prosperity in society may be alluring, but they cannot compare with what God has to offer. We cannot save them; but we can claim them before the throne that God may have them and not the world.

Amidst this interchange with Joseph comes the touching reminder of Joseph's mother, Rachel, and the parting when "there was but a little way to come unto Ephrath." Jacob carried the grief of that parting with him until his dying day. There are griefs in life which cannot be erased but are indelibly inscribed on the heart.

The blessing which Jacob bestowed on Joseph's two sons represents the double portion of the birthright which Jacob gave to Joseph (1 Chron 5:1-2). What is significant in the event is the reversal of order. Ephraim was placed above Manasseh when Jacob crossed his hands, "guiding his hands wittingly" (v 14). Here again the lesson being taught throughout Genesis is being underlined for us a final time: the first is set aside and the second is brought in for greater blessing. While not desiring to suggest any flaw in the character of Joseph, here is one time when he erred in his judgment. His "Not so, my father" (v 18) was answered by Jacob's "I know it, my son." Jacob was placing Ephraim ahead of Manasseh and prophesying that he would become a great nation.

The final words of Jacob to Joseph in this section have caused discussion over when Jacob took a portion from the Amorite with his bow. While nothing is recorded and speculation abounds, we have the comfort of knowing that the portion referred to is seen in John 4 when a greater than Joseph came to a well in Shechem, his "branches running over the wall" to meet the need of a Samaritan woman.

Jacob and his Sons

The deathbed scene of Genesis 49 can be appreciated in several ways. Jacob is a prophet who gives a glimpse into the future history of the 12 tribes of Israel. He is a patriarch who, in typical eastern style, gathers his family around for final words of blessing and admonition. There are also practical and personal considerations in his words.

Several chapters in our Bible have a "judgment seat" motif. Romans 16 is often a source of ministry to this end. David's review of his mighty men as given in 2 Samuel 23 is another instance. In these records, secret and unknown deeds are brought to light and, in the case of Jacob and Genesis 49, it was done in private. Egypt knew nothing of it.

Prophetic Utterances

Do we have any Scriptural basis for claiming that in these blessings, there is a foreview of the history of the nation? Jacob's use of "last days" in verse 1 allows us to see this line of truth. This is the first of 14 times that "last days" is mentioned in the Old Testament. It points beyond the sons to the end times.

Notice the progression of the names and their link with the history of the nation.

In Reuben, Simeon, and Levi, we see their moral history up to the first advent of Christ - instability and defilement, cruelty and anger, actions which brought dishonour on the name of God.

Next is Judah and with him there are titles which speak of the appearance of the Messiah. Shiloh came but was rejected by the nation.

Zebulun, dwelling at the haven of the sea, and Isaachar, bowed down to tribute, are suggestive of their dispersion and subjugation to Gentiles. This followed their rejection of the Messiah and subsequent events from AD 70 onward. Dan with the prophecy of the adder in the path and the longing for salvation points to appearing of antichrist, the cry of anguish, and the deliverance which only the second advent of Christ to earth can bring for the nation.

Gad with the promise of ultimate victory, Asher with royal dainties to nourish the nations, and Naphtali with goodly words, confessing the glory of God, are a reminder of a remnant as victorious, nourished, and becoming true witnesses with goodly words.

Finally, Joseph and Benjamin suggest the coming of Messiah in Glory, the blessing for Gentile nations, and a kingdom at rest and blessed.

Patriarchal Blessings

Some might justifiably object to the title "blessings" in consideration of some of the utterances of Jacob.

Even though blessing is not obvious in each case yet blessing exists in the acknowledgment of sin and in repentance. So, all that Jacob spoke was either a direct blessing, or had the potential to lead to blessing if recognized and confessed in the presence of God.

Reuben heads the list as the firstborn, and we are reminded of the dignity which should have been his. If we can imagine the scene, as Jacob began speaking of Reuben, his initial utterances in verse 3 may have caused a bit of pride in Reuben. You might be able to imagine his chest puffing out a bit and his eyes looking around in pride and disdain on his brothers. But then came verse 4: "Unstable as water, thou shalt not excel." The Dignity that should have been his was marred by a Defect in his character. He was unstable, a word which is used only once in Scripture and is suggestive of ungoverned passions. He was not able to rule his own spirit. The privilege and potential of his life was marred by a problem which he never addressed and corrected.

The thought of being unstable is touched on in at least three portions in the New Testament:

- Instability in a trial in James 1:8

- Instability morally in 2 Peter 2:14

- Instability doctrinally in 2 Peter 3:16.

The Defect in his character led to Defilement (35:22); the sad incident of perhaps as much as 40 years prior is suddenly brought to light. Did Reuben think it had been forgotten? Did he think his father's silence was approval or dismissal of the foul deed? Joseph, the true firstborn, had stood and remained morally pure, albeit at great cost.

Reuben's instability led to the Denial of firstborn status and forfeiture of great potential. His future was blighted for no-one from the tribe of Reuben ever excelled. Moral character determined usefulness and destiny.

Simeon and Levi occupy verses 5-7. They do not fare much better than Reuben. Something of their character can be seen in thrice repeated mention of their fierce anger (vv 6, 7, 7) and their cruelty (vv 5, 6, 7). They may have had just cause for righteous anger, but it soon developed into a personal vendetta against the men of Shechem. Their anger brought them into secret counsels, counsels to which Jacob was not privy. The result of their anger and cruelty was a curse from Jacob their father.

Jacob was not indifferent to what had happened years earlier. They had made his name to stink among the nations and brought him to a point where he feared for his life and that of his family. Only the sovereign intervention of God preserved them.

The result of their sin was a curse which he placed upon them. Simeon was to be scattered in Judah. It appears that, eventually, the tribe was assimilated into Judah.

By the second census, just before the Israelites entered Canaan, the Simeonites had become the smallest tribe (Num 26). Moses passed over the Simeonites in his blessing of the Israelites (Deut 33). This tribe received only a few cities within the allotment of Judah, rather than a separate geographical territory (Josh 19:1-9) The Simeonites eventually lost their tribal identity, and lived among the other tribes, especially in Judah's territory (1 Chron 4:27, 38-43).

Levi was to be scattered in Israel. While initially meant as a curse, the behaviour of Levi (the use of the sword again) in Exodus 32 enabled Moses to use their scattering as a blessing to them and the nation (Deut 33:7-11).

By demoting Reuben for his turbulence and uncontrolled sex drive, Jacob saves Israel from reckless leadership. Likewise, by cursing the cruelty of Simeon and Levi, he restricts their cruel rashness from dominating.

In the prophecy concerning Judah (vv 8-12), we come to another of those climactic moments in Old Testament revelation. The prophecy concerning the coming redeemer, Messiah, now reveals to us that this will be through the line of Judah. If we consider that it is not until 2 Samuel, approximately 700 years in the future that we learn anything further about the line through which He is to come, and then a further 300 years to Isaiah and Micah for additional information, we begin to appreciate the significance of the "blessing" of Judah. Here we are made aware of the tribe from which He is to come; in 2 Samuel 7 and the covenant with David, we learn of the very family. When we get to Isaiah, we are taught that it will be through a virgin. Finally, Micah reveals that His birth will be in Bethlehem.

The blessing of Judah, praise, is of course a play on his name. He rises to the full potential of his name. While his beginning was not so praise-worthy, he appears to have changed and matured under the hand of God. In the words of Jacob, we learn of his Supremacy (vv 8-9). He will be the object of praise from his brothers and his hand will be on the neck of his enemies in triumph. The imagery of a lion is employed, linking with the "lion of the tribe of Judah." As such He is seen devouring the prey in youth and resting in victory as an old lion. "Shiloh" could well be a variant of the Hebrew "Shalom" or peace. He will, as such, be the center of gathering for the nation: "unto him shall the gathering of the people be" is not only true in the Church age, but in every dispensation.

The Sceptre will be his of universal rule and authority. "Binding his foal unto the vine" may suggest the radical changes which will occur in the "regeneration," that the vines will be so sturdy that a colt can be tethered to it without fear of its loosening. Certainly, He will be the Source of Joy and nourishment to a redeemed earth and to the restored nation (vv 11-12). The vine and its wine are the joy He will bring to all.

The "until" of verse 10 is one of the many crucial "untils" of the Word of God. It is a constant reminder of God's prophetic calendar and the certainty of His purposes.

It is remarkable that a man on his deathbed is giving such revelations of the coming Christ: Christ is known as the Sceptre and Shiloh, and later Salvation, and the Stone and Shepherd. Jacob ended his days with his eyes filed with the glory of a coming Christ. Could a man have a better end?

Notice that here we have a lion as well.

Prosperity and blessing will be so abundant that even the animals will be tethered to the choicest vines, and the very best wine will be as commonplace as wash water. Verse 12 returns to the picture of the king of Judah. Everything denotes a king marked by strength and power.

Zebulun's name means "dwelling." While not the same word, he is seen "dwelling" at the haven of the ships. Zebulun's territory would eventually include Nazareth of Galilee. There is little evidence that Zebulun ever reached as far as Zidon, the Phoenician centre. It is more likely that this is all prophetic and pointing to a Millennial fulfillment.

Issachar was marked by great potential. He had strength as a strong ass. He was given two burdens to bear for God, but his potential was marred by his perception. He "saw" that the land was good (Lot), that rest was good, and he lost his pilgrim character. He settled down and compromised to be able to enjoy the "good life" of comfort and ease. He became a servant, the sad results of compromise. See Deuteronomy 33:18-19 for the blessing of Moses on the tribe. Judges 5:12 16 tell of Issachar's response in the day of Deborah. In Judges 10:1 we learn of a Judge from Issachar, Tola. And in 1 Chronicles 12:32, the men of Issachar were men with spiritual understanding.

We all face the danger of emulating Issachar and settling down to a comfortable lifestyle. Our material prosperity is a constant source of temptation. We need frequent reminders from the Word of God of the pilgrim character and sacrificial living which ought to mark us.

The blessing on Dan is brief but very suggestive. Dan was the son of Bilhah, one of Rachel's handmaidens. From him came Samson, the Judge of the nation. The imagery of the "serpent by the way" and "the adder ... that biteth" has been likened to the evil of idolatry which the tribe of Dan introduced into the nation in the days of the Judges. Whitelaw in his book mentions that the bite of the adder is extremely poisonous and dangerous. But the mention of the Serpent turns the attention of Jacob immediate to the Salvation of God. This is the first mention of "salvation" in Scripture. If we allow a futuristic interpretation, it could suggest the tribulation period and the longing of a faithful remnant for the salvation of God to come.

Gad is marked by conflict and defeat at the onset, but victory at the end. The tribe knew lots of conflict and battles. Recall that they chose the Transjordan area, east of the Jordan, as their possession. This area made them more vulnerable to attack. They were among the first to be carried captive.

His troubles are likened to troops coming in waves. Many of God's people know "troops" of troubles, problems which are not from wrong decisions or failure. But Gad reminds us of the possibility of victory in the end.

> *Though the day may be dark, and the road may be rough,*
> *And the troubles increase when there's trouble enough ...*
> *In the day of adversity never forget*
> *Habakkuk's "Though" and Habakkuk's "Yet."*
>
> (Isaac Ewan)

Asher was blessed with a portion of the land which was marked by fertility and abundance. He was placed in an area of great potential and he proved faithful and a good steward. Personal prosperity marked him, and his bread was "fat." Such was the character of the produce of his land that it is here labelled as "royal dainties," food fit for the king. One New Testament individual from the tribe of Asher is Anna of Luke 2. Certainly, she did not enjoy a fertile field in which to work. A widow and probably childless, nevertheless she yielded royal dainties. She is a reminder that our circumstances do not necessarily have to define us or limit our potential for pleasing God. The word "dainties", which has the thought of that which brings delight, is employed in several other places in Scripture: 1 Samuel 15:32 – delicately; Proverbs 29:17 - delight to the soul; Lamentations 4:5 – delicately. If Asher used his opportunity to bring delight to God, Anna certainly did the same. As a woman she could not serve in the temple, but she could be there in prayer and fasting. She did what she could!

Naphtali is pictured as a hind let loose which speaks of his liberty. But as a result of liberty, he speaks goodly words and provides Light to Nations. While this will ultimately be true in the Millennial period, it is spiritually true now of all who are redeemed and set at liberty. All those who have been touched by the work of Christ and know the liberating power of His redemption, are expected to be light to the world around.

The blessing conferred upon Joseph is the longest in the chapter. Here is Messiah's blessing to the world. As we travel through Genesis, "blessing" is one of the key words, from Genesis 1 through to this chapter. It occurs some eighty-eight times in the book. Here in verses 25 and 26 the root occurs six times (once as a verb, and five times as a noun) like a grand finale, making a climax to the last words of Jacob.

Note five things about the blessing of Joseph:

He is a Branch in fruitfulness

- Wealth – We are told that he was a fruitful branch. Here is the summation of his life. Everywhere he went and everything he did was fruitful. He is like the man of Psalm 1 who brings forth fruit in season. If we were to look for the nine-fold fruit of the Spirit (Gal 5) in Joseph's life, it would be very easy to see all the virtues displayed in him. This is why he reminds us so much of the Lord Jesus Christ.

- Well – We discover the source of his fruitfulness. He was a fruitful bough by a well - the literal word is fountain. Here is the source of his fruit. He dwelt by "the rivers of water" (Ps 1:3). All fruit is the result of abiding in Christ and His Word abiding in us. There is no true fruit-bearing apart from the well.

- Wall – Here we are reminded of the scope of his blessings. They ran over the wall as Gentile nations were blessed as a result of Joseph's administration. Once again, this points onward to a future day of Millennial glory. But we cannot read it without being reminded of a day when the Saviour sat at a well and the branches ran over the wall to a Samaritan woman.

Bitter treatment he received

- Archers showed bitterness toward him. The archers, his brothers, the salve traders, and Potiphar's wife, sorely grieved him. There were days and nights of sorrow which Joseph experienced. Here, perhaps, is the first intimation that Jacob had some understanding of what Joseph had passed through.

- The archers had shot at him in an attempt to destroy him and derail God's purposes. How encouraging to see that a man who leaves his future in God's hands cannot be frustrated. God will always bring him to the goal He has for that life.

His Bow abode

- His bow "abode in strength"; they could not bring him down.

- His hands were made strong. Another translation says that "he did not shoot back." All their provocations and attempts never succeeded in Joseph retaliating. Whether to his brothers, Potiphar's wife, or the prison keeper, Joseph left all in God's hands. A believer never needs to defend himself. In the case of a misunderstanding, we can certainly provide information to clear up the issue (Acts 22:25-26). But if falsely accused or maligned, we can leave our vindication to God, difficult though it may be.

- His hands were made strong by the "mighty God of Jacob." This is the first time Jacob refers to God as the God of Jacob. The expression, "from thence" could mean from the pictured death and resurrection by the power of God as seen in the life of Joseph. The descriptions of the Shepherd and Stone could link with the first and second advents of Christ.

Blessings that endure and surpass

- The Dimensions of the Blessing – above, beneath, from the womb to the everlasting hills. It seems as though Jacob cannot contain himself as he thinks of how great the blessings of Joseph, and of the One whom Joseph prefigured, will be. They will fill an entire globe with blessings beyond measure.

- The Duration of the Blessings – they will be eternal. The Millennial blessings will merge into the eternal day, the blessings not cancelled but enhanced and made unchangeable.

Basis for his exaltation

- Separation – the basis for the blessings which are Joseph's is his separation from the evil all around. Here, in Genesis, the separation was on his part. He separated himself from the evil of the day, from his brothers and from Potiphar's wife. When we read a similar statement in Deuteronomy 33:16, the voice is different. Here it is his brothers who separated from him. Such was his life that they did not wish to have much to do with him. He separated himself from them; they kept apart from him. A separated man will usually find that those who do not share his convictions will soon separate themselves from his company.

- Suffering – but separation also meant suffering for Joseph. His suffering brought blessing for him but also for his brothers, Egypt, and all the nations which came up to buy corn. An interesting observation is that Genesis began with God's intent for a man, Adam, to be a blessing to the entire creation. It all appeared to fall apart due to Adam's fall. But the book ends with God's purpose fulfilled in another man, Joseph. He was a blessing to the entire world.

The final blessing is for the youngest son, Benjamin. Many have likened the blessing to the life of the Apostle Paul, a Benjamite, who ravaged the church in his youth but who divided the spoil in his mature Christian years. That may be permissible and applicable.

It is more likely, however, that the first half of the verse refers to the aggressive and war-like attitude of the tribe as demonstrated in Judges 20 and elsewhere in Scripture.

Practical and personal application can be made from Jacob's words to Benjamin reminding us that unless we gather in the morning of life we will not have spoils to enjoy in the eventide.

The remainder of the chapter deals with:

- The Charge - Canaan, not Egypt, is where all his hopes were
- The Cave – a reminder of resurrection and the Land
- The Completion of his pilgrimage.

All of this has been covered elsewhere. Suffice it to say that Jacob went home "looking his best." We are reminded of what God can do with a man whom He takes into His school. Jacob's last days were his best. He went out in a blaze of glory. He:

- Conferred blessings on Pharaoh (47:7-10)
- Communed in worship (47:31)
- Claimed a generation for God (48:5)
- Confessed God as his (49:24).

CHAPTER 13

The Burial

Nowhere else in Scripture do we have such a full description of a funeral. Jacob was buried with full military honours as though he had been commander-in-chief of Egypt's armed forces instead of a nomadic shepherd who had wandered into the land late in life

(John Phillips)

The Guarantee Extracted (49:28-33)

The Charge

Now for the second time (see ch 47), Jacob gives explicit instructions concerning his burial. Canaan, not Egypt is where all his expectations were. This was a confession of hope. The prospects in Canaan were greater than all the wealth of Egypt. Jacob had grasped by faith the promises of God, and they were linked with the land and not with Egypt. The events in these final chapters of Jacob's life were his finest hour. He went home to heaven in a blaze of glory.

Believers can also give expression to our hope in the manner in which we die, and in the arrangements concerning funerals. No one enjoys thinking of his or her own death, but it is an opportunity for witnessing to the hope we have.

The issue of cremation is often raised in this context. There are countries where cremation is mandated by law. Believers need to bow to the dictates of the government; God is able to raise their bodies from ashes. But when there is a choice there is a confession of both the dignity of the body and its ultimate resurrection which is seen in the burial of the body. Devout men carried Stephen to his burial as a testimony to the future hope of resurrection.

The Cave

Jacob was to be buried in the cave at Machpelah. There the patriarchs had been buried and he was to lie with them awaiting a future day of resurrection and the "city ... whose builder and maker is God" (Heb 11:10). It was a testimony to resurrection and the guarantee of the Land.

The Completion of his Pilgrimage

When he had finished speaking and charging his sons, we read that "he drew his feet up into the bed and breathed his last" (ESV). He was gathered to his people. With grace and with patriarchal dignity he came to the end of his pilgrimage. This is what the inspired writer highlighted in Hebrews 11:22 - "Jacob ... worshiped, leaning upon the top of his staff." His death bed became a platform for worship. How different is the Jacob of Genesis 49 from that of Genesis 27!

Several lines of truth should be noted here. This is the first mention of the expression, "these are the twelve tribes" (v 28). The descent into Egypt had served to solidify the nation and develop its distinct character. The record of their time while in Canaan was a history of flirting with the Canaanites and intermingling. They were separated from all that in the land of Goshen in Egypt and developed into a nation with a distinct identity.

Also, the name of Leah is once again introduced into the story of his life, but it is mentioned in connection with the burial spot in Canaan. In that sacred cave lay Abraham and Sarah, Isaac and Rebekah, and Leah. We are not told when she died but it was obviously prior to the departure of Jacob and his household for Egypt. But what is significant is that the woman who was given a second place status in life received a first place status in burial - "There I buried Leah" (49:31). Jacob was buried by her side in death.

Leah had opportunity to stay in Laban's house and to avoid the stigma of her lowlier standing. But she remained with Jacob and was honoured by the Lord for her fidelity. She had more children than the favoured Rachel; she bore Judah and Levi, the princely and priestly lines; she came into the genealogy of the Messiah; and she rested by Jacob in death. God honoured her, and there is little question that she will look back from eternity's shores and feel the sacrifice she made in obeying her marriage covenant was nothing compared to the honour the Lord gave her. Was Leah the bride God intended for Jacob? Very possibly!

In a similar manner, believers who have sacrificed and endured difficulties for the name of the Lord and in obedience to His Word will find that the compensation far exceeds the cost.

The Grief Evidenced (50:1-3)

Jacob expired. At 147 years of age he ended his pilgrimage. He had spent the first 77 years in Canaan; there were 20 years of education in the house of Laban; then 33 in Canaan once again; God graciously gave him another 17 years with Joseph in Egypt. At the completion of the first 17 years Jacob wept over the loss of Joseph (37:2, 35). At the close of the last 17 years Joseph wept at the loss of Jacob.

With the death of Jacob, the grief of Joseph gives vent to tears and a parting kiss. Joseph honoured and loved his father both as a boy and now as a grown man; the honours which Egypt had bestowed upon him did not hinder Joseph from expressing his genuine affection for his father. Joseph allowed the culture in which he resided to dictate the burial process, as long as it did not contradict Scripture. He shows respect for the body of his father and is going to fulfill his request as to his burial place.

There was an elaborate and detailed process which the Egyptians had developed for the embalming of a body. Some estimate that the process could take up to two months.

Something of Egypt's regard for Joseph is seen in the mourning for Jacob: all the land mourned for the father of Joseph.

The Granting of the Entreaty (50:4-6)

Joseph's wisdom is seen in the manner of his approach to Pharaoh. With typical humility and politeness, Joseph asks the counsellors to intercede for him with Pharaoh as to obtaining permission to leave to bury his father. Joseph gives assurances that he will return if allowed to travel back to the land of Canaan. To all of this Pharaoh gives ready assent.

The Greatness of the Honour Expressed (50:7-12)

The Cortege

Egypt sends an honour guard and Jacob is afforded a state funeral. This is even more remarkable when contrasted with the scarcity of detail given about Joseph's burial at the end of the chapter. The pilgrim is given a royal burial. It is the grandest state funeral recorded in the Bible, and was entirely appropriate since Jacob's story spans more than half of Genesis. The Egyptians mourned for Jacob "seventy days," just two days less than they normally mourned the death of a Pharaoh.

The Mourning

At the threshing-floor of Atad, there is a "great and very sore lamentation" for seven days. This is the first of at least six threshing floors of Scripture. Separation is evident in each; something is left at each threshing-floor.

Is there possibly here a foreshadowing of a future day when Gentile nations will escort Israel back to the land (Isa 66:20)?

The Graveside and the Interment (50:12-13)

The sons of Jacob now come to the forefront; they leave the Canaanite and Egyptian behind. These nations have nothing to do with the burial and hope of Israel. Egypt can mourn death but cannot expect resurrection.

The right to the burial place is again emphasized. There is another repetition of the purchase which Abraham made, almost as though it is once again restating Israel's right to the burial ground.

This was Joseph's first visit to his homeland in almost 40 years. It would be the route for the Exodus eventually, but for now they would retrace their steps into Egypt.

JOSEPH

M. CAIN

Contents

JOSEPH

In these Character Studies, unless otherwise indicated, verses referred to are taken from the Book of Genesis.

Joseph

Few Old Testament stories are as well-known and well-loved as that of Joseph, the favourite son of Jacob. Who doesn't know the story of the "coat of many colours"? Joseph, loved by his father and hated by his brothers, is thrown into the pit and then sold to become a slave. Years later he becomes the prime minister of Egypt — a story of good triumphing over evil!

But there is far more to his life than simply a great children's story for a Sunday School class! There is tremendous value in taking time to ponder his experiences. Perhaps no other Old Testament character presents us with such a lovely picture of the Lord Jesus. While some would hesitate to use the word "type" to refer to Joseph, it is clear that he is part of a pattern we see in the Old Testament of those who were raised up by God to be a means of salvation for His people. Some have counted well over one hundred similarities between the lives of Joseph and the Lord Jesus! Another interesting point of reference is to follow the story from Joseph through David and then to the Christ — for example, both Joseph and David were shepherding the flocks of their aged fathers, and both were hated by their brethren. Both ascended to high places and, in a certain sense, "saved" the nation. But we must get back to Joseph. As we move through Genesis we will notice many occasions where our minds are taken to One far greater than Joseph, and our hearts are drawn to worship Him.

Consider his *trials*: hated of his brethren, sold for a few pieces of silver (supposedly never to be seen again), and then accused, condemned and imprisoned unjustly. Peter reminds us that we can rejoice, even when "in heaviness through manifold temptations (or, better, trials): That the trial of your faith, being much more precious than of gold that perisheth, though it be tried with fire, might be found unto praise and honour and glory at the appearing of Jesus Christ" (1 Peter 1:6-7). We hope to learn some lessons about trials from the life of Joseph.

We will think of his *tears*: in the world tears are often considered to be a sign of weakness, but were shed by our Saviour on more than one occasion without shame. A few examples will make the point, although there are seven instances when Joseph wept. Instead of reacting harshly when his brothers arrived in Egypt to purchase corn — the very same brothers who had sold him into slavery more than a decade earlier — he had to "turn himself about from them" (42:24). When he finally revealed himself to his brethren there was no hiding his tears as on previous occasions, but open weeping at this happy reunion (45:1-2). Imagine the overwhelming joy when in the next chapter he fell on his father's neck and "wept on his neck a good while" (46:29). Are you a believer going through a time of tears? Look to Joseph, but look beyond him and see the Saviour, weeping at Lazarus's tomb as He considered the awful effects of sin; weeping over the unrepentant city of Jerusalem as He contemplated the rejection of a privileged people; and finally offering up "prayers and supplications with strong crying and tears unto him that was able to save him from death" (Heb 5:7) as He counted the cost involved in providing our salvation. Remember, He is not only our Saviour, but also our Great High Priest, touched with the feeling of our infirmities.

When we look at Joseph's *temptation* by Potiphar's wife we witness a God-fearing attitude later seen in the Lord Jesus too. Joseph recognized the inherent wrong in the temptation and said, "how then can I do this great wickedness, and sin against God?" (39:9). Years later the Lord would respond in a similar way, referring to God in each response he gave to Satan.

As we go through Genesis we will see a *transformation* — from a son who brought delight to his father's heart to the despised brother in the pit; from the forgotten prisoner to a favoured prince. Thankfully, we will also notice a transformation in his brethren as they go from rejecting Joseph to reverencing him. One day "they shall look upon me whom they have pierced" (Zech 12:10), and the One who was long-rejected by the nation will be accepted and reverenced.

When the time comes that he has to deal with his brothers to bring them to a place of repentance, Joseph's conversations are marked by *tenderness*. True, he does deal in a way that brings them to recognize their evil works from years before, but his heart was always tender, as we noted above in relation to his tears. How often we see this same characteristic in the life of the Lord Jesus as we read of His dealings with so many individuals in the gospels! He showed the perfect balance between grace and truth!

The ultimate manner in which right *triumphs* over wrong, finishing with Joseph exalted on the throne, also makes us appreciate what happened with the Lord Jesus. In those early days, back in Canaan, no one would have expected that this second-youngest brother would one day be on the throne in Egypt, just as very few believed that the child born in Bethlehem would be the Sovereign on the eternal throne.

There is also much practical teaching that we can find in following Joseph through the different stages of his life. Joseph did not live in easy times, nor do we! Nonetheless, we do serve the same God, and can follow his example of steadfastness and faithfulness, even amidst difficult circumstances. There were times of *training* and *testing*, first in his father's home where he learned how to care for the sheep, later in Potiphar's household when he learned much about administration, and finally in the prison when God continued to mould him for His purposes. With great reverence we marvel at the words written about the Lord Jesus: "Though he were a Son, yet learned he obedience by the things which he suffered" (Heb 5:8). All of life's experiences were necessary for Him to pass through - suffering even before He came to the events surrounding the cross.

We can ask ourselves what helped Joseph through all the challenges in life, and the simple answer is: his *trust* in God. They were not living in days of either full or frequent revelation from God. But Joseph had received one revelation from God at the age of seventeen, and he trusted that God would somehow, sometime fulfill His promise. God also calls us to a life of faith. We have far more revelation from God, and thus are more responsible to respond to His truth. At the same time, we live in full confidence that what God has promised for His people He will fulfill. The Lord Jesus is called "the author and finisher of our faith" (Heb 12:2); He trusted in His God and lived His life in full dependence upon Him, and thus is the perfect Example of a life lived by faith.

We see a very comforting *truth* as we move through Joseph's life: the providence of God. "Providence", although not a Bible word, is God's ability not only to foresee, but also to control the circumstances of our lives so that His purposes are fulfilled. Remember that, after his father Jacob had been buried in the land of Canaan, Joseph's brothers feared that he would no longer be kind to them. He responded: "But as for you, ye thought evil against me; but God meant it unto good, to bring to pass, as it is this day, to save much people alive" (50:20). God had allowed the years of darkness and difficulty in his life in order to bring about "good". No one in the family could have seen this decades before when Joseph had his dreams, but God did — He foresaw, and then directed circumstances in order to bring about His plan to save His people, a very small nation of seventy individuals, from famine and destruction. From this same nation our Saviour would one day be born! In so many ways we can trace God's providential hand, leading our Saviour to the cross. He was "delivered by the determinate counsel and foreknowledge of God", yet at the same time "wicked hands" were responsible for His crucifixion (Acts 2:23).

Why should we study the life of Joseph since we live in such different times, in a different culture, and with different challenges? Paul tells us that "whatsoever things were written aforetime were written for our learning, that we through patience and comfort of the scriptures might have hope" (Rom 15:4). The Word of God is indeed an *ancient* Book, but let's remember it is the only *living* Book, the Author of which has a real desire to communicate with us today!

First of all, it cheers our heart as we look at Joseph's life, because we will learn much about the *people* of God — God had chosen the seed of Abraham, and now He is caring for this same people, small in number though it may be. Hundreds of years later, the same remains true — He has called out a people for Himself, a people for His possession (Acts 15:14).

There is a challenge with which we are faced as we read about Joseph's dealings with his brothers when they arrive in Egypt. He had the power and authority to imprison them all, thereby taking revenge on them for their cruelty to him thirteen years before. But what we see is a full and free *pardon*. Is our attitude the same when we are wronged, or do we wait for the moment when we can take revenge?

Consider, too, the commencement of the fulfillment of a *prophecy* given to Abram in Genesis 15:13: "Know of a surety that thy seed shall be a stranger in a land that is not theirs, and shall serve them; and they shall afflict them four hundred years". As we come towards the end of the story, we see Joseph's father and family coming into a "land that is not theirs." Once Joseph died, there would arise a king that did not know him and would begin to "afflict them four hundred years."

The New Testament references to Joseph are also instructive. In Acts 7 Stephen refers to Joseph to charge his hearers with resisting the Holy Spirit just as their fathers had done. Then in Hebrews we read that "By faith Joseph, when he died, made mention of the departing of the children of Israel; and gave commandment concerning his bones" (Heb 11:22). This tells us that Joseph died in hope, a word consistently used in regard to believers living today.

We can easily divide Joseph's life into three phases:

1) There were seventeen Years of Difficulty (30:24-37:2)
2) Then followed thirteen Years of Obscurity (37:2-41:46)
3) Finally, we see eighty Years of Prosperity (41:46-50:26).

Another possible way to look at his life is as follows:

In his Parents' Home:	The Position of Affection
In the Pit:	The Pain of Affliction
In Potiphar's House:	The Purity in his Associations
In the Prison:	The Propriety in his Actions
In the Palace:	The Power in his Ascension.

It is not for naught that the story of Joseph takes up a quarter of the book of Genesis. He shows us what a life of distinction is truly like - a life that pleases God. Not only was his conduct different from that of his brothers when he was at home, but we also notice how distinct it was from that of the Egyptians with whom he had to live for many years. More importantly, we will observe that his character was distinctive — he was truly a man of integrity. This was part of the reason his father loved him "more than all his children" (37:3).

May God help us to appreciate even more this man, and at the same time consistently turn our eyes to the Man on the throne, our blessed Lord Jesus.

CHAPTER 1

The Circumstances were Adverse

Problems should not be an Excuse

There are times in the lives of believers when we wish we lived in a different place, or in a different period, or with different people. We can quickly come up with reasons, or perhaps excuses, for the absence of progress in our Christian experience. We sometimes focus on the many problems in our lives, and we can quickly complain about how unfair our life is compared to others. What we hope to see in this chapter is that circumstances, whether favourable or frustrating, are no reason not to live our lives to the glory of God.

So look at Joseph's life! We hear no excuses despite the fact that his experience was not what we would consider to be easy. The places where he lived were not easy; the period was difficult, and it will quickly become apparent that not all the people in Joseph's life treated him as he deserved. However, we don't find a long list of complaints coming from his mouth. Do we too quickly blame our difficult circumstances for almost any failure or lack of progress in our own lives? We see none of that in Joseph. Adverse circumstances often bring out the worst in us: frustration, anger, or even bitterness, none of which are seen in him. Part of our negative reaction is due to the realization that we cannot control all that happens to us.

Meekness is not a common characteristic in the world in which we live, nor has it ever been. It is, however, exemplified in Joseph, as it later would be in the Lord Jesus. Meekness is one's deliberate decision to accept the circumstances in which one finds oneself, even when these are adverse, recognizing that they all are part of God's wise plan for character formation, and the accomplishment of His will in our lives. Joseph realized that only God could see the end from the beginning; only God was aware of the big picture. He understood that the unfolding of circumstances was all in God's control. Remember the words of the Lord Jesus in Matthew 11:29: "Take my yoke upon you, and learn of me; for I am meek and lowly in heart: and ye shall find rest unto your souls." Meekness is something we need to learn from Christ, to practice in our daily lives. Why? In part the answer has to do with "rest". When we realize that God in His all-wise plan has allowed certain circumstances to come into our lives, and we do not resist, but rather request grace, we find rest to our souls. Fighting against God's plans for us causes us to become agitated and angry; the meekness of acceptance brings quietness and tranquility.

Paul, thousands of years later, wrote these words, already cited in the Introduction: "For whatsoever things were written aforetime were written for our learning, that we through patience and comfort of the scriptures might have hope" (Rom 15:4). We do well to consider Bible history for many reasons, but Paul here speaks of the hope we find as we study the Word of God. Are you passing through adverse circumstances? Does it seem that everything, and maybe everyone, is against you? Have you got your eyes on your own problems? Take a good look at Joseph, and you will find hope through your patient endurance, and the comfort of the Scriptures.

Before we get into the actual development of the story of Joseph, note the following points with me, and see how, humanly speaking, we maybe wouldn't expect to see Joseph amount to much for God. We will see some of these points in more detail once we get into the story, but I want us to consider how God graciously works to bring about His purpose, even when things seem very bleak and dark. On more than one occasion in Joseph's life, things indeed *did* seem very bleak and dark, but through it all God was moulding Joseph in order one day to exalt him and use him to save the nation from which the Messiah would eventually come.

The Past and its Consequences

In order to understand some of the background in Joseph's upbringing, we need to take a brief survey of the family history. We will look in more detail at his childhood in the next chapter, but for now consider these few details.

After a period of barrenness, God had promised to Rebekah that, of the twins in her womb, "the elder shall serve the younger" (25:23). When Isaac and Rebekah's twin boys were born, Jacob, the younger, took hold of Esau's heel, thus gaining the name "Supplanter", or "Deceiver". In the same chapter, we read how Jacob purchased the birthright from Esau in a cunning manner. Esau returned home from hunting, and he was faint. Seeing, or perhaps smelling, the stew that Jacob had prepared, Esau was willing to sell his birthright for "one morsel of meat" (Heb 12:16). Jacob took advantage of the situation and showed how his name was true to his character. We turn to chapter 27 and find that not only does Jacob have the birthright, but now he is receiving the blessing from his father Isaac. Again he used deceit, by pretending to be Esau, to obtain what God had clearly promised to his mother Rebekah years before, that the older would serve the younger. This clearly does show a lack of trust in God's ability to fulfil His promises and to bring about His purposes.

Jacob then had to flee from his parents' home due to the fear he had of Esau, who said in his heart, "The days of mourning for my father are at hand; then will I slay my brother Jacob" (27:41). Rebekah, who favoured Jacob, upon learning of Esau's intentions, told Jacob to flee to "Laban my brother to Haran; And tarry with him a few days" (27:43-44). Those few days turned into twenty long years, and Jacob would never see his mother on earth again. Although we are not studying Jacob's life, let us learn that what results from deception is more deception, and regrettable consequences. Someone has well said: "We can choose our decisions, but we cannot choose their consequences."

The Pattern of Cunning

Jacob, who early in his life had learned deceit, will soon become the deceived one. He arrives in Haran and meets Laban, his uncle, who seemingly appreciates Jacob's service, and asks what his wages should be. Only a month has passed since Jacob's arrival, but he now loves

Rachel, who is "beautiful and well favoured", and he offers to serve Laban seven years in order to marry her (29:17-18). However, on the wedding night, Laban gives his older daughter Leah to Jacob instead of Rachel! One needs to take the customs of the land into account, as well as the darkness of the night, to understand how it was possible for Jacob to be beguiled in this way. But such was his love for Rachel that he was willing to fulfill Leah's week, and then work for Laban for a further seven years in order to marry Rachel who would eventually become Joseph's mother.

In the coming years, we see more of Jacob's and Laban's cunning, one always trying to outwit the other. Remember the speckled and spotted sheep and goats, the rods, and the gutters in the watering troughs (30:32-42). Jacob was constantly attempting to get the upper hand, to enrich himself. Then, at the end of the twenty years that Jacob served Laban, tending his flocks, Jacob says, "thou hast changed my wages ten times" (31:41). Laban constantly tried to circumvent Jacob's prosperity in regards to the flocks.

On this same occasion, Joseph is six years old, surely old enough to understand that something is not right about his mother's being sealed on his grandfather's gods, having not only stolen them, but now deceiving her own father (31:31-35). Unfortunately what she had learned, not only from her father but also from her husband, she is now practising. A word of counsel to the wise: make sure you marry someone of godly character who will influence you for good, instead of leading you down a path of deceit and harm.

His Parents were somewhat Carnal

When we think about the time of Joseph's birth, the sad truth is that we do not see a high level of spirituality in his parents. Jacob has been doing things his way, without showing much trust in God, for a good number of years. His mother, although not yet in possession of her father's gods, obviously had some attraction to them. We will see in the next chapter that she did know God and saw that Joseph's birth was an answer to her prayer. However, this episode indicates that not all was right in her relationship with the only true God.

Lest you think that I am being too hard on Jacob, let us note that even Laban realized that his own blessings had to do with Jacob's presence. He said, "I have learned by experience that the LORD hath blessed me for thy sake" (30:27). So Jacob was not entirely silent about his faith in God, yet there was obviously much self-confidence, too. The Apostle Paul warns the Philippians about the dangers of having "confidence in the flesh" (Phil 3:3-4). He explained that he would have far more reason to have confidence in the flesh than anyone else, but all these things he once treasured he now counted as loss "for the excellency of the knowledge of Christ Jesus my Lord" (Phil 3:8).

The works of the flesh were manifested in Jacob's life, and Joseph would have witnessed this in his childhood. May God help those of us who are parents to crucify the flesh and allow the Spirit to develop His fruit in us so that we can live well for God before our children.

God was soon going to do a work in Jacob's life, and things began to change when Joseph was born. At this point, he had served his father-in-law fourteen years, and he said to Laban, "Send me away, that I may go unto mine own place, and to my country" (30:25). Something about Joseph's birth in particular made Jacob long for his true home.

It isn't until six years later, however, that they actually left Haran for home, and it is then that Jacob has real dealings with God (32:24-32). His name is changed to Israel, and, although he is not a perfect man after that, we begin to note a real change in his character.

The Polygamous Confusion

Go back with me to the beginning, some two thousand years before Jacob's day, to the Garden of Eden. Our Creator made it very clear that marriage was designed to be the union of one man and one woman. Listen to these plain and simple words:, "Therefore shall a man leave his father and his mother, and shall cleave unto his wife: and they shall be one flesh" (2:24). The Lord Jesus repeated these words in the gospels, helping us to understand that this is an abiding principle, still applicable to us in our modern culture.

When we look at today's society, we wonder how its moral bearings have changed so quickly. David asked the question: "If the foundations be destroyed, what can the righteous do?" (Ps 11:3). As we see the foundations of society being attacked generally, let us remember some truths expressed by David in response to his own question: "The LORD is in his holy temple, the LORD's throne is in heaven: his eyes behold, his eyelids try, the children of men" (Ps 11:4); and, "the righteous LORD loveth righteousness" (Ps 11:7). First, remember He is holy; next, He is still on His throne in heaven; then, He is not ignorant of what is happening around us; and finally, He still loves righteousness. Let us be like Him, let us trust Him, let us love what He loves.

But even four thousand years ago, mankind had deviated from God's original and perfect plan. Jacob not only had Leah and Rachel as his wives, but both of them had given their own handmaids to Jacob, by whom he also had children. Joseph was the penultimate son of twelve. At the time of his birth there were four mothers, twelve children, and one father. This is a sure recipe for conflict, conniving and confusion, and we will see some of that as we go through Joseph's life story.

What is termed a "dysfunctional family" has become increasingly common in the last fifty years. Joseph's family would surely fit into that category in any age, yet he did not allow that to stop him from becoming the man of God he was shown to be.

The Pain of Calamity

Joseph knew sadness in his life. When he was a little boy, Deborah, who was Rebekah's nurse, died (35:8). Although she was not his mother, she was an important part of the family. Then we move further down the chapter and we find there is great joy. Joseph will have a full brother! Tragically, during the labour, Rebekah, Joseph's mother, died, and was buried (35:19). Come with me to the end of the chapter, and we learn that his grandfather "Isaac gave up the ghost, and died" (35:29).

We often consider pain, suffering and calamity to be negative things. Nobody enjoys suffering. Nobody seeks out pain. Nobody wants calamity to come into their life. But life's sad events are used by

God. Remember what the prophet Isaiah penned years later: "I have chosen thee in the furnace of affliction" (Isa 48:10). It may not be what a believer would choose, but God knows best, and He is in control of life's circumstances. Why does He allow certain things to happen to His children? Consider our last point.

God's Purpose in Forming Joseph's Character

Joseph could not see the big picture. As a little boy, then as a young lad, and even as a teenager, he was not aware of the great purposes God had for his life. But God, through all of these adverse circumstances of life, was moulding and shaping Joseph; he was forming his character, a character that reminds us so much of our Lord Jesus Christ.

Let's think about the Lord Jesus for a moment. Obviously there are many differences when we consider His background, but at the same time we would have to conclude that, again, humanly speaking, what would be expected of a man coming out of Nazareth? Remember that was Nathanael's question: "Can there any good thing come out of Nazareth?". Philip had the right response, to which we have taken heed as well: "Come and see" (John 1:46). There is none as lovely and perfect as He; but the leaders of His day did not expect that He would amount to much. He came from a despised place, from a poor family, and even His own brothers did not believe in Him. The circumstances were difficult. But think how God, as He had with Joseph, used Him mightily for His purposes. No one ever brought such glory to God — either here on earth, or in heaven.

Paul helps us to consider God's purpose, His providence, His people, and His power. He writes, "And we know that all things work together for good to them that love God, to them who are the called according to his purpose" (Rom 8:28). How applicable this is to Joseph we have already noted in his statement to his brethren: "ye thought evil against me; but God meant it unto good, to bring to pass, as it is this day, to save much people alive" (50:20). What confidence! What rest! Remembering that God had a purpose in his life gave him a sense of peace that the world surely could not understand then, nor does it today. He could look back and see how God's purpose was for him to be the saviour, not only of his family, but also of the nation of Egypt, and beyond.

Think of God's providence. The beginning of the verse in Romans says, "... we know that all things work together." God skillfully intertwines the hardships of life with the happinesses of our experience in perfect balance, making them work together to form our character, that we might be "conformed to the image of his Son" (Rom 8:29). He did it with Joseph, and He is doing it in us, His people, those "that love God".

Paul says, "we know". Knowing that God "meant it unto good" helped Joseph bear the separation from his family, the sadness and the suffering. He trusted in God's power to fulfill His purposes. God had revealed His objective in a special way through dreams, and this revelation helped Joseph carry on through all the adverse circumstances that came his way. We don't have that type of revelation from God, but we do have a clear Word from the Lord, and can rest assured that He is forming and shaping us through the circumstances in our life.

Our vision of the future is very limited, but we can do as Joseph did and trust in the very same God, who sees perfectly what the end purpose is that He has in mind.

So, as we move into these important chapters of Genesis, let us keep in mind that even when all appeared bleak, when Joseph's eyes blurred with tears, when the burdens seemed too heavy to bear, he did not allow the adverse circumstances in which he found himself to take away his trust in God. Nor did he use them at any time as an excuse for not following after God, even while living in a very pagan society.

It is not difficult to see that there are lessons for us. Many who read these pages have had the privilege and blessing of being brought up by godly parents, modelling Christ-likeness in the home. But there are other believers who have a different life story. So, we can ask ourselves these questions: Are we dealing with the consequences of others' decisions or of our own? Have we observed the ugly effects of cunning behaviour in ourselves or others? Has carnality reared its ugly head in us? In our family is there some conflict or confusion? Have calamities come knocking on the door of our life? Remember three simple lessons: God is still in control; we cannot use our unfavourable circumstances as an excuse for not growing in grace; and, finally, we must meekly accept what comes our way as part of God's plan for building Christ-like character in us.

William Cowper wrote the following lines in 1774, but they have lost nothing of their power.

God moves in a mysterious way
His wonders to perform;
He plants his footsteps in the sea,
And rides upon the storm.

Deep in unfathomable mines
Of never-failing skill
He treasures up His bright designs,
And works His sov'reign will.

Ye fearful saints, fresh courage take;
The clouds ye so much dread
Are big with mercy, and shall break
In blessings on your head.

Judge not the Lord by feeble sense,
But trust Him for his grace;
Behind a frowning providence
He hides a smiling face.

His purposes will ripen fast,
Unfolding ev'ry hour;
The bud may have a bitter taste,
But sweet will be the flow'r.

Blind unbelief is sure to err,
And scan His work in vain;
God is His own interpreter,
And He will make it plain.

CHAPTER 2

His Childhood and its Advantages

The Seriousness of Parenthood

Having considered the fact that Joseph faced much adversity even at a young age, we now want to look at his childhood and upbringing in more detail. Joseph had the advantage, at least in early life, of living with both parents. Jacob was not by any means a young man when Joseph was born, but he did still have many productive years before him. After a long wait, Joseph became Rachel's firstborn, and was her only child for a number of years.

The importance of a mother's role in the life of her children cannot be overemphasized in the day and age in which we live. The Bible speaks plainly about this in both the Old and the New Testaments, by means of exhortations and examples.

The Legacy and the Learning

Think of what the psalmist writes: "Lo, children are an heritage of the LORD: and the fruit of the womb is his reward" (Ps 127:3). Many believers look back on life and marvel at the legacy that is theirs in having godly parents. They perhaps left little, or nothing, behind of this world's wealth, but passed on something of far more value, a proper perspective on life, one based on the Bible.

Remember "the words of king Lemuel, the prophecy that his mother taught him" (Prov 31:1). He had obviously sat at his mother's feet and learned much, not only about the character of a spiritual woman, but also about the wise way in which one should live. We could consider the same in the life of Timothy, who not only had the blessing of a godly mother Eunice, but also a God-fearing grandmother, Lois. In them dwelt "unfeigned faith" (2 Tim 1:5), but also a wealth of knowledge that they shared with Timothy. Paul reminded Timothy of this blessing in 2 Timothy 3:15: "And that from a child thou hast known the holy scriptures, which are able to make thee wise unto salvation through faith which is in Christ Jesus."

Consider Jochabed and Hannah, both of whom had a very limited time with their respective sons before turning them over to the care of others; Moses would go to the pagan palace in Egypt, and Samuel to the tabernacle where the priesthood was faltering and failing. Surely before they let them go they poured into their sons' minds all they knew about God and His care for His people.

So, mothers, take heart! You can leave an important legacy, having had your children on your knees so they could learn what you know about our great God and Saviour.

The Loving and the Leading

Paul writes to Titus the following exhortation: "The aged women likewise, that they be in behaviour as becometh holiness ... That they may teach the young women to ... love their children" (Titus 2:3-4). One would think that the love of children would come naturally, but Paul suggests there is something in this sphere that older women can teach to the younger women. Life is not always simple; the road is sometimes rough; the children can, at times, become a bit of a challenge. Thus we have this brief word from Paul: Love your children. They will be exposed to plenty of other sentiments in the world - hatred, contempt, rejection, and perhaps prejudice - but a child should always feel secure in a mother's love.

Both parents need to know their children and take note of their tendencies and leanings. They will then be able to lead and to guide them in the right path: "Train up a child in the way he should go: and when he is old, he will not depart from it" (Prov 22:6). This would apply, too, to their career path. We don't want them to become what we perhaps always wanted to be, and did not obtain, but rather our desire is for them to follow a path that will be God-honouring and in keeping with their own character and tendencies.

Where does Joseph fit into these thoughts? Look with me first of all at:

The Supplication of his Mother

"And God remembered Rachel, and God hearkened to her, and opened her womb. And she conceived, and bare a son; and said, God hath taken away my reproach: And she called his name Joseph; and said, The LORD shall add to me another son" (30:22-24).

God's Actions

God remembered — we ought not to understand from this that God had in any way forgotten about Rachel. We have the same expression used several times in the Old Testament, first of all of Noah in Genesis 8:1: "And God remembered Noah, and every living thing, and all the cattle that was with him in the ark." The water had prevailed upon the earth for one hundred and fifty days; this after the initial seven days before the flood began followed by forty days of rain (see 7.9, 10, 12). Had God forgotten about Noah and his family inside the ark? Had He forgotten His promise to bring them safely through the flood? Certainly not! Years later, we read that "God remembered Abraham, and sent Lot out of the midst of the overthrow" (19:29). Again, Abraham had never been forgotten.

We understand, then, that God is always aware of His people's condition, but the right time comes for Him to act. Then He responds to their cry to Him. So, God had been aware of Rachel's condition, of Noah's location, and Lot's situation — but He would act according to His perfect timing.

God hearkened — it ought not to cease to amaze us when we read what seems to be a simple phrase such as this one: "God hearkened to her." It simply means that God heard her. But that in itself is an absolutely marvellous truth! The Almighty God of heaven takes the time to hear His people's cries. Earlier in Genesis, the angel of the Lord told Hagar, "Behold, thou art with child, and shalt bear a son, and shalt call his name Ishmael; because the LORD hath heard thy affliction" (16:11). In Exodus 2:24 we find these words: "And God heard their groaning, and God remembered His covenant with Abraham, with Isaac, and with Jacob." David wrote these beautiful words: "The eyes of the LORD are upon the righteous, and his ears are open unto their cry" (Ps 34:15), and they apply to us today. As God's children, we have His promise — His ears are open, He does hearken to our cry as He did so long ago to the deep cry from Rachel's heart for a child. We do not know the reasons behind any seeming delay, but we can trust that God is working out His purpose according to His perfect programme.

God opened her womb — Rachel is the third in line of notable women who were barren in the book of Genesis. First we recall that God had promised Abraham that He would make of him "a great nation" (12:2), but Sarah was barren. About twenty-five years later, "the LORD visited Sarah as he had said, and the LORD did unto Sarah as he had spoken. For Sarah conceived, and bare Abraham a son in his old age, at the set time of which God had spoken to him" (21:1-2). Now we know that there were some bumps along that long road, but, when the time was right, God opened Sarah's womb, and she bare a son, Isaac. Next, when Isaac married Rebekah, she was barren, too! Twenty long years of waiting passed before Esau and Jacob were born. The writer says, "And Isaac entreated the LORD for his wife, because she was barren: and the LORD was entreated of him, and Rebekah his wife conceived" (25:21). Finally, we find Rachel, Jacob's second wife, who is barren for several years after their marriage. What made it more difficult was that her sister Leah was bearing children on a consistent basis. So Rachel cried to the Lord, and "God hearkened unto her, and opened her womb." In two succeeding verses in relation to Hannah, we find that it was God who had control over her womb: "the LORD had shut up her womb" (1 Sam 1:5-6). She cried to God, too, out of her affliction, knowing of other similar cases, and "the LORD remembered her" (1 Sam 1:19), and she conceived. At the very least, we can understand this from the account of God hearkening and God opening the womb: it is very obvious that the conception of a son was a work of God in response to a cry to God.

God took away her reproach — this is the first mention of the word "reproach" in our Bible. It bears the idea of contempt, or scorn, or to use a more modern word, stigma. For a Hebrew woman, not being able to bear a son who would become an heir in the household was to be treated as an object of scorn. We see this again in the life of Hannah, when Elkanah's other wife, Peninnah, provoked her continually because she had not yet borne children. When we consider Jacob's family circumstances and read just a few verses prior to this about the infighting over mandrakes, it is not hard to imagine the reproach that Rachel felt every day.

Rachel's Attitude

She was content — one can only imagine the sense of relief and happiness that flooded over her when she realized she had conceived. Long before the days of ultrasound it was impossible to know if the child would be a boy or a girl, but imagine her joy months later when a healthy baby boy was born — "she bare a son." We see this contentedness in her words, "God hath taken away my reproach." Although we have already noticed that Rachel had some attraction to her father's gods, she obviously realized that Jehovah was the true God, and He was the One who had answered her cries for a son.

She was confident — having seen that she could trust God to answer her plea for the first son, she now names him "Joseph", meaning "Jehovah will add". She then expresses that thought very clearly, saying, "The LORD shall add to me another son." Her continued confidence and trust would be in the Lord Himself.

There are few details about those very early years in Joseph's life, but we know that he was Rachel's only child for a while. She did not know that her time with Joseph would be far briefer than she had ever imagined, but as is normal in the life of any mother, she surely spent every moment possible with him. We have dealt somewhat at the beginning of this chapter with the importance of motherhood, but let's remember that the time God grants us with our children will go far more quickly than we ever expected. We must take advantage of those precious moments, instilling the truth of God into their young minds and hearts. Their capacity to learn while very young is astounding, and what they learn will stand them in good stead now and in coming days if we take the time to "bring them up in the nurture and admonition of the Lord" (Eph 6:4).

The Sudden Change in his Father

"And it came to pass, when Rachel had born Joseph, that Jacob said unto Laban, Send me away, that I may go unto mine own place, and to my country. Give me my wives and my children, for whom I have served thee, and let me go: for thou knowest my service which I have done thee" (30:25-26).

Rachel had been Jacob's first choice for a wife, and even after he has married both Leah and Rachel, we find that she is the favoured bride. Genesis 29:30 makes this very clear: "He loved also Rachel more than Leah". It also is not difficult to see how this played out in the previous verses in this very chapter. Reuben, Leah's first son, had gone out in the time of the wheat harvest and found mandrakes in the field. While many different interpretations have been given to this particular word, the context indicates that they were thought to have some special power with regard to the conception of children. Thus Rachel was very interested in bartering in order to receive some of these mandrakes. The relationship between the two sisters is characterized by rivalry. Leah says, "Is it a small matter that thou hast taken my husband? and wouldest thou take away my son's mandrakes also?" Rachel responds, "Therefore he shall lie with thee to night for thy son's mandrakes" (30:15). The next verse gives more details: "And Jacob came out of the field in the evening, and Leah went out to meet him, and said, Thou must come in unto me; for surely I have hired thee with my son's mandrakes. And he lay with her that night."

Jacob obviously was living in an atmosphere of conflict, at least at times. This is not unexpected, given the choices he had earlier made. He does not seem to be a tremendous leader in regards to his family, and that is rather clear from the previous paragraph - pushed and pulled in different directions; somewhat controlled by his wives; and far from happy in his work for his father-in-law!

Now that Rachel has her first child, it seems that Jacob suddenly comes to his senses. He has been away from home for more than fourteen years, his mother has died in the meantime, his father is ageing, and he himself is already over ninety! But something about Joseph's birth in particular sparked this interest or desire for home in him. Remember something similar years before: "And Enoch lived sixty and five years, and begat Methuselah: and Enoch walked with God after he begat Methuselah three hundred years, and begat sons and daughters" (5:21-22). Looking into the face of this newborn baby, the first son of his favoured wife, the desire to leave Mesopotamia becomes increasingly strong. Considering the future needs of his ever-increasing family, he wants to go home, to Canaan.

The Sadness in Joseph's Experience

As mentioned in the previous chapter, there were adverse circumstances in the life of Joseph, and that from a very early age. As we consider these events, remember Paul's comforting words: "And we know that all things work together for good to them that love God, to them who are the called according to his purpose" (Rom 8:28). Joseph at this point had not had his significant dreams, but God already had a purpose for him, and was soon going to bring various circumstances into his young life that would be formative, although very difficult.

The Departure from Mesopotamia

Although Jacob had the desire planted in his heart to leave Mesopotamia for Canaan when Joseph was born, his father-in-law resisted. Laban said: "I have learned by experience that the LORD hath blessed me for thy sake ... Appoint me thy wages, and I will give it" (30:27-28). Jacob now felt even more the pressing need regarding the future of his family. It was acceptable for his father-in-law to be blessed, but now he asks, "... when shall I provide for mine own house also?" (30:30).

We know that the next six years were difficult for Jacob, as he and Laban continued to try to outdo one another in regard to their flocks, but finally, another crisis came. He realized that his cousins, Laban's sons, were jealous of his success, and saw that Laban's face was "not toward him as before" (31:2). The Lord graciously spoke to Jacob at this point, and confirmed his desire to leave: "Return unto the land of thy fathers, and to thy kindred; and I will be with thee" (31:3).

Jacob called his two wives out to the field, explained the situation to them, and told them about the divine directive. They understood that there was no portion or inheritance for them in their father's house. Indeed they were now considered strangers by their own father. So "Jacob rose up, and set his sons and his wives upon camels; And he carried away all his cattle, and all his goods which he had gotten" (31:17-18). You can imagine the questions in a young boy's mind: Where are we going? Why are we leaving? Why didn't we say goodbye to my grandparents? Why the big secret? Why the rush? What's happening? His world was being turned upside down.

Imagine the feeling that came over Jacob's camp when Laban finally caught up with them. Laban's accusations were strong, but he would not act against his son-in-law since God had warned him in a dream to speak no evil to Jacob. A covenant was made between the two, a stone was placed for a pillar, and a sacrifice was made. How must six-year-old Joseph have felt early the next morning when "Laban rose up, and kissed his sons and his daughters, and blessed them" (31:55), and then departed? This would not be the only sad separation that Joseph would experience in his life.

The Dread of Man

You will understand that oftentimes the mood of the father will set the mood for the family. Think about Jacob as he recalls the circumstances in which he had to flee for his life years before, believing that Esau was going to kill him because of the trickery he had employed in taking away the birthright and the blessing. Now he is going to be coming close to his brother again. So he sends messengers to Esau in the land of Seir, seeking grace in his sight (32:5). But now he begins to fear as he hears that Esau is coming to meet him, with four hundred men. And the dread that Jacob feels certainly cannot be hidden from his family. He was "greatly afraid and distressed", and so "he divided the people that was with him … into two bands" (32:7), thinking that if Esau struck one group, the other could surely escape.

Jacob pleads with God in the following verses, remembering His promise to him years before when he had passed over the Jordan. It is from here that we often rightly quote in relation to ourselves: "I am not worthy of the least of all [thy] mercies" (32:10). Joseph was old enough now to understand that something serious was going on. More serious yet would it all appear when Jacob caused all his family to cross over the ford Jabbok, and remained behind himself, and this at night! Can you envision the scene? Can you hear the questions again? Why aren't you coming along? What is happening? Surely a young boy of six would be alarmed by all of this.

The next day, Jacob sees Esau coming towards him. But something has happened in the meantime. Jacob has had wrestlings with God Himself! He has received a new name, Israel! He is halting upon his thigh or, as we would say today, he had an obvious limp. His family would have perceived that something had happened, but not know what had transpired.

We see again in this scene something of the preference that Jacob has for Rachel, and for Joseph too. As he divides the family up, he puts "Rachel and Joseph hindermost", at the very back, the most protected place. Joseph would recognize this distinction, even if he did not yet understand its significance.

God here, as at other times, had his hand upon Joseph, preserving and protecting him for future usefulness in His divine purposes. Esau and Jacob embrace and weep, a happy reunion. Many years down the road, Joseph will fall on his brothers' necks, kiss them and weep in a happy reunion, perhaps recalling this earlier restoration of a relationship fractured so many years before.

The Death of his Mother

After the defilement of Dinah in Genesis 34, God directs Jacob to "go up to Bethel, and dwell there: and make there an altar unto God" (35:1). At this point Jacob instructs all his household and servants to "put away the strange gods", to "be clean" (35:2), and then "they journeyed" (35:5). God's preserving hand was upon this family during the trek through enemy territory so that no-one pursued after the sons of Jacob, those that had taken revenge for the sin against their sister, decimating the city where Shechem resided. They all arrive safely in Bethel, where God again speaks to Jacob, confirming His promise and covenant: they are a people chosen by God, and He will provide a place for them to live. Joseph, although just a youngster, could not have helped being impressed with these happenings, a very positive turn of events in the spiritual life of the family. It was here that Jacob set up a pillar and poured out a drink offering and oil upon it. These spiritual practices would have remained in Joseph's memory years later when he was living in a very pagan country and culture.

The exciting family news was that Joseph was going to have a sibling. Since he was Rachel's only child, this surely would have been thrilling for him — to think he would have a younger brother, and he would no longer be the youngest in the family! There must also have been a definite spring in Jacob's step, despite his limp. Again, remember that the mood of a parent often sets the mood of the family!

As the day approaches, they are coming close to Ephrath, "and Rachel travailed, and she had hard labour ... And it came to pass, as her soul was in departing, (for she died) that she called his name Ben-oni" (vv 16-18). She was "buried in the way to Ephrath, which is Bethlehem" (v 19). Being familiar with the story from our youth, we perhaps miss some of the impact of these statements. Jacob has lost the love of his life, Joseph has lost his mother, and now there is a newborn child, named by his mother in her dying moments "the son of my sorrow", for another to bring up. Jacob shows his mettle, and insists on calling him "Benjamin", or "the son of my right hand".

There will be some who can all too readily relate to Joseph in this moment of sadness. Surely all he had heard and learned from his mother would become even more important to him now, and he would treasure these precious memories. Remember that God is the God of all comfort, and both Jacob and Joseph learned to carry on, even in their deep sorrow, one an aged man, and one very young. Surely the bond between them became even closer, and now Benjamin would be included in this circle of love.

By now you may be asking why this chapter is entitled "His Childhood and its Advantages", since we have dealt with some very challenging times in Joseph's life. Before looking at one more event, just think about what it meant for Joseph to be brought up by a father and mother who loved him. He had a mother who taught him, and surely would have told him how he was the answer to her prayers over the course of many years. He would have begun to understand something of God's workings in his life. How important it is to teach our children not only of God's care for them, but also His sovereign control over events in our lives.

The Significance of Grandparents

"And Jacob came unto Isaac his father unto Mamre, unto the city of Arbah, which is Hebron, where Abraham and Isaac sojourned" (35:27).

We live in an era when dates and times are recorded with great precision. As we go through the story of Isaac, Jacob and Joseph, however, we don't have that luxury, but we do find some markers to help us.

It seems that once Jacob left Haran, he spent some time in Bethel before moving on and spreading his tent beyond the tower of Edar, then later finally arrived at Hebron where his father was still living. The timing of Rebekah's death is not noted in the Bible, although most feel that Jacob never had the opportunity to see his mother again after having fled from Esau decades before.

Not every young lad can say that Isaac was his grandfather! A close look at the chronology will show us that Joseph had the privilege of spending a good number of years alongside his grandfather before being sold into slavery. He had been separated from Laban, his maternal grandfather, but now God was giving him the opportunity to learn from his paternal grandfather, Isaac. We can assume that he would hear from Isaac's lips some wonderful stories about Abraham, his father, and the father of the faithful. Can you imagine hearing the story we read in Genesis 22 from the very man who had once been placed on that altar? Would the story of God providing Himself a lamb for a burnt offering not have a great impact young Joseph? Would not the mentions of God's faithful care not be a help to Joseph in those dark and difficult days that were not too far down the road?

We bring to mind the story of young Timothy, sitting on the knees, not only of his mother Eunice, but also of his grandmother Lois. In them he had seen faith exemplified, and had learned the Scriptures. Thus Paul exhorts Timothy with these words: "But continue thou in the things which thou hast learned and hast been assured of, knowing of whom thou hast learned them; And that from a child thou hast known the holy scriptures, which are able to make thee wise unto salvation through faith which is in Christ Jesus" (2 Tim 3:14-15). Not only parents, but godly grandparents, can pour God's truth into young minds and hearts, praying that it will one day bear fruit, as it did in Joseph's life.

So, yes, there were moments of adversity, but Joseph did have many advantages in his childhood that would be a real blessing to him throughout his life. Let us remember that God weaves the difficult and the delightful moments together to work out His purposes. He asks us to humbly and simply trust in Him.

CHAPTER 3

The Conflict and Animosity

Genesis 37:1-11

Moses dealt briefly with the story of Esau and his descendants in Genesis 36, similar to his approach earlier in the book with Ishmael and Isaac. The brother who would not form part of the Messianic line was mentioned first, without great detail, and then the younger brother whose descendants would be in the Messianic line are written about in much greater detail.

As we begin this chapter in the story of Joseph, we find the family dwelling "In the land of Canaan" (37.1), the Promised Land. It commences with Joseph, a young lad of seventeen, tending his father's flocks, and ends with him being sold into slavery by his brothers who hated him without a cause. The whole chapter could be summarised by four words: Joseph is *serving*, he is *special*, he is *scorned*, and he is *sold*. We will, however, go into more detail, learning lessons along the way.

His Responsibility and Service

"These are the generations of Jacob. Joseph, being seventeen years old, was feeding the flock with his brethren; and the lad was with the sons of Bilhah, and with the sons of Zilpah, his father's wives: and Joseph brought unto his father their evil report" (37:2).

The Task of Tending

Joseph is the second youngest in the family, but immediately after mentioning the "generations of Jacob" Moses moves straight away into the story of Joseph. Although amongst the youngest of the family, this did not excuse him from working along with his older brothers. Dan and Naphtali were Bilhah's sons, while Zilpah's two sons were Gad and Asher. Bilhah was Rachel's maidservant, and Zilpah was Leah's. Jacob was a wealthy man and Joseph had learned how to shepherd his father's flocks. In Bible times and later, sons generally adopted the same profession as their fathers, but this has greatly changed in many cultures in recent centuries. Nonetheless, teaching our children how to carry responsibility from a very young age remains part of bringing them up "in the nurture and admonition of the Lord" (Eph 6:4).

We should take a moment to bring to mind another who would call Himself "the good shepherd" (John 10:11). Joseph reminds us of the Lord Jesus, both in his willingness to tend his father's sheep, and in his interest in the wellbeing of others, as we will notice shortly. The Lord Jesus spoke of His willingness to lay down His life for the sheep, an act that teaches us something about the value that God places on His own.

Another lesson we cannot ignore here is found in the word "feeding", elsewhere translated in Genesis as "keep", or "shepherd". If in the Lord Jesus we see the supreme example of one who shepherds the flock, can we not also understand something of the burden that godly overseers bear in a local assembly? They are to feed the people of God; be aware of dangers that are present, or that soon will come; be cognizant of the believers' needs, especially, but not only, in the spiritual realm; and also ensure that the sheep are growing. We could summarize their responsibility this way: pasture, protection, provision, and progress.

Telling the Truth

Although many have commented that Joseph should not have brought to his father the report of the conduct of his brothers, Biblical principles tell us otherwise. Although not yet written when Joseph lived, consider Leviticus 5:1: "And if a soul sin, and hear the voice of swearing, and is a witness, whether he hath seen or known of it; if he do not utter it, then he shall bear his iniquity." Joseph was thus duty bound to relate to his father what he witnessed in his brothers.

We can see two sides to what happened with Joseph bringing to his father "their evil report." It is quite possible that Jacob, knowing his sons' character, was looking for an honest report of their behaviour when they were far from their father's house. Or, it is also possible that Joseph felt a real burden to tell his father that his sons' conduct, at least when they were absent from him, was far from prudent. In either case, there is no blame whatsoever to be laid at Joseph's feet. He simply and truthfully reported what he had observed.

Consider the Lord Jesus' words: "The world cannot hate you; but me it hateth, because I testify of it, that the works thereof are evil" (John 7:7). He knew what was in man, not only observing their conduct, but also knowing their character. Their works were evil because their heart was evil. It is interesting, in contrast, to consider the Lord Jesus in John 17 praying to His Father and mentioning many things about His disciples as He nears the end of His earthly sojourn, but there is nothing negative. The disciples surely had failed on many occasions, but the Lord Jesus simply brings before God their faithfulness: they had kept God's word, they had known, they had received His words, they had believed that He had been sent by the Father (John 17:6-8), and then He says, "I am glorified in them" (v 10).

On a practical note, we should ask these questions: What would be said about us in reference to our faithfulness in the tasks that God has placed into our hands? Can our Saviour observe us and give a good report to our Father?

Another inherent warning we find here has to do with the challenge of a young person being far away from the influence of his parents. There does indeed come a time when the arrow needs to be released from the quiver (Ps 127) and sent out into the world of studies or employment, a world that is full of pitfalls and problems, of temptations and testing. Remember that, as parents, we are given a very brief time to instill the fear of God in their hearts, by both education and example. We are not blaming Jacob for his sons' evil behaviour, but at the same time he cannot be entirely excused.

But before leaving this point, take a look at talebearing in Proverbs.

"A talebearer revealeth secrets" (11:13); "the words of a talebearer are as wounds" (18:8); "where there is no talebearer, the strife ceaseth" (26:20). So we are not condoning a free-for-all telling of tales, a sharing of every little detail we may know about others, a rumour mill, or anything of the sort. But Joseph did what was right in this situation, sharing the truth about his brothers' behaviour as part of his responsibility to his father. Sin should not be ignored or covered, but rather exposed and dealt with.

His Robe of Superiority

"Now Israel loved Joseph more than all his children, because he was the son of his old age: and he made him a coat of many colours. And when his brethren saw that their father loved him more than all his brethren, they hated him" (37:3-4).

We can easily see two reasons why Joseph had a special place in the life of his father - age and affinity.

His Advanced Age

As we have previously noted, Jacob was over 90 years of age when Joseph was born. Moses clearly states here that "he was the son of his old age". While it is true that Joseph was not the last son born to Jacob, he was the penultimate, and then there was a pause of six years before Benjamin came along.

This chapter shows us that Jacob was now remaining at home as his sons worked, tending the flocks far from their normal habitat. Because Joseph was younger than his other siblings, his father likely had doted on him more than he would have been able to do with the other sons in earlier days when Jacob himself was completely responsible for the flocks, not only his own, but also Laban's many sheep. This is not meant in any way to be a criticism of Jacob, as it is normal for people to go through different phases in life. It could be a warning, however, to us to be aware of any possible dangers related to our current stage in life.

Their Affinity and Affection

In another sense, we can understand the place of superiority that Joseph received in the family as there would be an affinity between Jacob and this son. He was, after all, the first-born son of his first love, Rachel. Jacob had waited many years to have a son with his favoured wife, and finally Joseph had come along. The two of them shared in the heartbreak of losing Rachel — a dearly loved wife and mother.

Jacob, although not a perfect man, was a work in progress at this point in his life. God had renamed him "Israel" during the trek from Mesopotamia to Canaan (32:28), and he was starting to live up to the meaning of this new name: "a prince with God".

Perhaps Israel was looking to the future and pondering the needs of his growing family. Reuben had sinned, as we read in Genesis 35:22: "And it came to pass, when Israel dwelt in that land, that Reuben went and lay with Bilhah his father's concubine: and Israel heard it." Jacob did not act at the time but kept in mind this grave error in judgment. As he considers who could be a leader, Joseph, although young, is the obvious choice. The writer of the Chronicles sheds more light on this: "for he [Reuben] was the firstborn; but forasmuch as he defiled his father's bed, his birthright was given unto the sons of Joseph the son of Israel" (1 Chr 5:1).

The relationship between Jacob and Joseph was so very special, but our minds are drawn to the eternal relationship between the Father and the Son. The Lord Jesus was the Son of the Father's love; the One who brought delight to the Father's heart; the One who always did those things that were pleasing to the Father. When He came into the world, the Son said, "Lo, I come to do thy will, O God" (Heb 10:9). The Father, on two occasions, opened the heavens to declare, "This is my beloved Son, in whom I am well pleased" (Matt 3:17; 17:5).

It is true that Jacob loved Joseph more than his other brethren, but:

The Apparel made it Apparent

There are two dangers that we need to consider at this point - favouritism and forgetfulness.

The writer says: "And when his brethren saw that their father loved him more ..." (37:4), they hated him. How did they see this? Well, possibly they had observed many actions over the years, and heard words of intimacy between the father and the son, but here what comes to the fore is this phrase: "he made him a coat of many colours" (37:3). What they perhaps had always suspected was now very apparent.

Whatever the exact form the coat took (the Hebrew is a little obscure), it was, no doubt, beautifully crafted, it was not only lovely to look upon, but had a special meaning — it spoke of leadership. This type of leadership would not normally belong to one of the youngest in the family, but when Jacob gave this coat to his favoured son Joseph, his other sons understood the message: "Joseph is the chosen one; Joseph will be the leader. I am giving Joseph a superior place in this family." It is even possible that while in the field, his responsibility was, in part, to supervise the labours of the others.

We are not saying it was wrong for Jacob to give this place to Joseph, but at the same time he was showing favouritism, and that in itself is always problematic. God is no respecter of persons (Acts 10:34; 1 Peter 1:17), and we ought to live with this in mind. Showing favouritism in our family circles will always bring sad consequences. The same can be said about local assembly life. We are not saying that all have the same responsibilities in a local assembly, for God has gifted each believer differently. However, let us recognize the folly of favouritism, whether towards a family member or someone else in the "right" circle of friendships. The assembly is no place for excluding believers who perhaps are from a different social class or background than many others in the fellowship. It is also not the place for the baton to be passed from generation to generation with no regard to calling and gift.

But how quickly Jacob had forgotten this fact! He was his mother's favourite, and Esau his father's. We noted earlier that this brought conflict, deceit, separation and heartache to Isaac's household. Will we not see the same happening now in Jacob's family? A lesson we will notice again later comes from Paul: "Be not deceived; God is not mocked: for whatsoever a man soweth, that shall he also reap" (Gal 6:7).

When it comes to the Lord Jesus, we recognize that His position as the Son of God is not the same as our position as sons of God. There is no rivalry nor favouritism. He has been given "a name which is above every name" (Phil 2:9); "And he is before all things, and by him all things consist. And he is the head of the body, the church: who is the beginning, the firstborn from the dead; that in all things he might have the preeminence" (Col 1:17-18).

The Revelation was Special

As we read through the life of Joseph, we find five dreams, of which only two were personal, and they came in close succession. Later, when he was in Egypt, we read about Joseph interpreting the dreams of the baker, the cupbearer, and Pharaoh.

"And he said unto them, Hear, I pray you, this dream which I have dreamed: For, behold, we were binding sheaves in the field, and, lo, my sheaf arose, and also stood upright; and, behold, your sheaves stood round about, and made obeisance to my sheaf ... And he dreamed yet another dream, and told it his brethren, and said, Behold, I have dreamed a dream more; and, behold, the sun and the moon and the eleven stars made obeisance to me" (37:6-7, 9).

The Recognition of the Facts

The dreams were not in need of any special interpretation, but they were a special revelation from God for Joseph. His brothers and his father quickly understood the meaning behind them both — that Joseph would have a very high place, and that the rest of the family would recognize and honour him. There was no mistaking the significance of these two dreams — but it was not a fact that was easy to accept, even though it was simple to recognize.

The Reason regarding his Future

Why were these dreams so important at this juncture in Joseph's life? Although he did not know it, he soon would be separated from his family, which, despite the conflict and confusion that existed amongst them, at the same time did exert some positive influence on him. There were God-fearing people with whom Joseph had daily contact. But all of that would soon end.

God, therefore, in His kind and providential care of Joseph, revealed what would surely have been a blessing and an encouragement to him in coming days and years. Think of Joseph in Potiphar's house, working as a slave, or later when he was cast into prison. What would have sustained Joseph? The hope that one day God would fulfill what He had revealed to him years before in two simple dreams: he would reign, he would see his family again, and they would bow down to him. Joseph quietly lived his life in faith, seemingly without hearing God's voice on a regular basis, but rather simply relying on what God had plainly revealed to him.

Years later Jeremiah would write concerning hope both in his prophecy and in the book of Lamentations. Five times in Lamentations 3 he mentions hope, starting by saying, "My strength and my hope is perished from the LORD" (v 18). As he begins meditating on the Lord's mercies, however, he writes, "This I recall to my mind, therefore have I hope" (v 21). What had he recalled? God's mercies, compassions, and faithfulness: "It is of the LORD'S mercies that we are not consumed, because his compassions fail not. They are new every morning: great is thy faithfulness" (vv 22-23). What comfort this brought to him! It did not mean that the trial wasn't going to remain, but in the midst of difficult circumstances he continues, "The LORD is my portion, saith my soul; therefore will I hope in him. The LORD is good unto them that wait for him, to the soul that seeketh him. It is good that a man should both hope and quietly wait for the salvation of the LORD" (vv 24-26). While it is true that these words were written years after he was born, they describe Joseph's hope, based on what he had learned from his forefathers, as well as the direct revelation he received in dreams from God. True, he did not have the privileged experience that Abraham, Isaac and Jacob had - that of hearing God speak directly to them on different occasions - but what he did know about God, and what he had received from God directly, brought him through a very long trial when he was sent to his brothers by his father and then sold into slavery. We, too, may go through seeming periods of silence in our experience, with nothing outstanding occurring, but God is pleased and honoured when we simply trust Him, following what we have learned from His Word.

We, too, as New Testament believers, have a living hope. Hope is mentioned by Paul, Peter, and John, as well as the writer to the Hebrews. Biblical hope is not something we are trying to obtain, or something we are grasping after, but a sure thing that awaits us in a coming day, and this cannot be taken away from us by anyone. We "have a strong consolation, who have fled for refuge to lay hold upon the hope set before us: Which hope we have as an anchor of the soul" (Heb 6:18-19). An anchor of the soul! This is no light matter! Or consider these words: "Christ in you, the hope of glory" (Col 1:27). Glory will be attained in that coming day, when Christ will share even more fully with us His glory. Remember His words as He prayed to His Father: "And the glory which thou gavest me I have given them" (John 17:22).

The Response from his Father

Upon hearing the second dream, Jacob first of all rebuked his son. He wondered how it could be possible that not only Joseph's brothers, but also his parents, would bow down before him in a coming day. "But his father observed the saying" (37:11). This means he kept it in remembrance. He did not ignore it, he did not push it from his mind, but kept it before him, pondering its meaning, and meditating upon its significance.

Remember that many years before, Jacob, too, had dreamt: "And he dreamed, and behold a ladder set up on the earth, and the top of it reached to heaven … And, behold, the LORD stood above it, and said, I am the LORD God of Abraham thy father, and the God of Isaac: the land whereon thou liest, to thee will I give it, and to thy seed … And, behold, I am with thee, and will keep thee in all places whither thou goest, and will bring thee again into this land; for I will not leave thee, until I have done that which I have spoken to thee of" (28:12-15). Jacob, when he awoke, said, "Surely the LORD is in this place; and I knew it not" (28:16). So now, looking back, Jacob realizes that what God had promised to him in a dream He had fulfilled: he was in the Promised Land again! While we are not recounting Jacob's story in this book, it is useful to note that this dream had an impact on his life, and thus he was not so quick to dismiss the importance of Joseph's dream.

Perhaps there were times in the next two decades when to Jacob's memory would come these dreams. Perhaps, as many parents do, he would ask: "Why?" If God had promised by means of a dream to make Joseph great, what had gone wrong? But we remember that God is patient, and in His providence He was working out the means for these dreams to become a reality.

But consider also:

The Reaction of his Family

Some would perhaps criticise Joseph for telling his brothers about his dreams, but there is no sense of condemnation in the Bible for this action on his part. They refused to heed God's revelation to them by means of Joseph, and thus the whole family would eventually suffer through a famine before coming to recognize the veracity of the dreams given to their young brother two decades before.

We notice their doubt: "Shalt thou indeed reign over us? or shalt thou indeed have dominion over us?" (37:8). How could it be possible that this young stripling of a lad would somehow have such a position in relation to his older brethren — they scoffed at him. But they also despised him: "And they hated him yet the more for his dreams, and for his words" (37:8). Notice, however their measure of discernment: "And his brethren envied him" (37:11). They obviously were able to discern that there was some truth behind Joseph's dreams, otherwise there would have been no reason to envy him.

The Lord Jesus was in fellowship with His Father, with no need of "special revelation". In prophecy we hear the Lord say that "he wakeneth morning by morning, he wakeneth mine ear to hear as the learned" (Isa 50:4). We observe in the Gospels that the Lord went often into solitary places to pray. This surely emphasizes the close relationship He had with His Father.

The Resentment and Spite

"And when his brethren saw that their father loved him more than all his brethren, they *hated* him, and could not speak peaceably unto him. And Joseph dreamed a dream, and he told it his brethren: and they *hated* him yet the more ... And they *hated* him yet the more for his dreams, and for his words ... And his brethren *envied* him" (vv 4-11)

The Motivation behind the Hostility

As we move down the brief section of this chapter we note animosity and hostility time and time again. There were two things that motivated their hatred for Joseph: the position he held in his father's heart, and the revelation given him in the dreams received from Heaven itself. Had their attitude been different, instead of resentment there would have been recognition and acceptance of what was truly the will of God. Resisting the will of God will always bring difficulty and distress, sadness and sorrow.

The Manner in which the Hatred was Expressed

Hatred is very difficult to contain and control, partly due to the fact that it is a work of the flesh (Gal 5:20). Remember, too, the words of the Lord Jesus: "for out of the abundance of the heart the mouth speaketh" (Matt 12:34). They were acting in the power of the flesh, and their heart was not right with God. The same can happen today when we resist God's working in our lives.

First of all we see that they "could not speak peaceably unto him." We do not have a record of their actual words, but there were certainly no kind words spoken to him. Perhaps they were words of mockery, or of ridicule. In today's society we read much about "bullying" — that which happens when another is perceived as vulnerable, so unkind words are spoken to intimidate, harm or coerce the "weaker" person. This has no place in a Christian's life. Solomon wisely writes concerning the power of words: "The words of the wicked are to lie in wait for blood"; then later, "Seest thou a man that is hasty in his words? there is more hope of a fool than of him" (Prov 12:6; 29:29). Joseph's brothers perhaps did not realize they were on a slippery slope, a downward path, that commenced with words. Paul writes: "Let no corrupt communication proceed out of your mouth, but that which is good to the use of edifying, that it may minister grace unto the hearers" (Eph 4:29). Our words will either tear down or build up — when our heart is right, our words will follow as we seek to bless those around us.

Then we see that they "envied him". This, too, is a work of the flesh, a mark of carnality, as Paul writes: "for whereas there is among you envying, and strife, and divisions, are ye not carnal, and walk as men?" (1 Cor 3:3). Solomon helps us understand the seriousness of envy, writing: "A sound heart is the life of the flesh: but envy the rottenness of the bones"; and, "Wrath is cruel, and anger is outrageous; but who is able to stand before envy?" (Prov 14:30; 27:4). Envy, as W. E. Vine aptly defines it, "is the feeling of displeasure produced by witnessing or hearing of the advantage or prosperity of others". How true this is in Joseph's case! It was evident to his brothers that he was prospering, and their displeasure soon became clear.

Why is it that human nature finds it particularly challenging to be happy when others do well? Paul deals with this in two epistles: "Rejoice with them that do rejoice, and weep with them that weep" (Rom 12:15); "And whether one member suffer, all the members suffer with it; or one member be honoured, all the members rejoice with it" (1 Cor 12:26). We all come together to help the weak and wounded, but envy and jealousy oftentimes keep us from rejoicing when others are honoured or promoted in any way.

As believers, we need to be constantly on our guard against the flesh - "Walk in the Spirit, and ye shall not fulfil the lust of the flesh" (Gal 5:16). It never is satisfied, and although "they that are Christ's have crucified the flesh with the affections and lusts" (Gal 5:24), it attempts to raise its ugly head on a regular basis. We need to be continually walking "in the Spirit" (Gal 5:25) in order to please God, and avoid these manifestations of our flesh. Would to God that we would heed Paul's exhortation to the Ephesian believers: "Let all bitterness, and wrath, and anger, and clamour, and evil speaking, be put away from you, with all malice: And be ye kind one to another, tenderhearted, forgiving one another, even as God for Christ's sake hath forgiven you" (Eph 4:31-32).

The Lord Jesus was misunderstood by His earthly family. They said to Him, perhaps as a challenge, "Depart hence, and go into Judaea, that thy disciples also may see the works that thou doest" (John 7:3). Why was this? John continues, "For neither did his brethren believe in him" (John 7:5). Later in the same book, although in the context of the broader circle of the nation, the Lord Jesus says, "They hated me without a cause" (John 15:25). Never was there such a lovely man who walked upon this earth, but never was such hatred displayed as that which He faced throughout His life.

You will recall that one of the words in the list of works of the flesh in Galatians 5:21 is murder! But we will have to leave consideration of that until the next chapter.

CHAPTER 4

The Cruelty and Abuse

Genesis 37:12-36

Having seen the spiteful attitude of Joseph's brothers in the previous chapter, we now turn to see how important it is to keep our thoughts in line with the Word of God, for "as he thinketh in his heart, so is he" (Prov 23:7). These men who hated Joseph were only waiting for an opportunity to show how cruel they could truly be. As we go through the rest of Genesis 37 we will see Joseph sent by his father, spotted by his brethren, stripped of his special robe, and finally sold to the merchantmen who were going to Egypt. It does not do us any harm to remember again that God, in His sovereign plan, was going to work all these things out for His purposes, even though the circumstances that would take Joseph to that place were very difficult.

Jacob's Desire

The Request

Jacob, being fully aware of his sons' behaviour, decided to send Joseph to Shechem to check up on them and the state of the flocks: "come, and I will send thee unto them" (37:13). Although we know what happened, surely had he known what would befall Joseph he would not have sent him, but Jacob was not cognizant of the depth of the hatred his other sons felt towards his favoured son Joseph. He did not know that twenty years would pass before he would lay eyes on Joseph once more.

Consider the wisdom of sending his seventeen year old son this distance — he was a trusted son, and Jacob was giving him increasing responsibility on the "family farm". This would not be seen as such a positive thing from the other brothers' perspective, but it remains wise today to teach responsibility to our children, obviously dependent on their age. On the other hand, we do wonder if Jacob was fully aware of the perils that faced Joseph. Not only from the hostility of those who dwelt nearby, but also the envy and anger that existed in his own sons' hearts towards their brother.

Partings can be difficult times — sending a son or daughter off to university, or to a different city for employment purposes, not knowing what perils and challenges they may face, can be a test of the emotions. All that time and effort invested, and the question remains: What will happen to my boy?, or, How will my daughter fare? One can only trust that what has been poured into their child will bear fruit. Many partings are sadder yet, but here Jacob likely had no undue concerns and no inkling that later he would have longed for it never to have happened.

The Response

Joseph's response was brief, but sincere: "Here am I". Does this interchange not make us think about another favoured Son who was sent? Even though Joseph said, "Yes", it is quite likely that there was some sense of trepidation in his heart, and along the road he would think of the cruel and abusive words that his brothers had heaped upon him on previous occasions. He possibly would not be aware of how deep was the hostility that resided in his brothers' hearts. But not so in the case of the Lord Jesus — both He and His father knew full well that when He came to His own, His own people would not receive him (John 1:11). Nonetheless, the words that came from the mouth of the Lord Jesus are precious: "Lo, I come to do thy will, O God" (Heb 10:9). We see perfect and knowing submission to the Father's will in the Lord Jesus. On a practical note, we should ask ourselves the question: Am I as quick in bowing to God's will in my life as He was? When something from His Word comes to mind, do I readily submit? Joseph asked no questions, and did not delay.

The Road

"So he sent him ... and he came to Shechem" (37:14). The distance was about 50 miles, and there would be perils and loneliness along the way. But Joseph continued until he reached Shechem. Think about the Lord Jesus, who travelled a much longer and more difficult road, leaving Heaven itself. Both of these sons enjoyed times of closeness with their fathers, yet both were so entirely devoted to their fathers' will that they were ready to leave his side to accomplish their fathers' plan.

> *From heaven He came and sought her*
> *To be His holy bride;*
> *With His own blood He bought her,*
> *And for her life He died.*
>
> (S. J. Stone)

Joseph's Diligence

When Joseph arrived in Shechem, his brothers were nowhere to be found. It would have been easier for Joseph to return home, tell his father that his brothers were not where they were supposed to be, and thus give up. But Joseph showed diligence with regard to what had been committed to him. We can far too easily become distracted or discouraged, or we can delay our obedience — but not Joseph, and certainly not our Lord Jesus!

The Direction

As Joseph wandered in the field, God sent a man to guide him in the right direction. When asked, he responds, "I seek my brethren" (37:16). This was his duty, and he wanted to please his father. We don't see Joseph as a cynical young man, looking for a route of escape from responsibility, but rather a guileless son. One doubts that Joseph at this point had any fear that his brothers would actually abuse and harm him, much less kill him, so he moved along, continuing his search.

This is one of those apparent coincidences that we find not only in this chapter of Genesis, but in many parts of the Holy Scriptures. God is sovereign, and He has given to us, His mortal creatures, the ability to choose and made decisions, to respond to Him in faithful obedience. We should not err on the side of over-emphasising God's sovereign control nor on the side of placing too much weight on man's free will. The former would make us into mere robots; the latter would rob God of His glory. The Word of God presents both sides, and here, as in many other instances, we find a man being used of God to fulfill His purposes, but with no indication that he was doing something outside the realm of normal human activity.

The Dependability

Jacob, who knew Joseph well, understood that he could count on him to complete the task. This takes us to the truth of stewardship, where Paul tells us that, as stewards of the mysteries of God, "it is required ... that a man be found faithful" (1 Cor 4:2). Joseph, like the Lord Jesus who would come years later, was faithful. The question today is: Are we faithful in all those things that God has graciously placed into our care? Are we discharging our duties diligently?

His Brothers' Disdain

The Cause

Stephen, while giving his defense in Acts 7:9, says, "The patriarchs, moved with envy, sold Joseph into Egypt". We looked at the sad truth about envy in the previous chapter, but allow me to mention one other verse: "For he knew that the chief priests had delivered him for envy" (Mark 15:10). Pilate, an ungodly man, could quickly recognize that this man Jesus had been the object of envy by the Jewish leaders. Joseph, centuries before, was in the same position.

Joseph was not even close when his brothers recognized him, surely due to the coat of many colours that he wore, the object that had only served to fuel their envy even more. What had been a token of his father's love to him became not only a renewed cause for their cruel abuse of Joseph, but also a ready means by which they could identify him.

The Conspiracy

Thus, as he came closer, they conspired against the dreamer. "Come now therefore, and let us slay him, and cast him into some pit, and we will say, Some evil beast hath devoured him: and we shall see what will become of his dreams" (37:20). Although we are only surmising, it is quite likely that this idea of killing their brother had come up on previous occasions, and now would appear to them to be the perfect opportunity — far from home, and under the watchful eye of no-one. Or so they thought — God Himself would bring all this day's events back to them almost twenty years later, when they would repent of the evil they had done.

This would not have been the first case of fratricide in Genesis. We think back to the first two brothers, Cain and Abel, and how jealousy had then caused Cain to rise up against his only brother and slay him. It also ought not to seem to us to be outside the realm of possibilities for these men to behave thus, when we remember that Levi and Simeon had slaughtered many in order to defend their sister Dinah's honour.

But while men conspired to do their worst, God had other plans, and had a man at the ready who would save Joseph's life.

The Compassion

Reuben had some level of compassion on Joseph and could not bear the idea of slaying him. His suggestion was meant to save Joseph's life and then return him to his father. Reuben is the same brother who "went and lay with Bilhah his father's concubine" (35:22), and although we must use utmost care when thinking about people's motives, two possibilities come to mind: he was trying to win some favour with his father, as he would know that this previous sinful act could have repercussions later in regards to the inheritance; or, there was a change of heart in Reuben. We prefer to think the latter is true, and there is some evidence to support this when we later come to the conversation between the brothers in Genesis 42:22 — "Spake I not unto you, saying, Do not sin against the child; and ye would not hear?" Further evidence is seen when he is trying to convince his father to allow Benjamin to travel with them to Egypt to buy corn — "Slay my two sons, if I bring him not to thee: deliver him into my hand, and I will bring him to thee again" (42:37).

While Reuben was showing some compassion, the agreement of his brethren does not show any kindness on their part. What they were thinking was that they would be free from the guilt of actually laying a hand on Joseph to kill him, but leaving him to die a slow death in a dry cistern would certainly not have been an act of mercy!

The Concern

What Reuben wanted to accomplish on this occasion was to "deliver him to his father again" (37:22). Being the firstborn of all Jacob's sons, his word obviously had some weight, and he convinced his brethren to put Joseph in a pit, with the desire to later save his life. Reuben, being a father (46:9), could well imagine the feelings of sorrow that would overwhelm any father knowing their son had been slain. Nonetheless, we will see that his plan did not work, and sadly, he did not have the courage days later to tell his father the truth about what had happened to Joseph.

Joseph's Despair

The Humiliation

Being stripped of the coat that his father had lovingly made for him would have been humiliating and disheartening to Joseph. Being cast into the empty pit would have caused him much grief. We do not read about his reaction here, but come with me to Genesis 42:21: "we saw the anguish of his soul, when he besought us, and we would not hear." Years later, in Joseph's hearing, this is what his brothers remembered and spoke of about his reaction to their cruelty.

We can only imagine what Joseph would have felt through all of this — wondering, waiting, weeping. Wondering if someone would have pity on him. Waiting to see if someone, perhaps his father, would come to rescue him. And weeping — "the anguish of his soul". This young lad would pass through many more trials before God would bring him to the throne.

Deep anguish of soul and the humiliation that accompanied it make us consider once again our blessed Saviour. Regarding the anguish of His soul, we read that he "began to be sorrowful and very heavy. Then saith he unto them, My soul is exceeding sorrowful, even unto death" (Matt 26:37-38). Reflect on these words: "they stripped him", then later "they took the robe off from him", and finally, "they crucified him, and parted his garments" (Matt 27:28, 31, 35). He had humbled Himself, "and became obedient unto death, even the death of the cross" (Phil 2:8), but it was another thing to be humiliated by His own creatures.

Wondrous Thy humiliation
To accomplish our salvation:
Thousand, thousand praises be,
Precious Saviour, unto Thee.
                              (E. C. Homburg)

The Hardness

At times it is difficult to understand how so many horrific things happen in this world. It makes us recall the words of the weeping prophet: "The heart is deceitful above all things, and desperately wicked" (Jer 17:9). The human heart can easily become hardened, and in the case of Joseph's brothers this is precisely what we see.

Let these words have their full impact on your soul: "And they sat down to eat bread" (37:25). Such hardness. Such cruelty. One can almost hear them mocking Joseph as they sat near the pit and enjoyed a meal: "Let's see what becomes of his dreams now! This is what he deserves for becoming such a daddy's boy". All the while he besought them, and they would not hear.

Matthew writes, "and sitting down they watched him there" (Matt 27:36). This perhaps makes a bit more sense to us, as these were hardened soldiers who were used to crucifying criminals, not the behaviour of the Lord's own brothers in the flesh.

We see such a contrast in the life of the Lord Jesus, for as we read through the Gospels we find Him "moved with compassion" time and time again; He would lift up His eyes, see a need, and have not only the desire, but the ability to meet that need. May God grant each one of us tender hearts, hearts like that of the Lord Jesus, ever open to meet the needs of the people we meet.

The Brothers' Decision

Their Eyes

As the brothers were enjoying their meal together, they lifted up their eyes and saw a group of merchantmen moving through the area, heading down to Egypt. Listen to Solomon's wise words: "Wilt thou set thine eyes upon that which is not? for riches certainly make themselves wings; they fly away as an eagle toward heaven" (Prov 23:5). Their indifference leads to an idea of how to profit from all this.

Their Eagerness

"What profit is it if we slay our brother, and conceal his blood?" was Judah's question (37:26). Judah, although not the firstborn, will later show leadership when speaking with his father before making the second journey to Egypt and in his dealings with Joseph in Egypt. On this occasion he shows some level of compassion, saying, "Let not our hand be upon him; for he is our brother and our flesh" (v 27). Their eagerness to rid themselves of their own brother is quite evident when we read that "his brethren were content" with his suggestion to sell him to the Ishmeelites. This group, also descended from Abraham, were distant cousins of Jacob's sons.

The Estimation

They engaged in some bartering over Joseph and settled on the amount of twenty pieces of silver. Years later, Judas Iscariot's eyes were wide open to the opportunity at hand. He, a descendant of Judah, went to the chief priests, as he knew they wanted to rid themselves of the Lord Jesus. "What will ye give me, and I will deliver him unto you? And they covenanted with him for thirty pieces of silver" (Matt 26:15). In Bible times, the death of a slave would be compensated by just thirty pieces of silver (Ex 21:32). What truth we find in Isaiah's words, "He was despised, and we esteemed him not" (Isa 53:3). Men underestimated the value of Joseph, then, centuries later, men underestimated the value of Christ Jesus. We, as true believers, can say, "My beloved is white and ruddy, the chiefest among ten thousand ... yea, he is altogether lovely" (Song 5:10, 16). Joseph was sold, and his life was preserved. The Lord Jesus was sold, and His life was taken from him.

The Brothers' Deceit

The problem with sin is that one is never enough. They would now have to deal with their father, and what appeared to be the easiest tactic was deceit.

Reuben's Desperation

Reuben's plan fell apart as he was obviously not present when the deal was made with the Ishmeelites. When he returned to the pit, he rent his clothes, obviously greatly moved by this turn of events. In desperation, he said, "and I, whither shall I go?" More than twenty years later he still will feel the burden of guilt for not having done more to save his brother's life.

Jacob's Despondency

They concoct a plan of deceit, taking Joseph's coat, killing a kid of the goats, and dipping the coat in its blood. They then return home with the coat and utter a complete lie: "This have we found" (37:32). Although it is true that the law had not yet been handed down to Moses, knowing the importance of telling the truth would have been impressed upon them. Sadly, however, the man who had deceived his father was now being deceived by his own sons. He and his mother Rebekah had killed a goat in order to make a meal for Isaac, and to clothe Jacob with its skin in order to deceive his father. Recall Paul's words to the Galatian church: "Be not deceived; God is not mocked: for whatsoever a man soweth, that shall he also reap" (Gal 6:8). Jacob would eventually learn this lesson, but the process would be protracted and painful.

Nonetheless, our heart is moved when we listen in to the conversation. When they ask him to identify the coat, "he knew it, and said, It is my son's coat; an evil beast hath devoured him; Joseph is without doubt rent in pieces" (37:33). The men standing around him listen to their father who is convinced that his favoured son has been torn apart, and they say nothing at all. What hypocrisy - pretending to care for their father, likely "mourning" with him, yet secretly glad that they would not have to deal with Joseph again. What hardness - seeing their own father mourn with such deep anguish, yet remaining deceitful for many years. One wonders if Jacob ever did find out the truth about what had happened to Joseph.

Jacob then rends his clothes, and mourns for many days, refusing to be comforted. He understood death was coming, but would continue mourning until that day, "for I will go down into the grave unto my son mourning" (37:35). There is some hope in that statement that we ought not to overlook — "unto my son". So although there had not been a full revelation of truth concerning life after death, he had the confidence that he would see his son once more on the other side of the grave. Would the last conversation they had, as he sent his beloved son off to Shechem, not ring through his ears every day? Let's make sure that our partings are always sweet!

What he did not know is that he would see him in Egypt long before he went to the grave, yet those twenty years would be difficult ones for Jacob! That leads us to our last point in Genesis 37, reminding us that God was, and is, in control of every circumstance.

God's Determination

It certainly was not chance or coincidence that Joseph ended up being sold. The first thing we read is that "they brought Joseph into Egypt" (37:28). Not only had he been delivered into the hands of the Ishmeelites, but now "the Midianites sold him into Egypt unto Potiphar" (37:36). God had His hand in all of these things, knowing precisely what Joseph later learned: "God meant it unto good" (50:20). At the time, however, we can only begin to imagine what the son of his father's love felt as he stood in the slave market, waiting for the highest bidder to take him, not understanding the language that was spoken, and surely confused about what life was all about.

When we consider the life of Christ, we realize the same thing - these happenings were not by chance, and they were not a coincidence, but rather God was controlling the circumstances in order to glorify Himself by providing a Saviour. Peter explains it on the Day of Pentecost in Jerusalem in this manner: "Him, being delivered by the determinate counsel and foreknowledge of God, ye have taken, and by wicked hands have crucified and slain" (Acts 2:23). Man was responsible, but God was in control. Man made his decisions for which he is responsible, but Peter clearly taught that the Son of God was delivered by God's determinate counsel. We marvel at the love and grace of God, providing salvation for us at such a cost.

God, with complete knowledge and in complete control, willingly gave His Son, sending Him into a world that would hate Him, and eventually crucify Him. Jacob, too, in a lesser sense offered up his son for the greater good. Jacob, however, did not do it willingly, nor knowingly. Yet we see in the sending of Joseph a beautiful picture of our Saviour coming to save that which was lost.

CHAPTER 5

The Challenges were Abundant

Genesis 39

We now move into the second division in the life of Joseph. This thirteen year period of his life, which in the introduction we entitled "Years of Obscurity", is the shortest of the three periods, but surely felt like the longest to Joseph.

He has gone from the position of affection which he held in his father's heart, through the pain and affliction caused by the hatred of his own brethren, and now we will see him in the purity of his associations in Potiphar's household.

Of course, we know the end of the story, but put yourself for a moment in the position of someone who is reading this account for the first time. Perhaps as we come to the end of chapter 37 we are made to wonder: What can become of a young man like this? Sold into slavery and living in a foreign country, will he become bitter? Will he even survive?

Joseph, like any other young man, would continue to face challenges in his life, and this chapter has four which we will look at in detail:

> The Challenge of Prosperity: vv 1-6
> The Challenge to his Purity: vv 7-12
> The Challenge of Persecution: vv 13-19
> The Challenge of the Prison: vv 20-23.

The Challenge of Prosperity

Perhaps the first thought that comes to someone's attention is this:

"I don't think I would find prosperity to be a challenge!" Well, keep in mind the fact that Joseph was a slave, yet called a prosperous man. So Moses, as he wrote this book, was not thinking about monetary issues but rather about something far better. The other fact that we need to recall is that the chapter ends with Joseph prospering, although at that point he is below the status of a slave — he is a prisoner. Finally, remember that it was the Lord, both in Potiphar's house and in the prison, who caused Joseph to prosper.

Potiphar

The captain of the guard was an officer of Pharaoh, and thus would be a wealthy man with both a large home and large tracts of land. Servants, or slaves, would not be scarce in such circumstances. He was in charge of protecting Pharaoh from any overt or covert attacks. We would not be likely to choose him as our employer. But Joseph had no say in the matter.

However, Joseph was going to be a source of blessing for this ungodly man. Potiphar would soon realize why. "His master saw that the Lord was with him" (v 3). Once Joseph learned the Egyptian language, did he share with his master something about his background, his faith and his God? It would certainly seem that way, but more than Joseph's words, it was his works that convinced Potiphar. Are not people today looking for consistency between what we as believers profess and how we act?

Yet we have to understand that Joseph accepted his circumstances, living far from home in an ungodly land, and obviously decided to make the best of them. Daniel, taken to Babylon hundreds of years later, would do the same. The Apostle Paul was imprisoned, yet he did not languish there, but made the best of it, writing letters, praying, singing praises, and seeing people reached by God's grace! Do we have the tendency to blame our lack of growth and spirituality on our present circumstances? God *is* in control, and He knows exactly where He has placed us in order that we can accomplish His will for His glory.

God's Presence

You will have noticed that "the LORD was with Joseph" is an expression we find in verses 2 and 21, and then it also says in verses 3 and 23 that "the LORD was with him". We ought not to pass over this lightly or quickly, but rather remember that we, too, have the promise in the New Testament from the Lord Jesus: "I will never leave thee, nor forsake thee" (Heb 13:5). This presence is not only comforting to us, but also challenging — we will notice this later when Potiphar's wife tempts Joseph (v 9). Remember that not only was Joseph conscious of the Lord's presence with him, but "his master saw that the LORD was with him" (v 3). Is it possible that our neighbours, co-workers, fellow-students, or unsaved family members come to that same conclusion about us? Is there any outward evidence, or expression of our link to Christ? Do people notice that we know much of God's comfort and control in our lives? Are we ever asked for a reason of the hope that is within us?

Notice that what is true in Joseph's life can be traced in the lives of many other believers from Bible times, and especially in the life of the Lord Jesus: God does not always deliver us from the difficult circumstances, but He is always with us, even in those difficult moments. Remembering that He is in control ought to have a positive effect on our attitude as we go through life's trials. Peter puts it this way: "ye greatly rejoice, though now for a season, if need be, ye are in heaviness through manifold temptations [or better, trials]" (1 Peter 1:6). The word of the Lord that came to the nation brings us comfort as well: "Fear not: for I have redeemed thee, I have called thee by thy name; thou art mine. When thou passest through the waters, I will be with thee" (Isa 43:1-2).

Joseph surely had days, and maybe even more nights, when he wondered, "Why?" His desire had always been to be with his father, with his younger brother Benjamin, and to live a normal life. What about his dreams? How would they ever come about now? But even if these questions and doubts flooded his mind from time to time, we never read about a poor attitude in Joseph. There is no resentment mentioned; no hint of self-pity; and therefore no bitterness. He trusted in God, and, although his words may have been different, surely what was in his heart was the same as the Lord Jesus prayed centuries later: "nevertheless not my will, but thine, be done" (Luke 22:42).

His Prosperity

So, what is prosperity? The word actually means "to accomplish satisfactorily what is intended" (TWOT, 1917). It may appear that the wicked prosper, as Asaph wrote in Psalm 73. He was confounded and writes: "When I thought to know this, it was too painful for me: Until I went into the sanctuary of God; then understood I their end" (Ps 73:16-17). Sometimes we also need to adjust our perspective as we consider those around us who do not know God, but their lives seem to be more "successful" than ours. Whenever we get into God's presence, however, things become clearer — their prosperity is temporary, and their portion will be terrible.

How do we become prosperous? Psalm 1 gives tremendous teaching on this theme. We need to be careful with whom we walk, where we stand, and where we sit. What delights our heart cannot be the things of the world, but rather the law of the Lord; that which is our meditation day and night. We need a source of nourishment, planted by rivers of water, so that we are fruitful, with no withering leaves. Then says the Psalmist: "whatsoever he doeth shall prosper" (Ps 1:3).

Although it may sound like a conundrum, prospering can be a costly thing. Consider the Lord Jesus in Isaiah 53 — all that He was willing to suffer was with this great desire: "the pleasure of the LORD shall prosper in his hand" (Isa 53:10). The verse begins with this stunning phrase: "Yet it pleased the LORD to bruise him; he hath put him to grief".

Amazing pity! Grace unknown!
And love beyond degree.
                              (Isaac Watts)

We need, then, to make sure that we don't get caught up with the world's way of thinking about prosperity. Earthly possessions and bank accounts will all be left behind one day. Let's remember that we noted that the biblical significance of the word "to prosper" is to "accomplish satisfactorily what is intended". Our circumstances may be far from what we consider to be ideal, but that ought not to stop us from being prosperous. It certainly did not hinder Joseph's accomplishments! Before God we need to ask ourselves these questions: Are we prospering as believers? Are we accomplishing, with God's help, what He intends us to do?

His Promotion

Joseph was a slave, yet Potiphar made him an "overseer over his house" (39:4). This indicates a trust, or a stewardship; a responsibility given to Joseph to look after Potiphar's possessions, with the understanding that he would have to give account to Potiphar for what he did with his time, his talents and Potiphar's treasures.

The Apostle Paul, too, understood the truth of stewardship, but of something far more important than Potiphar's treasures. He wrote: "Let a man so account of us, as of the ministers of Christ, and stewards of the mysteries of God. Moreover it is required in stewards, that a man be found faithful" (1 Cor 4:1-2). Potiphar found Joseph to be faithful and diligent, fulfilling his responsibilities in a conscientious manner.

Let us challenge our own hearts in the sight of God: How are we doing as His stewards?

His Power

"He left all that he had in Joseph's hand" (39:6). Joseph was in complete control. He had power. In 1887, Lord Acton wrote these words: "Power tends to corrupt, and absolute power corrupts absolutely." Thank God there are exceptions, and Joseph surely was a wonderful example of a man who had great power in the household of one of Pharaoh's officers, yet remained loyal and faithful in his responsibilities. Such was the confidence Potiphar had in Joseph that he "knew not ought he had, save the bread which he did eat" (v 6). For the Egyptian people, food was very important, and they thoroughly enjoyed their meals, so for Pharaoh to have the liberty to do so would make him appreciate the loyalty and dedication of a man like Joseph even more.

The Problem

This section ends with a short phrase that alerts us to a pending problem, although Joseph bears no blame whatsoever. "And Joseph was a goodly person, and well favoured", or as Darby puts it: "And Joseph was of a beautiful form and of a beautiful countenance" (v 6), or "Now Joseph was handsome and good-looking" (RSV). His grandmother Rebekah "was fair to look upon" (26:7) and his mother Rachel "was beautiful and well favoured" (29:17), so it is not surprising that Joseph was considered to be handsome.

We remember that Abraham was concerned about others being attracted by the beauty of his wife while they sojourned in Gerar, and told Abimelech, "She is my sister" (20:2). This led to Abimelech taking Sarah, and God in a dream warning him, causing him to restore to Abraham his wife, Sarah.

Isaac, too, followed those footsteps of his father. We read that when he was in Gerar he said, "She is my sister: for he feared to say, She is my wife; lest, said he, the men of the place should kill me for Rebekah; because she was fair to look upon" (26:7). So, beauty can bring challenging circumstances, and when linked with an attractive personality, as in Joseph's case, it can lead to temptation.

Society around us is obsessed with appearance. God looks upon the heart, or, as Peter puts it, "the hidden man of the heart" (1 Peter 3:4). No matter the outward impression we give to people, let us allow God to form the character of Christ within each and every one of us.

The Challenge to his Purity

This section is intensely practical and applicable still in the 21st century. It does teach us that temptation to immorality is nothing new, but it also shows us that there is no need to fall into sin when tempted — God does make a way of escape possible.

Let us remember that although it is the woman who takes the initiative in this chapter in regards to sexual sin, the previous chapter recounts the sad story of Judah, now a widower, approaching a woman he believed to be a harlot. These two chapters, back-to-back, paint the genuine story of how fallen humanity can act — God does not make it all look lovely. The story of Judah ends in tragic sin; the story of Joseph ends in triumph over sin.

Since this world is at odds with the God of heaven, it serves us well to be aware of the perils that believers face every day, especially at school or in the work place. We also need to reject the idea that these temptations only affect those who are younger than us.

The Realization (vv 7, 11)

Between the time Joseph arrived in Egypt and became a servant in Potiphar's household until he was exalted by Pharaoh, thirteen years passed. It is difficult to know exactly for how much time he was imprisoned, but he was there at least two years after interpreting the dreams of the butler and the baker.

Married women in Ancient Egypt were better off than in many other societies over the course of history. They tended to have more freedom and responsibility. Adultery, however, could result in the death penalty, just as required in the Law later handed down to Moses.

At some point in Joseph's employment in the home, Potiphar's wife came to the realization that he was a fine looking man, a "goodly person, and well favoured" (39:6). Where did this temptation to sin begin? With her eyes, as she "cast her eyes upon Joseph" (v 7). The Lord Jesus said, "And if thine eye offend thee, pluck it out" (Mark 9:47), as He knew that the sight is one of the main ways that temptation comes to the mind. The first temptation in human history had to do, at least in part, with the eyes: "And when the woman saw that the tree was good for food, and that it was pleasant to the eyes ..." (3:6). Eve was attracted by what she saw. Soon after, Job said, "I made a covenant with mine eyes; why then should I think upon a maid?" (Job 31:1). He was not a young man by this time, but realized there was still a danger in what he could see around him.

The Request (vv 7, 10, 12)

"Lie with me." She was nothing if not direct in her request. This would surely have come as a surprise to Joseph, but it certainly was not subtle. It was a surprise in part due to the difference in social standing between them; a surprise also to a young man who understood the need for purity. Sadly, today's culture is becoming more and more overt with regard to illicit and immoral relationships, and we need to be not only aware of this, but alert to the danger, well prepared to act as Joseph did.

Without trying to read too much into one phrase, a question does arise in verse 10 - "or to be with her". Is it possible that what Pharaoh's wife longed for was not just the physical relationship, but companionship also? Is it possible that her husband, with all of his responsibilities of being the "captain of the guard" had little time for her? Now that Joseph was "over all that he had" there was perhaps less need for him to be at home, looking after those affairs. Whatever the reasons she may have had, we are not defending her actions!

Can we be practical for a moment, and suggest that men, as believers, need to exercise the utmost caution in what we would call "platonic relationships"? Likewise sisters who are in the workplace can face the same temptation. Many a marriage has been ruined by one of the spouses getting too close emotionally to someone of the opposite gender in the workplace, or the playground, for example. They begin to share their struggles, their hopes and desires; baring their heart more than they would even do with their own spouse, and "suddenly" an emotional attachment is made, while their marriage is being undermined. Emotional infidelity can be devastating to a marriage and must be guarded against. It can happen, too, between believers in an assembly context — perhaps when seeking counsel from an older believer. It is true that our deepest satisfaction is found in Christ, but all believers need to understand the deep emotional connection between spouses and do all they can to preserve and respect their own marriage relationship, and that of others.

This sometimes happens with an unsaved co-worker, who sees something in the believer that is very attractive, a different spirit, a gentleness perhaps not found in others in that environment. Isn't that what we noticed with Joseph in regards to Potiphar? He saw in Joseph a man who lived in the presence of God. Surely his wife had noticed not only Joseph's physical attractiveness, but also his pleasant demeanour.

"And it came to pass about this time" (v 11) that she seized what she saw as an opportunity, as "about this time ... there was none of the men of the house there within", and "she caught him by his garment, saying, Lie with me" (vv 11-12). Calling what came to pass this day a "request" perhaps seems a bit tame. She was astute, and she was aggressive.

The Refusal (vv 8, 10)

"But he refused." He was nothing if not direct in his refusal. A woman in her position would not be used to being rejected, especially by a mere slave. And it wasn't just a one-time refusal; "she spake to Joseph day by day" (v 10). It is one thing to say "No" once, but when the temptation just will not go away, it can wear you down. But Joseph was just as firm in his refusal as she was in her persistence: "he hearkened not unto her" (v 10).

We can learn much from just those three words. Joseph did not stop to consider his options; he did not try to reason it through by saying, "If she is my boss, I have to obey"; nor did he focus on the fact that for an unmarried man, intimate relations were normal and accepted by society. The more one delays in resisting the temptation, preferring rather to deliberate the pros and cons, the more the danger of falling into sin increases.

The Respect (vv 8-9)

But why did Joseph refuse to yield to the sustained temptation? We read about three clear reasons: a respect for his master, a regard for the sacredness of marriage, and reverence toward God.

First, Joseph respected his master. He understood the value of loyalty, and realized he was accountable to Potiphar. "My master wotteth [knows] not what is with me in the house" — Joseph saw that Potiphar trusted him, and trust is extremely valuable while being at the same time very fragile, and easily broken. "He hath committed all that he hath to my hand" — Potiphar's household was Joseph's stewardship, and he felt the weight of being accountable to him. Joseph indicated that everything within Potiphar's household was available to him, but there was one clear exception. Another temptation, at the beginning of time, was similar. Everything in Eden was at Adam and Eve's disposition, except for one tree. Adam and Eve failed; Joseph did not.

Second, we see that Joseph had a high regard for the vows of marriage. In Egypt there may not have been a ceremony such as we have today, but there was a contract that the couple entered into, and it came into force when the woman entered her husband's home. "Neither hath he kept any thing back from me but thee, because thou art his wife." While it is true that his father did have more than one wife, the truth of Genesis 2:24 was not unknown: "Therefore shall a man leave his father and his mother, and shall cleave unto his wife: and they shall be one flesh." The same remains true today, despite the myriad of attacks against what God established from the beginning, and the Lord Jesus repeated when here on earth. There was no way that Joseph was going to do something that would harm their marriage.

The third phrase we notice is at the end of verse 9: "how then can I do this great wickedness, and sin against God?" Who established what is good and what is evil? God Himself. So again, although Joseph did not have a Bible, nor a copy of the Law (for it had not yet been given), Paul tells us that even Gentiles have "the law written in their hearts" (Rom 2:15). Joseph knew that this would be wickedness — a "sin against God". Joseph lived in the fear of the Lord — there was a consciousness of living in God's presence, and this had a preserving effect on him.

More than a dozen times Solomon writes concerning the "fear of the Lord" in Proverbs. Take just two examples: "The fear of the LORD is the beginning of wisdom" (9:10), and, "by the fear of the LORD men depart from evil" (16:6). Both of these can easily be seen fulfilled in the life of Joseph: he was young, yet wise; and he knew what it meant to depart from evil. May we know more of the fear of the Lord in our lives!

Today people are capable of reasoning away the plain teaching of Scripture, but Joseph, even without the Scriptures in his hand, was capable of rejecting this temptation outright, recognizing it would be, first of all, a sin against God. True enough, it would be a sin "against his own body" (1 Cor 6:18); it would defraud Potiphar (1 Thess 4:6); it would be a sin against Potiphar's wife, but what stopped Joseph in his tracks was his reverence for a Holy God. Joseph did not fall into the modern trap of situational ethics, rather making his decision based on absolute moral standards. He took into account the will of God, rather than the context and culture in which he lived and laboured. Would not more of the fear of God stop us today from falling into diverse temptations, bringing constantly to mind what God wants, not what is culturally acceptable?

The Resource

This helps us understand a basic, yet important truth: your convictions need to be formed before the moment of crisis comes. In the heat of any type of temptation there most probably will not be enough time to consider the pros and cons, to weigh up the various factors, and come to a biblically based decision. The Psalmist wrote: "Thy word have I hid in mine heart, that I might not sin against thee" (Ps 119:11). We are at a tremendous advantage in this regard in comparison with Joseph who did not have a Bible to open, yet he had biblical truth hidden in his heart.

When we consider the Lord Jesus, He responded to a direct

temptation from Satan himself with the Word of God that was hidden in His heart. Three times over He said, "It is written" (Matt 4:4, 7, 10). May God help us to treasure up His holy Word so that we can resist each temptation that comes our way.

The Ruse (vv 11-12)

Potiphar's wife was nothing if not astute. Seeing one day that there was no one else in the house, she "caught him by his garment, saying, Lie with me". Is it possible that she had deliberately sent everyone else out of the house so that she could be alone with Joseph for this last ditch effort to tempt him?

We certainly cannot blame Joseph for going "into the house to do his business" (v 11). We have seen the diligence that resulted in his prosperity. He certainly was not looking for temptation, but obviously was ready to act if it did rear its ugly head.

However, on a very practical note, bring to mind Paul's warning: "let us therefore cast off the works of darkness, and let us put on the armour of light ... Let us walk honestly, as in the day ... But put ye on the Lord Jesus Christ, and make not provision for the flesh, to fulfil the lusts thereof" (Rom 13:12-14). Remember that temptation in and of itself is not sin, for the Lord Jesus was tempted, too. It is the response of our heart and mind to the temptation that can lead to sin.

The Robe (v 12)

Joseph would have none of it, and "he left his garment in her hand, and fled, and got him out" (v 12). He ran from temptation! He did not stay around to have a discussion about it; he did not try to reason with Potiphar's wife; he ran! Paul wrote these plain words: "Flee fornication", and "Flee also youthful lusts" (1 Cor 6:18; 2 Tim 2:22). Is it possible that he was thinking about Joseph's experience as he penned them?

Running from her was going to cost him — first, he lost his garment, or robe; secondly, as we shall presently see, he was persecuted and placed in prison. But Joseph was going to preserve his character, even if it cost him much. While Joseph waited for all this to play out, would he have thought about the last time he lost his garment? That seemed to not end well for him either — he was then cast into a pit.

Temptations will come — we cannot avoid all of them. But going back to Paul's exhortation that we make no provision for the flesh, we understand that it is possible to place ourselves in temptation's way, and this we need to learn to avoid.

When the temptation comes, of whatever nature it may be, the best response is that of Joseph — Flee! There is no need to think twice — it's wrong, so run!

Temptation does come in a variety of ways. God is not the source of temptation, but "every man is tempted, when he is drawn away of his own lust, and enticed" (James 1:14). We can try to blame others around us, or blame Satan, but the bottom line is that our own desires are the problem. There are sexual temptations, like the one we have been examining, where there is a desire to enjoy outside of marriage what God has designed to be enjoyed only within a marriage relationship. There are personal temptations; by that we mean the temptation towards power, popularity or position. There are also material temptations, a strong desire to obtain the objects that others own. So let us beware that while we are still living in this body of flesh, temptations will abound, and we need to be ready to flee at a moment's notice.

The Challenge of Persecution

The Reason - An Accusation

Joseph disappears off the scene for a while, but Potiphar's wife quickly schemed, and came up with a story. She blames, at least in part, her husband who had "brought in an Hebrew unto us to mock us". She makes the racial distinction obvious, and also is inclusive in her accusation — "... unto *us* to mock *us*". She perhaps felt she needed the support of the other servants and reminding them that a foreigner was their "overseer", that is, the steward in charge of them, might strike a chord with at least some of them.

She held on to the "evidence", Joseph's garment, until Potiphar came home, and she repeated to him the same false accusation.

Consider the Lord Jesus. He did not have one person against Him, but many. "Now the chief priests, and elders, and all the council, sought false witness against Jesus, to put him to death" (Matt 26:59). The next verse says twice that they found none. Not to be deterred, the search continued until "At the last came two false witnesses" (Matt 26:60).

Paul wrote to Timothy that true believers, with a desire to live for God, will be persecuted (2 Tim 3:12). Paul knew what it was to be falsely accused and persecuted for his convictions, too. We ought not to think that we are beyond that in today's society — the motives may be different, but man is the same.

Peter, too, gives additional clarity on the subject of persecution: "For what glory is it, if, when ye be buffeted for your faults, ye shall take it patiently? but if, when ye do well, and suffer for it, ye take it patiently, this is acceptable with God" (1 Peter 2:20). "Acceptable" is the word "grace", and in this context means something that brings delight or pleasure to the heart of God. Our attitude in a world that is against us, the control of our tongue in our response to accusations, and suffering for doing good is that which delights the heart of our God. The Lord Jesus is the supreme example of this.

The Reaction - Anger

We read that Potiphar's "wrath was kindled" (v 19). It does not say with whom Potiphar was angry, but there are only two possibilities — his wife, or Joseph.

Consider the possibility that he was angry with his wife. Joseph was his most trusted and valuable employee; Potiphar had seen how his whole enterprise, both in the house and in the field, had prospered under Joseph's hand. He had seen how "that the LORD was with him";

never had he had a steward like Joseph. What would happen now? Who could replace a man like Joseph? It is quite plausible that he did not believe his wife; had he sensed an emotional distance between them? Was this why she wanted Joseph "to be with her"? Were this the case, a man in Joseph's position would not likely have just been put into prison. Men were often punished for the crime of violation with emasculation, mutilation or even death.

On the other hand, some would suggest he was angry with Joseph, having believed the accusation that his wife brought against his valued slave. Although this is possible, the punishment doesn't really fit the crime.

The Response - No Argument

What do we hear from Joseph's mouth? Absolutely nothing. Now, it is quite possible that he wasn't given an opportunity to defend himself. Potiphar was in a difficult situation, as he could not publicly believe a mere Hebrew slave over his own wife.

But Joseph in his silence brings our minds to think once again upon our Saviour. "Jesus held his peace" before the high priest (Matt 26:63). Before Pilate "Jesus yet answered nothing" (Mark 15:5). Herod asked him many questions, but "he answered him nothing" (Luke 23:9). This we see prophesied by Isaiah: "He was oppressed, and he was afflicted, yet he opened not his mouth: he is brought as a lamb to the slaughter, and as a sheep before her shearers is dumb, so he openeth not his mouth" (Isa 53:7). What grace! What patience! What pity!

The Challenge of the Prison

"Joseph's master took him, and put him into the prison, a place where the king's prisoners were bound, and he was there in the prison" (39:20).

As we come to the end of this chapter, we want to consider just three things.

The Captive

Moments before being put into prison, Joseph was in charge of Potiphar's affairs. Suddenly he finds himself thrust from importance to imprisonment. Perhaps the first thought that would go through our minds would be, "Why, Lord?" This was almost a flashback to some time before when his own brothers, for no fault of his own, had cast him into a pit.

Imprisonment in those days was not common, and was usually used for political reasons, such as we will see in the next chapter. There Joseph will call it a "dungeon" (v 15), and clearly conditions would have been far from luxurious.

But where is the complaint from this captive? You will be hard-pressed to find one. Two men that were deprived of their liberty in the New Testament also did not complain — the Lord Jesus and, later, the Apostle Paul. Joseph was a precursor to this attitude of meekness; accepting what comes to us as part of God's larger plan, and thus submitting to it.

The Compassion

We read at the beginning of the chapter on two occasions that the Lord was with him. Things then were going well, or at least as well as you can expect for a slave. But now conditions are far worse, and yet we read, "But the Lord was with Joseph, and shewed him mercy, and gave him favour in the sight of the keeper of the prison" (v 21).

Notice again with me the truth that God will never forsake us. He may allow us to pass through deep and long trials, but the Lord is always with us. The Lord moved the heart of the prison keeper. We would not expect kind treatment from a man like this, but the Lord "shewed him mercy".

Our God never changes. Remember Jeremiah's words, "It is of the LORD'S mercies that we are not consumed, because his compassions fail not. They are new every morning: great is thy faithfulness. The LORD is my portion, saith my soul; therefore will I hope in him. The

LORD is good unto them that wait for him, to the soul that seeketh him" (Lam 3:22-25). What more can we ask for? He does not change; His character today is the same as it was in Joseph's day.

The Commitment

Such was the work of God in the prison keeper, and the character and attitude that Joseph displayed, that it did not take long for Joseph to be in a position of responsibility. The prison keeper committed all the prisoners into Joseph's hand — he had no experience of looking after prisoners, but faithfulness and diligence were again seen in him.

This is the third person in this chapter who saw something unique in Joseph. Potiphar and his wife had both taken note of Joseph, albeit for different motives, and now the keeper of the prison notices Joseph's distinct character. They were ungodly people for sure, yet quite able to recognize a distinction when they saw it.

As Potiphar did not need to worry about household matters, the prison keeper was not perturbed about the running of the prison. In all that was done there, Joseph "was the doer of it" (v 23).

Can we say the same about us? Are we found faithful in our daily lives? Family, assembly, community and work all ought to show what we truly are, sons of God, and should manifest our God-fearing character.

As we close this chapter, we see the word "prosper" come up once again. No matter where Joseph was, he was cognizant of God's presence, and God's blessing was upon all he did.

CHAPTER 6

Joseph's Confinement and Attitude

Genesis 40

We left Joseph in prison at the end of the last chapter, accused by Pharaoh's wife of committing a lewd act, yet completely innocent of all charges against him. In his short life he had already faced many challenges, but through them all we understand that God was making him to be the man He would use in a marvellous way in the future. God's training ground can be difficult at times, yet we see in Joseph a wonderful example of His ability to bring good out of what we would consider to be bad.

Before we delve into this next section of Joseph's life, remember the important phrase, "The LORD was with Joseph". We read this in relation to his time of prosperity as he was promoted in Potiphar's household, but we also read it when he was in prison (39:2, 21).

We want to see in this chapter that although Joseph's life was not going well, at least from a human perspective, his attitude was always appropriate. Too often we can fall into the trap of blaming others, or the crisis at hand, for our poor attitude — not so with Joseph, and it was never so with our blessed Lord either.

The Companions (vv 1-4)

Prison, generally speaking, is not a pleasant experience in any country or in any age. But this is where God had allowed Joseph to be placed, even though the sentence was unjust.

The Butler and the Baker

These two men had tremendous responsibility in Pharaoh's court. Palace intrigue and assassination attempts are not new occurrences in human history. They had to ensure that both what the king of Egypt ate and what he drank were not only pleasing to his palate, but safe for his health. We are not told how, but in some way both of them "had offended their lord the king" (v 1), and he became "wroth", or angry, with them both and had them incarcerated.

We know that with God there are no coincidences, nothing that happens "by chance", or "by luck", so it is no surprise to us to see how one of these men is later used by God in the fulfillment of His purposes, not only for Joseph, but in an even greater way for the people of Israel and the surrounding nations. Surely this butler, or cupbearer, had no inkling that he would be recognized in Scripture and discussed for centuries!

Learning the Lessons of Leadership

When these men arrived at the prison, the "captain of the guard charged Joseph with them" (v 4). They were his responsibility. We read at the end of the previous chapter that "all the prisoners that were in the prison" were committed to Joseph's hand. We don't know exactly what age Joseph was at this point, but he certainly did not have previous experience of running a prison!

This was part of God's plan — if Joseph, beginning at the age of thirty, were to manage a nation, he would have to imbibe some important lessons. He had learned much while overseeing Potiphar's household and field operations, but this was going to be different. Handling prisoners would surely be more difficult as they are not generally content with the punishment meted out, and not happy with their current position and future prospects.

Consider these three words for a moment: "he served them" (v 4). This is the same expression as is used in the previous chapter when Joseph served Potiphar. The word here indicates it was menial service, although the same word is used in other Old Testament books to refer to priestly service. When we look at the teaching of the Lord Jesus to His disciples, we learn some relevant truths:

1) "For even the Son of man came not to be ministered unto, but to minister" (Mark 10:45). He Himself set the example of humble service.

2) "He that is greatest among you, let him be as the younger; and he that is chief, as he that doth serve" (Luke 22:26). After hearing the Lord Jesus speak about His betrayal, a conflict arose amongst the disciples concerning who would be the greatest. He needed to teach them, not only by His own example given on many occasions, including when He had washed their feet in this same upper room, but also very directly. He told them that leadership amongst God's people is not the same as worldly leadership, but completely contrary The chief amongst them would be the one willing to serve.

3) "If any man serve me, let him follow me; and where I am, there shall also my servant be: if any man serve me, him will my Father honour" (John 12:26). It is a wonderful privilege to be able to serve the One who came to serve all mankind. To serve Him, we must follow Him, and follow His example. There are also two promises that He gives us — His presence, as well as honour from His Father.

Joseph was not above serving; our Saviour was very willing to serve; and now the challenge remains for us — how willing are we to serve others? We could perhaps say that Joseph had no other option - it was required of him. Although this is true, what we want to notice is that his attitude was always right — there was no "root of bitterness" springing up that would not only trouble him, but also be the means that "many be defiled" (Heb 12:15). A bitter spirit is never content to be alone — it is contagious and needs to be cut off at the root.

So Joseph was given the opportunity to serve those who were not from society's highest class, but prisoners, some even condemned to execution. We ought not to think that we can choose whom we serve, but rather look for the opportunities that God places in our pathway.

Faithfulness in our daily responsibilities, no matter how menial they appear to be to us, is the best preparation for future service for God, in whatever sphere He has planned for us.

The Consideration (vv 5-8)

An Optional Observation

One particular morning Joseph noticed a change in the faces of the butler and the baker. The writer comments that he "looked upon them", he observed or considered them. He saw that they were sad — is it not true that most people in prison, if not all, are sad? But this sadness obviously was something distinct to the norm seen in such a place, and Joseph was both attentive and astute.

His job description surely did not include "Rid prisoners of all sadness", yet Joseph showed a genuine care and interest in these two men, and asked them, "Wherefore look ye so sadly today?" (v 7). Are we aware of what is happening in the lives of those around us? I am not speaking of being a busybody, but the expression of genuine concern when it is obvious that someone is going through a struggle. It is so easy in today's busyness to get entirely occupied with our own challenges and difficulties, and to forget that there are many around us who are suffering, or perhaps are simply lonely. They need to hear a caring word, an expression of interest in their wellbeing, whether that is emotional, physical or spiritual. It is quite possible that we cannot solve their issues, but remember Paul's words: "Bear ye one another's burdens, and so fulfil the law of Christ" (Gal 6:2). May God help us to have the heart of Joseph and reach out to others in need.

Remember also the two who were walking to Emmaus after the Lord's crucifixion. The Lord Himself drew near to them, well aware of their sadness, and said, "What manner of communications are these that ye have one to another, as ye walk, and are sad?" (Luke 24:17). He observed them, expressed a genuine interest in them, and was able from the Scriptures to encourage their hearts. Joseph is a wonderful example; the Lord Jesus is the supreme example — both are worthy of our imitation.

Ability and Amiability

Joseph heard their response: "We have dreamed a dream, and there is no interpreter of it" (v 8). A while before this Joseph's problems had increased because of his own dreams. Perhaps the logical response would have been something like this: "Dreams, you say? I'm here because of dreams I had — I'd rather not go down this road with you!"

We notice that Joseph's response reveals to us once again three characteristics that we see time and again in his life: his humility, his compassion and his dependence upon God: "Do not interpretations belong to God? tell me them, I pray you" (v 8). He was living in a polytheistic pagan country, and most certainly this mention of "God" would be something new to these two men who were deeply involved in the palace culture, dependent on many gods. However, Joseph clearly states his monotheistic beliefs here in this conversation.

Joseph knew that he himself had no ability to interpret dreams, but he was confident that God could do so, and he depended entirely upon Him. Going beyond dreams to other aspects of our life, can we not see that this is what God is looking for amongst His children today? "He hath shewed thee, O man, what is good; and what doth the LORD require of thee, but to do justly, and to love mercy, and to walk humbly with thy God?" (Micah 6:8). The prophet called for a humble attitude that leads us to complete dependence on Him, mercy or compassion shown to others, and a desire to do what is just, or right before God.

Joseph recognized his own lack of ability, but in an amiable fashion expressed his desire to again serve the butler and the baker: "Tell me them, I pray you" (v 8).

The Clarity (vv 9-19)

Telling the truth is easy when there is good news, but it can be much more difficult when we know that the truth is bad news. God requires us to be faithful when sharing His Word with others. That which He has revealed to the writers by His Holy Spirit is not ours to alter, but rather to impart just as it has been revealed. Joseph was such a man.

The Branches and the Blossoms

The chief of the butlers recounted his dream to Joseph. There was a vine with three branches that budded and brought forth blossoms. It was a fruitful vine, giving ripe grapes, which were then pressed into the king's cup, and placed into Pharaoh's hand (vv 9-11).

Joseph, dependent on God giving him the interpretation, gave the butler good news: the three branches represented three days, which meant that within three days he would be restored to his previous position. He would return to delivering the cup into the hand of Pharaoh (vv 12-13).

Joseph continues with a simple request which, given the circumstances, would be considered quite normal. "But think on me when it shall be well with thee, and shew kindness, I pray thee, unto me, and make mention of me unto Pharaoh, and bring me out of this house" (v 14). This request is followed by a very short summary of his current circumstances. There is no need to take this as a complaint; he was simply stating the truth - first that he had been wrongfully taken from his own land, and then that in the new land of Egypt there was nothing he had done to deserve being confined in this prison; his conscience was clear (v 15). The Lord Jesus once challenged the Jewish leaders to find a fault in Him: "Which of you convinceth me of sin?" (John 8:46). There would be nothing they could point to of which He would be guilty. Yet He, too, later suffered although innocent.

The Basket and the Birds

The chief of the bakers was obviously encouraged by this interpretation, and so, hoping for the best, he shared his dream with Joseph. There were three baskets on his head in which there "was of all manner of bakemeats for Pharaoh". Darby describes these as "victuals ... that the baker makes", but whatever form and flavour they had, the birds enjoyed them as well (vv 16-17).

Delivering bad news ought to be done in a respectful way, but also with clarity. Joseph would have taken no pleasure in giving the interpretation to the baker, but he had to be honest and tell him the truth. Sadly, the news Joseph delivered was really his death sentence. He had three days to prepare, and then he would be lifted up on a tree, and the birds would come to eat his flesh (vv 18-19).

Without too much reading between the lines, and with no desire to add to the Word of God, is it not quite possible that a godly man like Joseph would have spent considerable time with that baker during his last three days on earth? Would he already perhaps have explained to both of these men who the true God is? Would the sense of urgency increase now? Amos, centuries later, would speak clear and urgent words to the nation of Israel: "prepare to meet thy God" (Amos 4:12).

Being very practical for a moment or two, let's remember that we are stewards of the Gospel message. The good news of God's salvation includes a side that is becoming increasingly unattractive in the culture in which we live. Even if the people happen to believe in God, they certainly do not want to hear about sin and justice and condemnation and death, but we would be unfaithful to the Word of God, and to the Lord Himself, were we to be tempted to water down the message. Joseph did no such thing.

The Calm Confidence (vv 20-23)

Fully Forgotten

When we come to the end of chapter 40, we read these words: "Yet did not the chief butler remember Joseph, but forgat him" (v 23). One would have thought that after having been encouraged in such a way by Joseph, the least the butler could have done for him would have been to drop his name on any of the many occasions he took Pharaoh the cup. But Joseph was completely gone from his memory.

In the meantime, what would happen? Two years were going to pass during which we read nothing about Joseph's activities in the prison, but that does not mean that God was not with him. God was still working in Joseph's life, moulding and making him into the leader he would soon be.

Furthering his Faith

Remembering that the dreams he had while he still lived in his father's house had not been fulfilled would perhaps from time to time have made Joseph to wonder when and how might these things come to take place. Could Joseph not have sung, along with the psalmist David, "How long wilt thou forget me, O LORD? for ever? how long wilt thou hide thy face from me?" (Ps 13:1)?

But this particular experience of interpreting these two dreams and then quickly seeing them fulfilled would further his faith. God's timing is not always what we expect, or desire, but it is always perfect. These indications along his pathway were an encouragement to Joseph while he waited.

We perhaps like to think that we are patient people, but the Lord allows us to pass through learning experiences so that our patience, and perseverance, grow. They may not be experiences that we would have chosen, but they are for our good and God's glory. Paul writes, "... we glory in tribulations also: knowing that tribulation worketh patience" (Rom 5:3). The apostle James teaches something similar: "Knowing this, that the trying of your faith worketh patience. But let patience have her perfect work, that ye may be perfect and entire, wanting nothing" (James 1:3-4). God allowed these difficult moments to mature Joseph — this is part of allowing patience to "have her perfect work", not trying to take shortcuts.

There are others who had to pass through a long experience of waiting before they commenced the service for which they are best known. Consider Moses spending forty long years in the wilderness, learning to care for sheep before he would be responsible for the care of millions of people as they passed through the desert.

The Bible teaches us that there is a reward, or recompense. The writer to the Hebrews encouraged them with these words: "Cast not away therefore your confidence, which hath great recompence of reward. For ye have need of patience, that, after ye have done the will of God, ye might receive the promise. For yet a little while, and he that shall come will come, and will not tarry. Now the just shall live by faith" (Heb 10:35-38). Today, as we wait for the One who will come, we do so by faith, confident in God's Word, just like Joseph so many years ago.

The psalmist writes concerning Joseph, "He sent a man before them, even Joseph, who was sold for a servant: Whose feet they hurt with fetters: he was laid in iron: Until the time that his word came: the word of the LORD tried him" (Ps 105:17-19). This only confirms to us that the timing was in God's control, as was the trial itself. It was a word that came from the Lord Himself that tried Joseph — God's promise by means of a dream one day to exalt him was sure. Joseph did not know when this would happen, but it did finally come to pass.

Faithful in his Functions

Joseph was still a very young man but was again proving that he was dependable. For two full years he worked diligently, and never do we read a word of complaint.

Obviously Paul had not yet written his letter to the Colossians, but Joseph was the embodiment of his exhortation: "Servants, obey in all things your masters according to the flesh; not with eyeservice, as menpleasers; but in singleness of heart, fearing God: And whatsoever ye do, do it heartily, as to the Lord, and not unto men; Knowing that of the Lord ye shall receive the reward of the inheritance: for ye serve the Lord Christ" (Col 3:23-25). In your daily employment remember that you can honour and please God, as serving man in this manner really is service to Christ.

Joseph was serving where God had allowed him to be. From his attitude, it appears obvious that he understood the truth that in whatever sphere God has placed us we can serve Him.

Consider the Cross

Centuries later another innocent man would be grouped with two criminals. Luke tells us that there were two malefactors "led with him to be put to death" (Luke 23:32). One of those two received wonderful news while at death's door: "Verily I say unto thee, To day shalt thou be with me in paradise" (Luke 23:43). The other malefactor did not come to repentance and therefore died in his sins. The Lord Jesus, while suffering greatly Himself, manifested a genuine interest in, and had great compassion on, a man in need, and met that need as no other could possibly do. May we be challenged to be more like Joseph, and more like our Lord Jesus, showing compassion and kindness to those whom God places in our pathway.

CHAPTER 7

The Changes were Astounding

Genesis 41

We perhaps have all read, or at least heard of, rags to riches stories. Few of these can compare with the one we are about to consider, either in the speed at which it occurred or in the pinnacles reached. At the beginning of the chapter Joseph is in prison; at the end he is in power. Partway through the chapter Joseph changes his clothes in order to be presented before Pharaoh, but later he is clothed with a far finer robe. And let us not forget that he goes from being single to being married, and then becomes a father. Such a change in circumstances could cause a lesser man to become "wise in his own conceit" (Prov 26:12), but it was not so in Joseph's case.

The Conclusion (v 1a)

Although it seems odd to commence a chapter with a conclusion, the first verse brings to our attention "the end".

The Time

"Two full years." To some, two years seem to go by very quickly. Much depends upon the circumstances. Were you to have been in prison for "two full years", time would have dragged on very slowly. This time in prison was undeserved. Joseph was there because of false accusations, but God was obviously in no hurry for him to be released — the timing was not yet right.

Perhaps Joseph thought, as David did years later: "How long wilt thou forget me, O LORD? for ever? how long wilt thou hide thy face from me?" (Ps 13:1). As we continue reading that Psalm, David says, "But I have trusted in thy mercy; my heart shall rejoice in thy salvation. I will sing unto the LORD, because he hath dealt bountifully with me" (Ps 13:5-6). The time of sadness was about to conclude; the time of singing was soon to commence.

The Trial

The time in the prison was a continuation of the trial that Joseph had been steadfastly enduring. It is not inappropriate to repeat that in the midst of his long trial we do not find Joseph complaining about his circumstances or becoming bitter against God.

Life was routine in the prison, perhaps even monotonous. This in itself can become challenging in our lives, especially in a world that is so focused on distractions and diversions, pastimes and pleasures — the mundane can almost become meaningless. But much can be accomplished for God in the routines of our lives; developing helpful habits is essential. The Lord Jesus had routines in His life: "And he came out, and went, *as he was wont*, to the mount of Olives; and his disciples also followed him" (Luke 22:39). He had learned these holy habits in his home, observing His earthly parents go to the temple (Luke 2:41-42).

So, yes, life can seem tedious at times; the trial may go on for much longer than one expects or desires, but God has a purpose and plan in all of this, and He knows that making us wait causes us to grow, not only in our own character but also in our communion with Him.

The Teaching

God was teaching Joseph essential lessons about leadership, and these included the lesson of patience. James wrote, "Knowing this, that the trying of your faith worketh patience. But let patience have her perfect work, that ye may be perfect and entire, wanting nothing" (James 1:3-4). Trials teach us what we need to learn in the school of God, and that includes the truth of "patience", or steadfastness, as seen here.

A leader faces many perils — will they become frustrated with those who follow them? Will they abuse their leadership? Joseph was not suddenly thrust into leadership, but rather matured ("perfect and entire") under God's hand so that he could now, at the age of thirty, be a trusted and wise leader in Egypt.

Even amongst the people of God we see the same truth applied to leadership. Paul writes to Timothy about shepherds in the local assembly: "Not a novice, lest being lifted up with pride he fall into the condemnation of the devil" (1 Tim 3:6). God will raise up men who have matured under His guiding hand.

The Confusion (vv 1b-8)

If you were to search the internet for the word "dreams", over four billion possible pages would come up! It would take a lifetime to sift through them all, but it goes to show us how much people in today's society are fascinated by dreams. Experts say we all dream each night, and there are many who are searching for the meaning of these dreams even at this very moment! Not only is it big business, but it can lead into dangerous delusions — how many millions each day check their horoscope, or have their palms read, or delve into other mystical realms? It should go without saying that none of this is for the believer! Our guide is the Word of God in our hands, heads and hearts, and the Spirit of God dwelling in us.

Although we have issued a warning about dreams, we do understand that there are a number of occasions in the Bible when God did indeed speak in this way. But it certainly was never the usual way — God expected His people to learn His law, and to teach it to the next generation. He also sent prophets from time to time to deliver new messages from God. Today we have the blessing of having God's completed revelation in our hands.

But let's remember, the interest in dreams and the occult is nothing new! At times Egyptian leaders considered dreams to be the divine means of directing them, and that is quite possibly the reason that this Pharaoh was so concerned about the significance of his dreams.

The Double Dream

Pharaoh dreamt first about cattle and then about corn. Both dreams dealt with prosperity and then with adversity. Seven fat cows had come out of the river and were feeding in a meadow, but then were eaten by seven lean cows who had come from the same river. Then in the second dream he saw "seven ears of corn" that were full and good, but were to be devoured by seven thin ears that had been blasted by the east wind.

When we get to verse 32, Joseph will say, "And for that the dream was doubled unto Pharaoh twice; it is because the thing is established by God, and God will bring it shortly to pass", but at this earlier point Pharaoh understands nothing of the significance of the dreams.

The Troubled Thoughts

In verse 4, "Pharaoh awoke". This often can happen when a dream disturbs the dreamer. But it is even more obvious in verse 8 that these dreams not only confused him, but also concerned him: "his spirit was troubled". There were three things in the dreams that would have troubled him: the cattle, the corn and the river. These were an important source of prosperity and security for the Egyptian people, and suddenly Pharaoh had this perturbing dream. The importance of the Nile River to the Egyptian monarchy cannot be overstated. Ezekiel brought a message from God years later to another Pharaoh, saying, "Behold, I am against thee, Pharaoh king of Egypt, the great dragon that lieth in the midst of his rivers, which hath said, My river is mine own, and I have made it for myself ... Behold, therefore I am against thee, and against thy rivers, and I will make the land of Egypt utterly waste and desolate, from the tower of Syene even unto the border of Ethiopia" (Ezek 29:3, 10).

This Pharaoh wondered: What did it all mean? Why these dreams mentioning the river? He turned to the most likely source of Egyptian wisdom, the magicians and wise men. They failed him.

The Wisdom of the World

As Pharaoh recounts the dream to all these men, the sad conclusion is this: "there was none that could interpret them unto Pharaoh" (v 8). This was the sum of Egyptian wisdom, as "all" were called. God hid the significance of the dream from them entirely. There was not one word of wisdom from any of them. We will soon see the difference between worldly wisdom and divine wisdom, when God reveals the meaning to Joseph. Worldly understanding failed, much as James teaches in his epistle: "This wisdom descendeth not from above, but is earthly, sensual, devilish" (3:15). These men had nothing to say, perhaps very perturbed themselves as they considered possible meanings. It was obviously bad news, and they preferred not even to offer an opinion.

The Cupbearer (vv 9-13)

An Obvious Oversight

At the end of chapter 40 we read these sad words: "Yet did not the chief butler remember Joseph, but forgat him" (v 23). It wasn't his intention to push Joseph out of his memory, but it was obviously the divine intention as God was, as we have earlier seen, still working in Joseph's life during these two years. So again we see how divine providence works — just at the right time Pharaoh has a dream, as Joseph is now ready for the tremendous weight of responsibility that will come upon him. God was in control of the circumstances and of the timing.

His Wise Words

True confession is extremely hard to come by today. The butler, or cupbearer, gives us a good example of what confession ought to look like: "I do remember my faults this day" (v 9). There is no excuse offered, no explanation, no evading the truth. He assumes complete responsibility for his actions and calls them "my faults".

On a spiritual level, far beyond this court scene, we understand that true repentance is related to true confession. The cupbearer hid nothing, but rather told the whole truth. When there is sin in the life of the believer it needs to be confronted and confessed in order to see full restoration.

His Restoration leads to a Recommendation

The butler now recognizes publicly the ability that "a young man, an Hebrew, servant to the captain of the guard" had to properly and accurately interpret dreams. The baker had committed some fault and had thus offended Pharaoh, and ended up being hanged. The butler himself was restored to his office, and thus could highly recommend this young man's services to Pharaoh.

The Change and Certainty (vv 14-16)

Dignity and Humility

When Pharaoh heard these words, he immediately sent for Joseph, who, upon hearing this call, shaved his face and changed his raiment. A study of the changes in clothing in Joseph's life is very interesting, but we will leave that aside for now. He obviously felt that the clothes apt for the dungeon were not fit for the king, realizing something of the dignity of the person whom he was soon to meet. We then read of the meeting between a poor, foreign prisoner and slave in all his humility and Pharaoh, the most powerful man on earth at this time, in all his dignity, yet in his deep necessity.

This is not the only time that we see a lowly person used of God to bring a message of hope to someone moving in a higher stratum of society. Remember Naaman's wife's maid, whose message was short yet sufficient: "Would God my lord were with the prophet that is in Samaria! for he would recover him of his leprosy!" (2 Kings 5:2). It was enough not only to bring health to Naaman's body, but also hope to his soul. Too often we fear to open our mouths to share something that could possibly lead to eternal blessing for another.

The Reply to the Request

There is no indication that Joseph was forewarned about the reason for being released, but Pharaoh comes right to the point: "I have dreamed a dream, and there is none that can interpret it" (v 15). When Joseph hears the request itself, he could have stood a little taller and assented to what Pharaoh said: "I have heard say of thee, that thou canst understand a dream to interpret it" (v 15).

But Joseph was not going to presume, like so many might have done, that his own abilities would suffice. He takes full advantage of the opportunity to bring God into the picture, a God that Pharaoh surely did not know, and quite probably had never even heard mentioned before. I wonder if we take advantage of the opportunities that God places in our pathway to speak to people about our God and Saviour.

"It is not in me" — these words may have temporarily startled Pharaoh! He was expecting something more along the lines of "Yes, your majesty!" But Joseph was not done yet. He will express not only complete reliance upon his God to interpret the dream, but an absolute certainty that God would "give Pharaoh an answer of peace" (v 16). We, too, need to remember what the Lord taught His disciples: "without me ye can do nothing" (John 15:5). In our service for God, we truly are completely dependent upon Him and His grace.

Pharaoh then recounts the dream to Joseph in the next eight verses, before we return to see what Joseph has to say. Remember he is a thirty year old man at this point with no political experience, but very obviously endued with wisdom from above. Again recall James' words about this type of wisdom: "But the wisdom that is from above is first pure, then peaceable, gentle, and easy to be intreated, full of mercy and good fruits, without partiality, and without hypocrisy" (3:17). We need much of this wisdom today, and none of the worldly wisdom.

The Clarity and Counsel (vv 25-36)

As we saw in the previous chapter, Joseph was not one to confuse the issue but rather got right to the point. In contrast to modern day

dream interpretations, this one would be specific and measurable —
there would be no way to confuse what Joseph was telling Pharaoh.
Here he goes beyond the interpretation and he takes it upon himself
to give counsel to Pharaoh.

The Preeminence of God

Joseph has already mentioned back in verse 16 that God Himself
would give the interpretation. Now in verse 25 he says that "God has
shewed Pharaoh what he is about to do". He repeats the same thought
in verse 28, and then affirms it twice more in verse 32: "The thing is
established by God, and God will shortly bring it to pass". At the very
least Pharaoh was receiving a brief lesson on God's sovereign control.

This regular mention of God ought not to surprise us in the least.
Joseph lived a God-centered life, so it would be only normal and
natural to mention God. Perhaps he was beginning to see how God
was going to work out His purposes in his life at the same time.

The Point of the Dream

Joseph makes it clear that the meaning of the dream is one, even
though it was given in two different ways. The doubling of the dream
was to emphasize the certainty and imminence of its fulfillment.

He told Pharaoh that there were going to be seven years of "great
plenty throughout all the land of Egypt" (v 29), followed by seven
years of famine, such that all the plenty would be forgotten. The famine
would "consume the land" (v 30), and deplete it of all its productivity
and prosperity.

The Plan

Joseph wisely and seamlessly moves into the presentation of a plan
in verse 33: "Now therefore let Pharaoh look out a man discreet and
wise, and set him over the land of Egypt". Remember Pharaoh was over

the land already, but Joseph was suggesting a second-in-command who would take responsibility for this unique plan. He would have to be discerning and wise — this was not going to be about power or popularity, but rather about character. A man of integrity would be required, a man who would not act in a corrupt or prepotent manner.

This wise man would be over the officers who would be in charge of a twenty percent levy on all the harvested crops during seven years (v 34). The math would tell us they needed less to survive, but Joseph was wiser than that, and realized the famine would reach other countries as well. Egypt would not come to the end of the seven years of famine crushed and defeated, but rather with a good balance of funds on hand due to the sale of the grain.

It was also wise not to build the storehouses in one central area, but rather in every city (v 35). Due to its tremendous volume, it would be easier to transport the harvested grain to nearby depots during the seven years of plenty, and later much more convenient to purchase it locally during the seven years of famine.

Joseph laid the weight of this responsibility on Pharaoh. A king truly ought to be concerned about the welfare of his people, but Joseph was not suggesting a welfare state either. This was not going to develop into a give-away or a free-for-all. He was suggesting a way that the people would work so that there would be provision in a coming day, although managed by the state.

The Purpose

Very simply put, the purpose was "that the land perish not through the famine" (v 36). Joseph understood the gravity of the situation. Were we to relate all of this to our responsibility to share the gospel, we understand that we are currently living in a day of opportunity, when in many parts of the world there is an abundant availability of the Word of God. Such will not always be the case, and each one needs to prepare for the coming day. Open doors close, and closed doors open as God works in special ways in different areas and at different times.

Had Joseph simply suggested to Pharaoh that each family set aside a portion for the coming years of famine, Egypt would have been decimated. Many would not have believed, and many would simply not have had the will-power to set aside something for a coming crisis. Egypt would not have been able to provide for the other nations; his family would not have come down to Egypt, and the nation of Israel could perhaps have been wiped out before it really got established. Had his own people not survived, the Messianic line would not have been preserved, so we are again caused to marvel at God's providential care.

The Prophetic Message

We can clearly see here a picture of the dispensation of grace, represented by the plenteous harvest, and then a seven year period of trial, or tribulation. We are living in the day of grace when the gospel message can be freely presented, and the Lord Jesus offers life: "I am come that they might have life, and that they might have it more abundantly" (John 10:10). But this period will one day come to a close, and seven years of desperate trouble will come upon the world. May God help us to faithfully present the message of the marvellous provision of salvation to those around us who are lost and perishing before it is eternally too late.

The Charge (vv 37-49)

Having interpreted the dream, it was now Pharaoh's decision to implement Joseph's plan with someone in charge, or to reject it outright. However, he had been convinced while listening to Joseph that this was indeed from God, and "the thing was good" (v 37).

The Acknowledgment

The first comment from Pharaoh's mouth is telling: "Can we find such a one as this is, a man in whom the spirit of God is?" (v 38).

Pharaoh may not have known much about this God that Joseph had mentioned, but he realized that His spirit was dwelling in this Hebrew man. This a challenge to us today — does any unbeliever with whom we come into contact have any idea that the Spirit of God is indwelling us? Is the fruit of the Spirit evident in our lives? Do we manifest a heavenly wisdom, not in a haughty way, but rather in humility? May God help us to have such an impact on others as Joseph had.

It did not take a lot of thinking to come to the conclusion that Pharaoh expressed, with the agreement of the whole court: "Forasmuch as God hath shewed thee all this, there is none so discreet [discerning] and wise as thou art" (v 39). Despite having magicians and wise men on his payroll, Pharaoh, in one very brief meeting, had to acknowledge there was a real difference between them and Joseph. They were quick to recognize what we know to be wisdom from above, given directly by God for the moment of need.

There was no real evidence that Joseph was right in his interpretation. It was still all in the relatively distant future. There had been good harvest years before, and there had been famine. But a prediction this precise was not known. There are perhaps three factors to take into account when we consider Pharaoh's rapid acceptance of Joseph's message: his confidence in expressing the message, with no hesitation, humming or hawing; the Egyptian tendency to think that their gods did indeed speak to them in dreams; and the fact that the cupbearer had given testimony to Joseph's ability to interpret dreams.

Years later in Babylon another powerful king would acknowledge the same about other young men far from their homeland and far from any God-fearing influence: "among them all was found none like Daniel, Hananiah, Mishael, and Azariah ... And in all matters of wisdom and understanding, that the king enquired of them, he found them ten times better than all the magicians and astrologers that were in all his realm" (Dan 1:19-20). This, too, went far beyond any natural intelligence and capability, and was a clear sign that the God of heaven was with these young men.

Is it not true that even today godly young men and women can be proven to be far more prudent and trustworthy than their peers, whether at university or at work? May we strive to have a testimony like that of these early believers.

The Advancement

Joseph would now be promoted in the kingdom. Pharaoh said: "See, I have set thee over all the land of Egypt" (v 41). As we consider how Joseph made this seemingly sudden advance in the kingdom from prisoner to "prime minister", let us remember that in another sense it really was not sudden, for during the last thirteen years he had proven himself faithful in whatever sphere of service he was found. The Lord Jesus taught years later, "He that is faithful in that which is least is faithful also in much" (Luke 16:10), and Joseph had lived out that principle in his own life.

This was a very heady and thrilling experience, but we do not see it affecting Joseph's character or conduct. Too often power and influence do go to a man's head, and we need to be aware of this danger. Consider the different aspects of his advancement or exaltation in verses 42-45:

A ring. This speaks to us of complete **authority**. There was no second ring made for Joseph, but he had the full authority of the king behind him. Whatever law he needed to promulgate, whatever edict he had to enforce, he had the weight of the Egyptian throne behind him. The giving of this ring indicates that Pharaoh had complete confidence in Joseph, even though he had just very recently met him. He is not the first person in this story that had trusted Joseph: his own father trusted him to go and check on his brothers' behaviour, Potiphar trusted Joseph with all his goods, and the prison chief had left all the prisoners in his care. In every case, Joseph had been faithful and trustworthy, and as we continue to read the rest of the story, the same will still be true of him.

Remember the words of the Lord Jesus as He was about to stoop to wash His disciples' feet: "Jesus knowing that the Father had given all things into his hands, and that he was come from God, and went to God; He riseth from supper, and laid aside his garments; and took a towel, and girded himself" (John 13:3-4). He had authority, but yet He stooped to serve His own disciples. What humility seen in this unique Man!

Garments of fine linen. This new apparel was a drastic change from his prisoner's garb from hours before, and even from what he stood in before Pharaoh at this moment. It speaks to us of his **purity** — yes, it is true that he had been falsely accused of a sensual crime, but he was pure. The Lord Jesus was stripped of His clothing when going to the cross, dressed in a robe so that they could mock Him, and then wrapped in fine linen when He was laid in the tomb. Tracing the garments of the Lord Jesus is a lovely study that we will not occupy ourselves in at this point. Here we simply note the beauty and distinction shown to Joseph, a figure of the purity of our Lord Jesus.

A gold chain. Yet another symbol of honour and **dignity** was laid upon Joseph's neck. Remember the words of the Psalmist as he writes concerning Joseph: "Whose feet they hurt with fetters: he was laid in iron" (Ps 105:18). At one time Joseph was amongst the prisoners, shackled with iron, but now he had received a chain of gold. In Revelation John speaks of the Lord Jesus having a golden girdle on His breast (1:13) and a golden crown upon His head (14:14). What dignity we see in our Risen Lord!

The second chariot. From a practical standpoint this would be required for Joseph to fulfill his responsibilities, travelling across the land. However, if we were to compare it to our days we could think of the magnificent motorcades of dignitaries as they move from place to place. Joseph, too, had the honour of representing **majesty**. The Lord Jesus said concerning the relationship between Him and His Father: "All men should honour the Son, even as they honour the Father" (John 5:23). This is One who sat down at the "right hand of the Majesty on high" (Heb 1:3). He is the "express image of his person" and merits our praise and adoration.

The acclamation. "They cried before him, Bow the knee." He who had been despised, shamed and imprisoned was now receiving the **glory** he deserved. Possibly Joseph had bowed his knee before many during the previous thirteen years in Egypt, but now the tables had been turned. We can only wonder what others like Potiphar and his wife thought about this change in Joseph's status! Consider the words Paul quoted from Isaiah 45: "As I live, saith the Lord, every knee shall bow to me, and every tongue shall confess to God" (Rom 14:11). When Paul writes to the Philippians about the Lord's willingness to humble Himself, he also speaks about His exaltation, and writes: "Wherefore God also hath highly exalted him, and given him a name which is above every name: That at the name of Jesus every knee should bow, of things in heaven, and things in earth, and things under the earth; And that every tongue should confess that Jesus Christ is Lord, to the glory of God the Father" (Phil 2:9-11). We willingly do what the psalmist penned many years ago: "Give unto the LORD, O ye mighty, give unto the LORD glory and strength" (Ps 29:1). We will do it in eternity, but it is our privilege to do it here upon earth where our Lord is still rejected and despised.

A new name. Can we suggest that the giving of a new name gave Joseph additional **notoriety**, or fame? Although it is difficult to know with exactitude the meaning, we present a few possibilities: Zaphnath-paaneah has been said to mean "Saviour" by the Coptics; "Revealer of Secrets" by the Hebrews; or portraying the "Victor over Temptation" in the hieroglyphs. All three would show us something of the character and labour of Joseph — he would be used to save the nation from perishing; he had been the only one able to reveal the secret meaning behind the dreams; and if the third is accurately translated, there perhaps was some knowledge of Joseph's ability to not fall into temptation. This latter meaning would be a tremendous benefit in a leader of any nation — a propensity to flee from whatever evil or corruption exists! All of these are easily applied to the Lord Jesus, who not only came to save the world, but also knows the thoughts and intentions of our hearts — nothing is hidden from Him. He, too, was tempted, but directly by Satan, and was victorious over the temptation.

A wife. In a book with much polygamy, it is thrilling to see a man living in a foreign land with one wife, just as God established in the beginning. Joseph would be in good **company**, accepted in the highest levels of society. His wife was not a Hebrew, but rather an Egyptian, the daughter of Potipherah, the priest of On. He received Asenath upon his exaltation. Some would perhaps criticize Joseph for marrying someone outside of his own people, but in this case there are reasons that made this acceptable: no law had been given to the people of God to the contrary as of yet, and this marriage would picture a far more important future relationship, that of Christ and His bride. Recall that in Acts 1 the Lord Jesus ascends to His throne, and then in Acts 2 He receives a bride, the Church. We know that the day of the full presentation of His bride awaits Him, but He purchased her with His own blood on Calvary's cross, and the day will come when all of His bride will be at His side.

So Joseph was exalted in the kingdom, far above all others. Joseph had taken the low place for many years, causing us to consider the principle the Lord Jesus taught: "For whosoever exalteth himself shall be abased; and he that humbleth himself shall be exalted" (Luke 14:11). As we have seen, there was a greater Man who humbled Himself willingly, and then was exalted far above the heavens — our Lord and Saviour.

His Age

Although Joseph had been actively serving and working from a very young age, it is at the age of thirty that he began a public role in regards to service (v 46). There is no difficulty in seeing a reference to a coming Man who also would begin public service at the same age. We read, "Jesus himself began to be about thirty years of age" (Luke 3:23). This was at the time of His public presentation at His baptism, when He was openly recognized by His Father, and the Spirit of God descended in bodily form upon Him. The years before reaching the age of thirty were not wasted years in either case, but rather a time when God was preparing His chosen vessels to serve and honour Him in a special way.

The Assignment

Joseph, now exalted above all others, goes out from the presence of

Pharaoh throughout all the land of Egypt. It was time to implement the plan that the Lord had given to him. His purpose now would be to save the lives of the nation in the coming years through proper administration of what the land would produce in the period of plenty. He almost certainly did not know that he would also be used to preserve alive his own family, and that all of what was happening was part of God's greater plan to fulfill the dreams Joseph had shared with them, to his apparent detriment, some thirteen years before.

The abundance of what the earth brought forth in those seven years became such that Joseph stopped counting, or weighing, the crops. "And Joseph gathered corn as the sand of the sea, very much" (v 49). We mentioned earlier the wisdom shown even in the storage of the grains — it was in every city. During these seven years of plenty Joseph was leading well but, truthfully, it is easier to be a leader when there are no real challenges and no lack of provision. We soon shall see Joseph guiding the nation in times of famine, and this requires far more of a leader.

It is interesting to note what we do not read as well as what we do read. How often have many people in the world come to power and then done all they can to retaliate against those who may have mistreated them previously? In many parts of the world a change of government brings real chaos to many people's lives as jobs are lost and some from the former regime may be persecuted or prosecuted. But with Joseph we see none of this — there is no rancour or resentment towards the captain of the guard, the head of the prison, or even Potiphar's wife. "Who, when he was reviled, reviled not again" (1 Peter 2:23) helps us see the One far greater than Joseph who never used His power to mistreat anyone, but rather sought, as Joseph did years before, the good of others.

The Children (vv 50-52)

Into Asenath and Joseph's home came two bundles of joy. "Lo, children are an heritage of the LORD: and the fruit of the womb is his reward" (Ps 127:3). Two sons that Joseph would be able to teach the ways of the Lord — an exceptional responsibility in that pagan society then, and the same is increasingly true in our day as well. The lack of the fear of God in modern-day society is frightening, but the principles of the Word of God can give our children, or grandchildren, a firm foundation.

The Moment of their Birth

Both of these sons, Manasseh and Ephraim, were born "before the years of famine came" (v 50). Remember that when you are reading God's Word all these seemingly little details are actually important, sometimes helping us to understand the chronology better, or giving us a better grasp of the age of the people involved. They were born in the time of plenty, but would live through, and beyond the time of famine. By the time the famine was coming to its end the boys surely would have been old enough to appreciate the wisdom of their father in having administered the agricultural production of a whole nation for so many years.

The Meaning of their Names

The firstborn was called Manasseh ("Making forgetful"), as Joseph said: "For God ... hath made me forget all my toil, and all my father's house" (v 51). Forgetting is a human weakness, and often what we most wish to remember is precisely what we forget. The opposite can often be true as well — there are things we want to forget, to remove from our memory, but they are burned into it. In this case Joseph obviously had not actually "forgotten" his toil and family as he mentions both, but rather he is saying that the Lord had provided him with a source of joy, someone who would provide new memories and help him leave the past behind.

The second son was Ephraim ("Fruitfulness"), and Joseph now rejoiced, not in being able to forget the past, but rather in God's goodness to him: "For God hath caused me to be fruitful in the land of my affliction" (v 52). It was a land that had afflicted Joseph for thirteen years, but his confidence in God had not waned. He saw that the Lord had been good to him and made him fruitful, giving him descendants.

The Commencement (vv 53-57)

We began this chapter with a conclusion and now conclude with a commencement. "And the seven years of dearth began to come" (v 54). The years of plenty were over, and a dreadful and drastic change was about to come, just as Joseph had said.

The Prosperity

In a very brief way the writer notes that the "seven years of plenteousness ... were ended" (v 53). Although the Lord Jesus warned against laying up treasures on earth "where moth and rust doth corrupt, and where thieves break through and steal" (Matt 6:19), on the other hand we read, "Go to the ant, thou sluggard; consider her ways, and be wise" (Prov 6:6). Even the ant knows that holding back some of the harvest for a coming winter day is a wise and proper thing to do. While hoarding can cause us to become independent of God, in this case it was God Himself who had warned about the coming years, so Joseph was showing his wisdom in this particular plan.

Would some of the Egyptians perhaps have wondered whether such prosperity would ever end? Were they secretly hoping that this abundance would continue many more years?

The Paucity

The next period commenced, and the dearth was everywhere, not just in Egypt. This would not be a case of migrating to another part of the world to seek employment and sustenance as often happens today. There were no worldwide organizations that could counter this famine. "The dearth was in all lands; but in all the land of Egypt there was bread" (v 54). The only reason there was bread there was due to Joseph's diligent care, his ability to administer what the land had been producing.

The Pleas

The private stores of the people soon ran out of food, and so we hear them crying to Pharaoh for bread (v 55). Pharaoh's words are a wonderful commendation, a recognition of Joseph's position in the kingdom as well as his prudence. "Go unto Joseph; what he saith to you, do" (v 55). It makes us think of the Lord's mother in John 2:5, "Whatsoever he saith unto you, do it." What wise words from this woman's mouth!

The Provision

We then find that Joseph begins to open the storehouses across the land. This was not going to be a government handout, but rather the grain was sold to the people. As the famine became more severe, the provision remained available and constant.

The Providence of God

Finally we see again God's hand in all of this. He was moving behind the scenes in order to fulfill His purposes. The chapter ends giving us a little hint as to what will happen next: "And all countries came into Egypt to Joseph for to buy corn" (v 57). We have started to see what one man, by himself, can do for God, and thus be a blessing to others too. This man, along with many other believers both in the Bible and in subsequent history, lived in a world completely opposed to God yet pleased Him by standing firm on their convictions, trusting Him even when circumstances were extremely adverse. We still need men like Joseph today, willing to take a stand for God.

We know the story well, but if you can imagine yourself hearing or reading it for the first time perhaps you would wonder: "What will happen next? Who is going to show up at Joseph's doorstep? I wonder what's happening to his family so far away?" Well, we will soon find out the answer to these important questions!

CHAPTER 8

His Compassion and Astuteness

Genesis 42

Joseph not only was a very powerful man in Egypt, second only to Pharaoh, but, as we will notice in this chapter, he was also compassionate. His generosity in sending his brothers back with their silver in their sack was misunderstood by them, but it truly was an act of kindness. But before we get to that point, we will also notice that Joseph was astute — sometimes that word is used to mean cunning and clever, but here we are employing it in the sense of his keen discernment with regard to his brothers' true condition. How will full reconciliation be brought about? Could Joseph not just have revealed himself to them as soon as he saw them? No, he will want to probe deeply to ensure there is true repentance, and not just some lesser feeling of remorse.

As we read through this chapter we find four conversations, with the first and last being between Jacob and his sons. In the middle we listen to Joseph speaking through interpretation with his brothers, and then our hearts quicken as we hear the brothers speaking amongst themselves, recognizing their guilt over their treatment of Joseph some twenty years earlier.

The Father's Decisions (vv 1-5)

Jacob at this point is nearing his one hundred and thirtieth birthday. He is obviously still the authoritative patriarchal figure and has lost none of his faculties. He is fully aware that the family is in grave danger due to the famine that was "over all the face of the earth" (41:56). It is quite probable that there were caravans of people heading through his area towards Egypt, for he "saw that there was corn in Egypt" (v 1). He is not the least bit aware of how this initial decision is part of God's great plan for preserving the lineage of the Messiah, nor how it will be used to bring about reconciliation between his sons, nor even how it will put into action the steps to bring him to see his favoured son Joseph once again. All he understood was the present pressing need for food for his family.

Once he had this information about the availability of food he seems perturbed by the lack of initiative on the part of his sons, basically asking them why they are still sitting around staring at one another while there is provision in a neighbouring land. His instructions are clear: "... get you down thither and buy for us from thence; that we may live, and not die" (v 2).

The ten sons, those of Leah, Bilhah and Zilpah, dutifully prepared themselves for the long journey to Egypt, and they "went down to buy corn" (v 3). It probably would have taken them about ten days to travel the 200 miles, so there was plenty of time for conversation and contemplation along the way. Had the mention of Egypt from their father's lips stirred something in their souls? Go back in your mind to a day more than twenty years before when they "sold Joseph to the Ishmeelites for twenty pieces of silver: and they brought Joseph into Egypt" (37:28). "What would be the chances of running into Joseph now?" "Surely he's just one of thousands of slaves — we'll never see him." "It's a huge country; don't even think about it." We can't say for certain that these thoughts crossed their minds on their southerly trek, but it certainly is possible. Those memories we wish we could forget often invade our thoughts at the most importune or undesirable moment. At the very least we will see that they weren't in the land very long before their now distant treatment of Joseph did come to their minds.

Then we read these words: "But Benjamin, Joseph's brother, Jacob sent not with his brethren" (v 4). The last time we read about Benjamin was back in chapter 35 when he was born and his mother Rachel died (v 18); and then in the list of Jacob's twelve sons, "The sons of Rachel; Joseph, and Benjamin" (v 24). But Benjamin was now a grown man, in his early thirties. He was more than capable of assuming his share of the responsibility to find food for the family. But he was very near to his father's heart, and Jacob feared that some "mischief" (or calamity) would happen to him (v 4). At the end of the chapter we will again see Jacob's adamant stand against his son leaving his side.

The Family Reunion (vv 6-20)

You have likely been to many happy family gatherings, and it is possible that at some point a distant relative had turned up, and many have wondered, "Who is that?" But here we have a family reunion that was rather peculiar, as only Joseph understood what was happening.

Joseph's Position and his Brothers' Prostration

Although we know why "Joseph was the governor over the land" (v 6), it does us well to remember it was in God's providence that this was so. The Lord had been working behind the scenes for years in order to accomplish His plans. He had allowed Joseph to be sold by his own brethren; He had arranged for him to work in Potiphar's house; He had allowed the temptation by Potiphar's wife to result in Joseph's imprisonment; and He had brought the cupbearer to the same prison in order for him to be a tool, a full two years later, to bring Joseph out of prison and to this important position. All this was in order to preserve life. This very same God, in His infinite wisdom and power, is still in control in the circumstances of our lives today.

Now God was beginning to move other pieces in His providence. About two hundred years before this, God had said to Abraham: "Know of a surety that thy seed shall be a stranger in a land that is not theirs, and shall serve them; and they shall afflict them four hundred years" (15:13). What we read in this chapter is God fulfilling His word.

But God had also revealed something to Joseph in a dream when he was seventeen years old, and although he didn't perhaps understand what all it meant, and certainly did not know when or how or where it would be fulfilled, he did share it with his brothers: "For behold, we were binding sheaves in the field, and, lo, my sheaf arose, and also stood upright; and, behold, your sheaves stood round about, and made obeisance to my sheaf" (37:7). It ought not to surprise us when we read now that his brethren came "and bowed down themselves before him with their faces to the earth" (v 6). Remember that in his dream there were eleven sheaves bowing down, but now there were only ten men before him, but this partial fulfillment would have been a tremendous confirmation to him of God's working in his life.

The brothers were completely ignorant — "they knew him not" (v 8). How was that possible, given he was their own flesh and blood? While it is true that twenty years changes a person's appearance somewhat, that does not mean that a brother would be unrecognizable! They had heard his voice, but he spoke to them using an interpreter (v 23). He also spoke "roughly", or "harshly" to them (v 7) when he started to converse with them. Why was this? Certainly not because of any unkindness in his heart, but is it not possible that had he not acted this way he would not have been able to control his emotions? Being somewhat gruff would allow him to hide his feelings more easily. His appearance was changed too — the Egyptian custom was to be shaved, while Hebrew men would have been bearded; his clothing would have been that of a very high-ranking Egyptian official, a far cry from the work-robes his brothers were wearing.

The Probing and the Protests

Joseph was astute and realized that it was not yet time to reveal to them his true identity. He wanted to probe their thoughts and feelings, and he was able to do this with great patience and wisdom. He begins with a simple question, asking them about their origin, to which they give a truthful answer: "From the land of Canaan to buy food" (v 7).

We then read that "Joseph remembered the dreams which he dreamed of them" (v 9). God surely brought these dreams back to his mind at this moment, as we recall Joseph had decided to forget all his toil, and all his father's house (41:51). Now his tactic changes and he is not only speaking harshly to them, but he accuses them for the first time of being spies that had come from afar "to see the nakedness of the land" (v 9).

He repeats this accusation again and again (vv 12, 14, 16). As they protest against this, saying, "Nay, my lord", we realize that their responses are honest; "to buy food are thy servants come" (v 10); "We are all one man's sons; we are true men, thy servants are no spies" (v 11). They were adamantly denying any ulterior motives in relation to their arrival in Egypt. When Joseph again repeats the accusation of spying in verse 12, they give him additional information which he was no doubt anxious to hear. All he could tell up to this point was that there were ten living brothers, but what about his father? And what about Benjamin, his younger brother? They now admit that there are twelve sons in the family, but that "the youngest is this day with our father" (v 13). This would have brought great joy to Joseph's heart, hearing that his aged father and Benjamin were both still alive.

But think about the phrase "and one is not" (v 13). Back in verses 7 and 8 we are twice told that he knew them. He was obviously at a tremendous advantage as he commenced probing them. "One is not!" How strange it must have been for Joseph to hear these words explaining why now there were only eleven. This "one" was standing in front of his ten brothers, fully alive and aware of the circumstances that had led to his "being no more". Some would perhaps think that this was the ideal time to reveal himself, but they yet needed to be proved further in prison.

Spying — we are made to wonder why he emphasizes this particular charge. But go back to Chapter 37 where we read that "Joseph brought unto his father their evil report" (v 2). His brothers considered him to be a spy, sent by their father to check up on their behaviour, and they had developed a deep hatred all those years ago. Now the tables are turned, and Joseph is accusing them of the same act. Then they had taken Joseph and placed him in the pit; now he would place them in the prison. Spying, at any stage of history, has been a serious offence, and these brave men were surely trembling as they wondered what this powerful man would do to them.

The Proving in the Prison

The testing, or proving, would be difficult — a test of separation. But first they were all placed in prison for three days so that their words could be proved, "whether there be any truth in you" (v 16). They had claimed to be honest, or truthful, men back in verse 11. Joseph would need to be convinced.

After the three days Joseph changes the plan somewhat. He had said one could return to Canaan while nine remained incarcerated in Egypt. Now he decided to allow nine to return home and one would remain imprisoned. It would have been very difficult for one man by himself to take back enough grain for a family of around seventy people, so we see clear evidence of Joseph's kind heart here as well.

"I fear God", were certainly not words that were commonly uttered in Egypt. Joseph's brothers were possibly in such a state of mind that they did not sink in, but on the other hand it is quite possible that this passing mention made them start to think upon their present distress and the reasons behind it. The fear of the Lord is mentioned fourteen times in Proverbs and is shown to be "the beginning of knowledge" (1:7), "the beginning of wisdom" (9:10), as well as the motivation for men to "depart from evil" (16:6). Although these verses would not be written for many years, Joseph understood very well what it was to live in the fear of the Lord. And he surely desired that his own brothers would learn something of the fear of the Lord and how that controls a person's thoughts, words and actions.

Joseph is about to send them away in order that they might bring their "youngest brother" to him, thus verifying their account and preserving their life (v 20). Their willingness to do so is seen in the same verse, although before they leave Joseph is privy to yet another conversation.

The Frightening Recognition (vv 21-24)

Listen in as the brothers now talk amongst themselves while preparing to leave. It appears to be an honest and transparent conversation, and we get the idea that God is bringing them to some understanding of wrongs committed in the past, and their seriousness even now. They have had three full days to consider why they are found in this situation. First there is an acknowledgment of guilt: "We are verily guilty concerning our brother" (v 21). They had seen the anguish of Joseph's soul twenty years before but had simply sat down to eat a meal while Joseph was in the pit, crying out. They now accepted their lot in life, saying, "therefore is this distress come upon us" (v 21). This appears to be more of a fatalistic viewpoint than the kind of true repentance and acceptance of the Lord's will we find in the Scriptures.

Remember the biblical principles from both the Old and the New Testaments: "Be sure your sin will find you out" (Num 32:23), and "Be not deceived; God is not mocked: for whatsoever a man soweth, that shall he also reap" (Gal 6:7). Twenty years had passed since they hated Joseph so much that they stripped him of his robe, threw him in a pit and then sold him to the Midianites. God, in His patience and kindness, was beginning to work in their hearts as they accept that they are now bearing the consequences of their actions.

Reuben, however, then attempts to avert some of the blame, saying, "Spake not I unto you, saying, Do not sin against the child; and ye would not hear?" (v 22). He had saved Joseph's life, suggesting he be placed in the pit instead. He had had every intention of later coming back and rescuing Joseph, "to deliver him to his father again" (37:22). When the transaction was done with the Midianites, Reuben was absent, and when he returned to the pit and saw it empty "he rent his clothes" (37:29), completely broken. He said to his brothers: "The child is not" (37:30), very similar words to those we considered in this chapter as they recounted to Joseph something about the family: "And one is not" (v 13). All these years later Reuben does realize that Joseph's "blood is required", a principle established when Noah came out of the ark years before. Joseph would not have known this part of the story, namely, that Reuben had desired to save his life, and return him to his father Jacob, and that he had played no part in the sale of Joseph to the Midianites. Perhaps for this reason, although he is the firstborn, he returns home while Simeon, the second son, remains behind in prison.

What they did not know was how this conversation amongst themselves was affecting Joseph. Understanding everything they said and realizing that there were positive indicators of contrition and repentance, he had to leave the room to weep. This is not the first time Joseph wept, and it won't be the last. Weeping is not a sign of weakness, but it is an indication of a tender heart. Joseph was not a vindictive man, looking for an opportunity to exact vengeance. He was going to overcome their evil with his good, long before Paul penned these words: "Be not overcome of evil, but overcome evil with good" (Rom 12:21). Once he regained control over his emotions, he had some further communication with his brothers before taking Simeon to be a captive as surety for the others. This particular section cannot be seen as the true confession that would be necessary, however, since it was not made to Joseph. That will come later on.

The Full Provision (vv 25-28)

Joseph showed much kindness to these men, even though they did not recognize him as being compassionate. He not only commanded that their sacks be filled with grain, but also that their money be placed inside their sacks. Beyond that we observe that he also gave them extra provision for the way.

Joseph was wisely working in their lives with the intention to bring them to full repentance. Likewise God works in people's lives today to bring them to repentance: "Or despisest thou the riches of his goodness and forbearance and longsuffering; not knowing that the goodness of God leadeth thee to repentance?" (Rom 2:4). Sadly, oftentimes the goodness of God is not recognized for what it is, and people take their blessings for granted.

Our God truly is good all of the time, and not only to His children. Remember the words of the Lord Jesus, "... he maketh his sun to rise on the evil and on the good, and sendeth rain on the just and on the unjust" (Matt 5:45).

These men, when they stopped for the night, were startled and their hearts sank, when they saw the silver in the sack of one of the brothers. Joseph's mention of God back in verse 18 perhaps had begun a work in their souls, and they now asked the question: "What is this that God hath done unto us?" (v 28). This was a very large step in their experience, realizing that God was intervening in their lives, and it struck terror into them. Joseph, sold for silver so many years ago, is now using silver to cause them to ponder what is happening to them.

What is missing in this story is gratefulness. There is not a word mentioned about these men being thankful. Paul wrote, "In every thing give thanks: for this is the will of God in Christ Jesus concerning you" (1 Thess 5:18). Our giving of thanks surely ought to extend further than the dinner table, but at the very least it needs to start there. God deserves to be thanked for His kindness and care, but "In every thing" goes beyond the times of abundance, and includes the challenging periods of life — even then we can be thankful to God for His love, His purposes, and the fact that He is in control of all things. These men had food and funds, but only were afraid, not recognizing God's goodness shown to them through Joseph.

The other noteworthy absence, but in a positive light, is the lack of vengeance. This would have been the ideal time for Joseph to take revenge on his brothers for their treatment of him in Dothan. We understand that Joseph lives prior to any of the Scriptures being written, but the truth of Leviticus 19:18 comes to mind: "Thou shalt not avenge, nor bear any grudge against the children of thy people, but thou shalt love thy neighbour as thyself: I am the LORD." There is no mention here of what he had already understood about being sent by God, but he was obviously well aware of God's purposes in his life. True meekness is seen in Joseph, not weakness, but an understanding that God is in control of every aspect of our lives. The mistreatment we receive at the hand of others may well be what God is allowing in our lives to form us and mould us into the image of His Son. I add a needed caveat to this: we are certainly not condoning illegal or corrupting activity, nor suggesting in any way that such should not be reported to the proper authorities. Meekness accepts God's will but shows strength in fulfilling it. Moses is the great Old Testament example - meek but never weak.

The Forthright Declaration (vv 29-34)

They finally come home again, probably having been gone for more than three weeks. We can almost imagine the scene as they all try to tell their father "all that befell unto them" (v 29). Some of the sons had disappointed and angered Jacob and so there may have been something of a strained atmosphere in the home. However, there was still a level of confidence between them all in which they could openly converse.

They recount how the "lord of the land" had spoken to them roughly and how he had accused them of being spies. They relate to Jacob what their defense had been and that they had told Joseph that there were actually twelve brothers in the family, although "one is not, and the youngest is this day with our father in the land of Canaan" (v 32). Finally, they tell dear Jacob that if they are going to buy more grain they will have to return to Egypt with Benjamin, his beloved son.

The Fearful Reactions (vv 35-38)

Joseph's compassionate act of kindness did not produce the desired effect in his brethren or his father. As they were emptying their sacks, each one found their "bundle of money" in his sack (v 35). This seemed like a very odd business transaction to this group of men! But beyond that we are told "they were afraid".

What causes fear to arise in the heart? Many times this can be due to a lack of knowledge. We are not dealing here with reverential fear, but rather of a fear that almost paralyzes a person. These men did not know who was "the lord of the land" and therefore they suspected the worst upon finding the money. They were well aware that they had to make a return trip, not only for more grain, but also to rescue Reuben. What would happen to them? Would they be accused of theft?

Jacob is not only fearful, but also in despair. He has lost Joseph, and obviously still missed him: "Joseph is not" (v 36). Now Simeon had been taken from him, and they were talking about taking Benjamin to Egypt on the next journey for grain. "All these things are against me", was his lament. Jacob had experienced much sadness in his life, much of it due to no particular fault of his own. He is now nearing 130 years of age, and troubles continue to come. It is almost too much for the old man to bear.

As Reuben illogically offers his two sons to his father to be slain if he doesn't return with Benjamin, we can almost feel the emotion in Jacob's voice as he answers: "My son shall not go down with you; for his brother is dead, and he is left alone: if mischief befall him by the way in the which ye go, then shall ye bring down my gray hairs to the grave" (v 38). Sadly, we don't see any trust in God in his words; indeed there is no mention of God at all in this whole discussion. The brothers had brought God into the conversation only when they opened the first sack along the way, but they still cannot see that God is working all this out for their good, and, more importantly, to fulfill His purposes in His people. The other sad thing to notice here is the favouritism still being shown by Jacob, declaring, "Benjamin is left alone", that is, he is the only one left. What about the other ten? What about Simeon left behind imprisoned in Egypt?

Some Final Reflections

Before we move on to the brothers' second visit to Egypt, let's think about some important lessons we learn from this section.

Although we will come back to the issue of confession and forgiveness, for now we will just note that one-sided forgiveness cannot repair or restore a relationship as long as true repentance and a full confession are lacking on the part of the offender. Joseph had forgiven his brothers years before, but there was not yet any reconciliation. He was wisely waiting to see the fruits of repentance in his brothers' lives.

Secondly, we note that God allowed the famine in the land of Canaan to bring these strong, proud men to their knees. Literally to their knees, in this case! This is not the only time we read of something like this. The Lord Jesus told the story of the young man in a far-off land who was brought to his knees in a time of famine (Luke 15). In Job's case, God allowed many disastrous events to happen in order to bring him to a fuller and deeper knowledge of Himself. When David had sinned, he penned Psalm 32, starting with "Blessed is he whose transgression is forgiven ...", but then he remembers the process that brought him to repentance, and writes: "When I kept silence, my bones waxed old through my roaring all the day long" (Ps 32:1, 3). We could bring many other examples to bear upon this truth — God is in control of circumstances, and never will allow a believer to pass through more than is necessary in order to teach us what we need to learn, but as a faithful Father He does want us to learn.

Next we noticed that God is able to bring certain events to the forefront of our minds and memories in order to start this process of repentance. Jacob mentioned Egypt to his sons at the beginning of the chapter, and it is possible that even the idea of going down to Egypt would have made them at least somewhat apprehensive. Once they experienced some hardship in the prison, their memories began working well, recalling their cruel treatment of Joseph twenty years before.

God was still moving in this family's life, but He was not in a hurry then, nor is He now. He rather was doing things according to His will, in His perfect timing and for His ultimate glory. We have the very same God today on the very same throne, in control of our lives, and we can patiently wait on Him.

CHAPTER 9

The Confession and Appeal

Genesis 43-44

Our section begins by reminding us of the tremendous trial that many were facing, "And the famine was sore in the land", but we are especially interested to see how God has been allowing difficult circumstances in the lives of His chosen people to bring about His purposes. We remarked in the last chapter that what God had told Abraham decades before was beginning to come to fruition. Beyond that, however, we want to notice how God is working on the character of this family: Even in Jacob we will see a transformation, for in Chapter 43 he is once again called Israel; his sons who had committed evil acts in the past we will soon see as broken men, having been brought to true and full repentance.

The Discussion and Departure (43:1-14)

Just as the previous chapter commenced with Jacob taking the lead in sending his sons to Egypt for food, we see the same again. Perhaps the sons were reluctant to broach the subject, even while facing a dwindling supply of food for their family. They were well aware of their father's determination not to send his youngest son back with them to Egypt. In Jacob's first words, "Go again, buy us a little food", is it not possible to see that he is demonstrating a defeatist attitude? "A little food." More than two years of famine, with the threat of five more years, would surely affect anyone's attitude. Along with that was the fact that one son was languishing in a prison far from home. And hanging over his head was the recollection from a few months earlier of the need to take Benjamin on the next trip to purchase grain. All these things were against him!

Judah is now taking the lead in the family's affairs in a very responsible and rational fashion. A transformation has commenced in his life, and although he was not the first born son, but rather the fourth, here he is dealing with his aged father, and later he will be the spokesman when they have to speak with Joseph. Judah is quite firm, yet respectful, with his father as he says, "But if thou will not send him, we will not go down" (43:5). Jacob is still obviously upset about the fact that his sons had told Joseph the truth about the family tree, saying they had dealt ill (or evilly) with him for having told the truth. Sadly, Jacob had shown in his past that being deceitful was a normal way of life for him, and he rather expected the same from his sons, but thankfully we see complete honesty now in them.

Judah becomes a bit more forceful as we continue reading the story, warning his father that if they do not go down with the lad Benjamin they will all surely die. He then offers himself as a surety and is willing to accept the "blame for ever" (43:9) if he himself does not return Benjamin to his father. This is a different Judah from the person of Chapter 37 when he had the idea of selling Joseph and indeed initiated the sale. Now he is willing to do all he can to protect his youngest brother. His heart has been changed; God has been working in him.

As they prepare to depart, Jacob prepares a gift for Joseph, only he does not realize it is for his own son. More importantly, in these two verses (vv 11-12) we see that neither he nor his sons appreciate or understand the gracious gift that this man in Egypt had given them, not only with provision for the return trip but also by placing the silver back in their sacks. You will recall the story of the time when Jacob was making his way back to Canaan and discovered that Esau, his brother, was coming to meet him with four hundred men: "And he lodged there that same night; and took of that which came to his hand a present for Esau his brother" (32:13). He assumed a present would take care of any problems between the two, and now again, many years later, he is thinking the same way. Fruits, balm, honey, spices, myrrh, nuts and almonds were all prepared for the return trip, as well as "double money" — first to repay what had been returned in their sacks, and then to buy more grain. In truth, the only requirement was to take Benjamin. So Jacob adds what we find in verse 13: "Take also your brother, and arise, go again unto the man".

Is it not true that today many people think that money, or some other gift, is the answer to life's problems? Drop a little here, help a little there, and all will be well. This may have some effect in our relationships with other mortal beings, but many consider that their giving will gain some merit with God. They have a difficult time accepting grace for what it is — God's undeserved favour towards us, meeting our every need. Thank God that His grace does not end when we receive salvation, but rather follows us throughout our Christian experience.

If we see both some fear and devious behaviour in Jacob's past, we now turn our sights to Israel's faith. When Jacob was about to meet Esau, "there wrestled a man with him until the breaking of the day" (32:24). He was then told: "Thy name shall be called no more Jacob, but Israel" (32:28). This name change was significant — so much so that God reminded him of this change in Genesis 35:10. After Joseph's disappearance we find no reference to Jacob being called Israel again until this chapter — his character had not been in keeping with the meaning of his new name, but now we see a man who will publicly express his trust in God, the same God with whom he had struggled years before. They are words of faith, not of fear: "And God Almighty give you mercy before the man, that he may send away your other brother, and Benjamin" (43:14). There was also an acceptance of what God would allow in His perfect will — it is not a fatalistic statement, but a recognition that God Himself is indeed in control of all these things: "If I be bereaved of my children, I am bereaved" (43:14). He had been bereaved of Joseph twenty years before; he well knew the sad and bitter experience of the loss of a loved one, but he was willing to leave all this now in the hands of the Almighty.

This mixture of fear and faith is also seen in the New Testament. When the Lord Jesus was asleep in the ship the disciples came to Him and awoke Him, saying "Lord, save us: we perish" (Matt 8:25). His response? "Why are ye so fearful, O ye of little faith?" (Matt 8:26). There may be times in our life when we act similarly, with a mixture of fear and faith; wanting to believe, to trust, but not quite able to take the step. May we be like Israel, who understood that he had to leave everything in the capable hands of God.

Wary of the Welcome (43:15-28)

It is quite evident that when Joseph sees his brothers return from Canaan he can hardly contain his excitement, quickly ordering the ruler of his house not only to invite them all to his home, but also to "slay, and make ready; for these men shall dine with me at noon" (43:16). Remember that Joseph was speaking in a language that his brothers could not understand. They were soon ushered into Joseph's own house. This treatment was not at all what they were expecting.

Then we read of their reaction: "the men were afraid" (v 18). These were brave and brawny men, but now they began to wonder what was going to happen to them, and they were only able to imagine the worst. They did not know Joseph, and they certainly did not know that his heart was full of compassion, but he still needed to put them through more testing.

They wrongly assumed that the reason for their being invited to Joseph's house was due to the money that had been found in their sacks. They figured that he was just waiting for the opportune moment to seize them and their donkeys, and make them all bondmen, or slaves. Once again, they are unable to recognize kindness and grace — is this possibly due to the fact that they were not brought up in an atmosphere of grace, but rather in one of antagonism and aggression?

This time of waiting obviously helped these men contemplate recent happenings. How are they going to get out of this problem? They tried to explain to the ruler of Joseph's house what had happened to their money on the way home: "And it came to pass, when we came to the inn, that we opened our sacks, and, behold, every man's money was in the mouth of his sack, our money in full weight: and we have brought it again in our hand" (43:21). But he insisted that he had their money.

Joseph's steward does make a very interesting comment at this point: "your God, and the God of your father, hath given you treasure in your sacks" (43:23). This is intriguing for two reasons: first of all, we can see that Joseph had obviously shared something with him about the one and only true God whom he served. We never read of anything that would be a point of blame on Joseph's character, and although his reputation, or testimony, would speak loudly to the steward, Joseph went beyond that to speak about his God and the "God of his father". Secondly, the steward not only started with the word "Peace", but also gave them a reason to calm their worried spirits: "the God of your father hath given you treasure in your sacks: I had your money." Without wanting to read too much into the passage, there is no reason to think that he was lying to them, and that gives us all the more reason to see that God had indeed blessed them, and had obviously used Joseph to be the channel of this blessing.

At this point the steward kindly brings Simeon out of the prison to be reunited with his brothers after what was probably a few months of being separated from his family (43:23). Simeon had been experiencing the loneliness that he had at least been partially responsible for in Joseph's life. The kindness now continues, with the steward not only giving them water to drink, but also washing their feet! Again we are caused to think of the kindness of God which leads to repentance, and this is what Joseph was wanting to see in his brothers' hearts. Not only did the steward care for the men, but he also provided feed for their donkeys. One can almost picture these men staring at each other, mouths agape as they considered this wonderful welcome to the ruler's house.

Still wary of what was happening, they "made ready the present" they had brought for Joseph, hoping perhaps to curry some favour, or at least to avoid any further problems with this man who had spoken harshly to them. "A gift in secret pacifieth anger" (Prov 21:14), and they were certainly hoping for some success on this visit.

It is rather striking to notice Joseph's arrival and where he focuses his attention. "And ... they brought him the present ... and bowed themselves to him to the earth" (43:26). There is no mention of his taking the gift from their hands, nor do the Scriptures indicate that he expressed gratitude for it. We are not suggesting he wasn't a grateful man, but when we consider his likeness to the Lord Jesus we are made to ponder the marvellous truth that we could offer our Saviour nothing to cause Him to look upon us more favourably. When one comes to Him for salvation, it is with a contrite heart and empty hands.

> *Nothing in my hand I bring,*
> *Simply to Thy cross I cling;*
> *Naked, come to Thee for dress;*
> *Helpless, look to Thee for grace;*
> *Foul, I to the fountain fly;*
> *Wash me Saviour, or I die.*
>   (Augustus Toplady)

Perhaps there was some concern in their hearts, but Joseph's questions ought to have dispelled many of their fears. He first asked about their own well-being, and then his next words surely would have comforted and encouraged them: "Is your father well, the old man of whom ye spake? Is he still alive?" (43:27). Why such interest in their father? But their response would have reciprocated the comfort, as the brothers responded that not only was he still alive, but he was in good health. Surely Joseph's heart would have taken at least a little leap as he realized there was still great hope that he again would see his father. As they answered Joseph, once again they prostrated themselves before him — not ten this time, as on the last visit, but rather eleven, just as he had dreamt. Many years before, the incredulous response to Joseph's dream about his family bowing down to him was, "Shalt thou indeed reign over us? or shalt thou indeed have dominion over us?" (37:8). Well, yes, here he was seeing the first dream fulfilled time and again, but the same God who had given him that assurance also gave him another dream that dealt with "the sun and the moon" (37:9) making obeisance to him. So seeing the first dream fulfilled again would instill new hope and confidence in Joseph that the other dream would also have its fulfillment — he would see his father once more.

Today God teaches us many truths in His Word - not new revelations, but rather truths that He brings us to understand; promises that have to do with His children in this dispensation. Do we take Him at His word, and make our decisions based on His promises to us? Do we live Joseph-like, patiently waiting for God to fulfill His promises to us? Although Joseph was certainly anxious to see his father, he was also willing to wait God's time. The psalmist wrote wise words about waiting: "Wait on the LORD: be of good courage, and he shall strengthen thine heart: wait, I say, on the LORD" (Ps 27:14). Waiting is difficult for most of us as we prefer to be doing something, but learning to wait on the Lord is needed since it shows us afresh our dependence upon Him.

The Wondering and Weeping (43:29-34)

The emotion is palpable in the three verses that commence this section. Joseph had recognized his other brothers on their first visit without any difficulty. Perhaps Benjamin had changed more than the rest, since he was only a lad of eleven when Joseph was sold as a slave, and now he is in his early thirties. Nonetheless, although he asked, "Is this your younger brother, of whom ye spake unto me?" (43:29), he fully knew it was Benjamin, and gave him a blessing: "God be gracious unto thee, my son" (43:29). Here is this "foreign" leader speaking to them about God again! When he sent them away the first time he told them, "I fear God" (42:18). His steward had reminded them about God's goodness to them, and now this man was blessing Benjamin, invoking God's name. Surely his brothers' minds were beginning to whirl as they wondered about the God of their father Jacob. Why was His name coming up so often?

Joseph had been able to maintain control over his emotions on their first visit, but something about seeing his full-blood brother, the only other child of his mother, brought all the memories he had tried to forget flooding back. The tears began to flow and he made a hasty exit to his chamber, or private quarters (43:30). Benjamin had played no part in Joseph being sold into Egypt. He bore no guilt, and thus the relationship was different with him; there was no need to see repentance in him. The writer tells us that Joseph's heart "did yearn upon his brother"; he was completely overcome by the affection he felt for his younger brother. Many of God's people know what it is to be separated for long periods from their loved ones, and have felt the emotions arise in their hearts, and the tears come to their eyes, when they lay sight on them after an absence.

Joseph was not yet ready to reveal the truth to them about himself. Although in the previous chapter there had been a testing of their character, more proving was about to happen on two distinct levels.

We find first of all a test of jealousy. These men had been very jealous of Joseph back when he was living amongst them, beloved of his father, and responsible to bring reports back to Jacob about his brothers' conduct. Not only the role he played in the household but also the special raiment his father had made for him were, to them, good cause to strip Joseph, cast him into a pit and then sell him. Joseph was not unaware, even at the young age of seventeen, of the reasons for his having landed in Egypt.

Joseph has all his brothers sit at a separate table, maintaining the distance required by Egyptian custom which held that as a nation they were superior to those living around them, and Joseph, as much as he would have loved to commune more intimately with his brothers, had to yet keep himself separate. But what would have caused them to wonder and marvel was the order in which they were seated. How was it possible that they could be seated in their birth order? They were astonished! Perhaps this incident helped them to accept the steward's claim that his lord could use a cup to divine matters (44:5-6, 15).

We don't know how much mathematics these brothers studied, but the reality is that there are 39,916,800 ways in which eleven men can be seated in different order each time. Even if they didn't know that number, they were well aware that there was something peculiar going on here.

Now they each receive their "mess" or serving. Their diet is unlikely to have varied much in the last couple of years, but there would be very little skimping in Joseph's house. Joseph astutely sends five times more food to Benjamin than any other (43:34). For these men in the past, this would have caused them to at least show, if not audibly express, some level of disgust and jealousy. Surely Joseph was carefully watching their facial expressions and body language to see their reaction. However, what we read shows us that God indeed was working on transforming their character: "And they drank, and were merry with him" (43:34). We know nothing about this part of their conversation, but the word "merry" helps us see that all is going well. Or is it? The next section will put them back into another test, having just passed this one. How will they fare?

We remember another table. One where our Lord Jesus was seated with His disciples. Along came Mary with a pound of ointment of spikenard, very costly, and anointed the Saviour's feet. It was another Judah, Judas Iscariot, who said: "Why was not this ointment sold for three hundred pence, and given to the poor?" (John 12:1-5). His heart was revealed at the table by his words, but there was no evil motive revealed as a lesser Joseph sat with his brothers and they "were merry with him". Joseph detected no jealousy or envy, which is "the rottenness of the bones" (Prov 14:30).

God alone knows everything about the trials in our lives. He knows their purpose and their end. He knows how much we can bear, as He Himself is the source of the grace we need during the trial. These men may have thought that all was about to end well, but things were going to get a lot worse before they got better.

The Silver in the Sacks (44:1-13)

As we move down through this chapter there is much excitement, and a sense of mystery as we read the order: "Fill the men's sacks with food ... and put every man's money in his sack's mouth. And put my cup, the silver cup, in the sack's mouth of the youngest" (44:1-2).

Thus begins the test of loyalty. How important was Benjamin to them? Was he dispensable, as they once considered Joseph himself to be? Included here was the testing of their honesty — Judah in particular had promised his father that he would return with Benjamin. So would he now fulfill his word, thus proving his honesty? He certainly had failed in this regard in other of life's experiences as we could read in Genesis 38 in regard to his daughter-in-law Tamar.

They were barely out of the city when Joseph sent his steward after his brothers' caravan with specific instructions and a challenging question: "Wherefore have ye rewarded evil for good?" (44:4). This is a theme we see repeated in other Scriptures - for example, "They rewarded me evil for good to the spoiling of my soul" (Ps 35:12). How often that can happen in the lives of believers! Paul exhorted the Romans in this way: "Be not overcome of evil, but overcome evil with good" (Rom 12:21). In this case, however, it was more of a challenge to Joseph's brethren as they were put to the test.

The next question about his silver cup has caused some deliberation: "Is not this it in which my lord drinketh, and whereby he indeed divineth?" (44:5). The accusation was clear: "... ye have done evil in so doing" (44:5) As we mentioned earlier, Joseph had seated his brothers in their birth order, so it is quite likely they would consider that act to be an indication of his ability to divine, in a way that involved the spirits. In no way do we see any possibility that Joseph actually did so, but rather was using these present circumstances to instill some fear in his brothers.

They were flabbergasted, and could hardly begin to make sense of the accusations against them. Darby translates their defense this way: "Far be it from thy servants to do such a thing!" (44:7). Certain they are not guilty, they remind the steward that they had returned from Canaan not only with money to purchase more grain, but the money they had found in their sacks upon their return. Their conclusion is then logical: "... how then should we steal out of thy lord's house silver or gold?" (44:8). They were suggesting that there was no financial lack amongst them, and thus no need to steal any of his lord's belongings.

Not only this, but they protest further, saying that if the cup was actually found in one of their sacks, that brother should die and the rest would become Joseph's slaves (44:9). There is a danger in speaking precipitously, as James reminds us: "Wherefore, my beloved brethren, let every man be swift to hear, slow to speak, slow to wrath" (James 1:19). The good news here is that Joseph was not going to keep any of them as a slave, and certainly had no thought of putting any one of them to death. But in their desperation they responded rather rashly. Their tongues had brought them into difficulties in the past as they considered Joseph's fate years before. Let us learn the lesson well — "swift to hear, slow to speak"!

Even the steward understood they had gone too far with their offer, and replied: "... he with whom it is found shall be my servant; and ye shall be blameless" (44:10). And with this they all quickly dropped their sacks to the ground, opening them from the oldest and finishing with the youngest. You can almost hear the sigh of relief each time another sack is opened and all is well. But at the same time they were probably holding their breath as the steward continued his search. Then very last sack was opened, "and the cup was found in Benjamin's sack" (44:12).

As we come to the end of this section, we read of the tremendous sadness that filled their hearts as they tore their clothes as a sign of deep contrition. Were they perhaps confused? Did the thought cross any of their minds about what they could do to get out of this mess? Did they wonder if Benjamin could possibly be guilty of this crime? With heavy hearts, they "returned to the city" (44:13), wondering what would happen to them now. Just when they thought that all was well, everything around them came tumbling down. Do believers today sometimes feel that way too? Recalling again James' words of wisdom as he writes about believers in times of trial, we read the following counsel: "Knowing this, that the trying of your faith worketh patience. But let patience have her perfect work, that ye may be perfect and entire, wanting nothing" (James 1:3-4). Patience in this context has to do with endurance and steadfastness, and this is one of the purposes that God has in allowing trials. We may wonder how we will get through, and James helps us there as well: "If any of you lack wisdom, let him ask of God, that giveth to all men liberally, and upbraideth not; and it shall be given him" (James 1:5). Wisdom from above will help us through the trial; God's unending grace will "be sufficient" for us. This is His promise to His children.

The Admission and Appeal (44:14-34)

The following conversation warms our hearts in a strange way as we consider the work of God in transforming Judah's heart. But before anyone opened their mouth, all the brothers once again "fell before him on the ground" (44:14). This simple, yet humble, act only shows us once more how God truly does accomplish what He promises, and this truth should always encourage us as we consider His faithfulness to us in our circumstances.

The Honesty Expressed

Joseph's words are few, and Judah's are many as he pours out his heart in honesty before Joseph, and in front of his brothers. Joseph's question is simple: "What deed is this that ye have done?" (44:15). We quickly notice that there are no words of defense, but there is an admission of responsibility, even though Judah was unaware of how the silver cup had ended up in Benjamin's sack. Generally speaking we are very quick to defend ourselves, especially if we feel the accusation is not actually true. Such was not going to be the tactic that Judah would use, but rather he would appeal to Joseph's goodness and grace.

Notice first of all the admission of guilt. "What shall we say unto my lord? what shall we speak? or how shall we clear ourselves? God hath found out the iniquity of thy servants: behold, we are my lord's servants, both we, and he also with whom the cup is found" (44:16). Judah was completely aware that there were no words that he could offer to clear him and his brothers of the obvious guilt. But what is encouraging to note here is Judah's mention of God; back in Genesis 42:28 we read that the brothers were saying one to another: "What is this that God hath done unto us?" Here it is Judah's first personal mention of God, and he realizes that God Himself is the one who has uncovered their iniquity.

Many of us learned Numbers 32:23 in our childhood days: "Behold, ye have sinned against the LORD: and be sure your sin will find you out". Sin can be covered from many for a very long time. Judah and his brothers had done just that with regard to Joseph's disappearance, deceiving their own father for more than twenty years, and they had hidden it well! But God, in His time, was bringing to bear upon their conscience their guilt, and now He had exposed their sin. It is quite probable that Judah was thinking beyond the silver cup, as we recall the conversation the brothers had among themselves in the presence of Joseph on the previous visit: "We are verily guilty concerning our brother, in that we saw the anguish of his soul, when he besought us, and we would not hear; therefore is this distress come upon us" (42:21). Their world of deceit was crumbling all around them. In dealing with sinful circumstances many, even at this stage, will attempt to prop things up, to make it all appear as best as can be presented, but the biblical example and exhortation is to confess the wrong done, freely and openly, without making excuses in any way.

There is confession to God, and this step is essential: "If we confess our sins, he is faithful and just to forgive us our sins, and to cleanse us from all unrighteousness" (1 John 1:9). But there is also confession to the offended party that cannot be skipped over if there is to be full reconciliation and restoration. More of this, in this case, will come in the next chapter of Genesis, but for now just notice what James writes: "Confess your faults one to another" (James 5:16), and what the Lord Jesus taught: "Therefore if thou bring thy gift to the altar, and there rememberest that thy brother hath ought against thee; Leave there thy gift before the altar, and go thy way; first be reconciled to thy brother, and then come and offer thy gift" (Matt 5:23-24). So there is a Godward confession and a manward confession, and both are necessary in the case of an offence against a brother or sister.

After the admission of guilt, we begin to listen to Judah's plea, or at least the first part of it: his offer shows that he has passed the test of loyalty, as he insists upon them all becoming Joseph's servants, including he "with whom the cup is found" (44:16). This would have been the ideal opportunity to hang Benjamin out to dry. "Let Benjamin handle the consequences — he's the guilty one; the rest of us are innocent, so we can just carry on with life." Perhaps in previous years Judah may have thought in that manner, but not anymore. He is at the very least retracting what had been the earlier offer, that the one who had the cup in his possession should die, and the rest become servants (44:9). This concern for his youngest brother, the object of his father's love, shows the work of God in Judah's heart. But the fact that none of the other brothers speak out at this point in protest is proof that not only Judah has been changed, but all the rest as well. They could have said, "No, let us go; keep Benjamin", but their silence speaks volumes about them.

Joseph is going to probe and push a bit deeper, a bit further. "Far be it from me to do so!" (44:17, JND). He insists that only the guilty party be retained as a servant and that the rest can go in peace to their father. One more opportunity to walk away from Benjamin has been presented to them. What will they do? There is no conversation between the brothers to discuss this offer, no hesitation at all on the part of Judah as he again assumes the leadership amongst them, draws closer to Joseph, and pleads as a servant to a lord.

The Humility Shown

Twice in verse 16 he refers to Joseph as "my lord", and then seven more times he does so as he begins to respond to Joseph's offer to leave Benjamin behind. Beyond that, we read twice in verse 16 the word "servants" and this word he will employ thirteen more times before he finishes his plea. What humility! What recognition of his own weakness to resolve this situation! What dependence upon this man, his brother, whom he was calling "my lord"! Is not this an appropriate way for us to draw near to our Saviour, recognizing His Lordship over us, and our humble place as His servants? When we move into the next chapter we will see that all of this greatly moved Joseph's heart. He became fully convinced that his brothers were indeed repentant, and that there had been a true change in their heart.

This humility is seen as Judah recognized Joseph's power and position, saying, "for thou art even as Pharaoh" (44:18). He feared this man's anger, perhaps recalling the harsh manner in which he had spoken to them on their first visit, as well as the authority he had. Joseph had the power and authority to take Simeon from them and leave him in prison during these months, so, very rightly, Judah approaches Joseph in a humble way. He begins to explain the whole story, returning to when they had first met Joseph and how he had questioned them about their family.

Their History Recounted

This time, as he recounts the story in what is the longest recorded monologue in Genesis, he is even more plain. He expresses the fact that Benjamin is the child of his father's old age, "a little one". Do we get a glimpse of tenderness here? Then he tells Joseph about the fact that "his brother is dead", an assumption that was very obviously untrue, at least to Joseph! But what Judah is saying is that these two, Benjamin and Joseph, were full-brothers, as he explains: "he alone is left of his mother, and his father loveth him" (44:20). This is said without any signs of jealousy or envy; he is simply stating the facts.

He rehearses more in Joseph's ears about how it was that, due to his insistence, Benjamin had travelled to Egypt with his older brothers, otherwise they would not have seen Joseph's face again. When Jacob told his sons to return to Egypt to "buy us a little food", they told him it would be impossible to do so if Benjamin did not go with them. Joseph is then going to learn something about his father that he could not otherwise have known: "And thy servant my father said unto us, Ye know that my wife bare me two sons: And the one went out from me, and I said, Surely he is torn in pieces; and I saw him not since" (44:28). For all these twenty-two years or so, Jacob had thought that Joseph had been torn in pieces, having seen his robe shredded. What sadness must have again pierced Joseph's heart as he considered his old father suffering in this way, mourning the loss of the son of his affection. Jacob had then warned his sons, "And if ye take this also from me, and mischief [or better, evil] befall him, ye shall bring down my gray hairs with sorrow to the grave" (44:29). Joseph's emotions are surely becoming more difficult to control, but Judah has more to say yet.

If they were to return to Canaan without Benjamin, Judah is convinced that their father will die, and that the brothers would be responsible for bringing the gray hairs of Jacob "with sorrow to the grave" (44:31). Judah again has expressed the place that Benjamin has in his father's heart, "his life is bound up in the lad's life" (44:30), but with no sense of anger, malice or envy.

The Heartfelt Appeal

Judah is about to wrap up his appeal in a personal way. He had become surety for Benjamin's life: "If I bring him not unto thee, then I shall bear the blame to my father forever" (44:32). Although we are certain Joseph has been convinced of a real and deep change in Judah's thinking, these statements would have hammered the truth home. "Now therefore, I pray thee, let thy servant abide instead of the lad a bondman to my lord, and let the lad go up with his brethren. For how shall I go up to my father, and the lad be not with me? lest peradventure I see the evil that shall come on my father" (44:33-34). Judah is pleading with Joseph to keep him as a slave and allow Benjamin to return to Jacob with the other ten brothers. He emphasizes once more that he could not bear to go back home and see his father were Benjamin not with him, certain it would be the end of Jacob's sojourn on earth.

A few concluding remarks will help us keep in mind some important principles.

Judah is manifestly repentant and is speaking on behalf of his brothers who are of like mind. Once we get into Genesis 45 we will tie repentance, reconciliation and restoration together, but for now we just remember that repentance is far more than regret. Regret and remorse stop far short of repentance and can be seen in the light of "being caught", but true repentance is a work of God.

Judah is being open, humble, honest and transparent, hiding nothing, as he realizes that nothing is hidden from God. Thus we apprehend that he is making no attempt to manipulate Joseph into coming to any particular decision. Attempts at manipulation express a lack of trust in God, and takes things into ones' own hands, endeavouring to bring about some desired end.

Judah has, in this appeal to Joseph, shown his maturity as well as his ability to be a true leader. He had no time to prepare a message, but was simply expressing what was truly on his heart, "... for of the abundance of the heart his mouth speaketh" (Luke 6:45).

Finally, let us remember that all testing and every trial is from God and is always with our good in mind. Letting God bring about His intended purpose may be difficult in the trial, but looking for escape routes and short cuts will not help the believer in the long run. "Behold, we count them happy which endure. Ye have heard of the patience of Job, and have seen the end of the Lord; that the Lord is very pitiful, and of tender mercy" (James 5:11).

CHAPTER 10

Confounded then Assured

Genesis 45

We recall these words found in the previous chapter: "Then Judah came near unto him, and said, Oh my lord, let thy servant, I pray thee, speak a word in my lord's ears" (v 18). Judah then begins to plead with Joseph and mentions the word "father" fourteen times, and actually finished his long plea with the word "father". Is it any wonder then that we read at the beginning of this chapter: "Then Joseph could not refrain himself"? Hearing so many mentions of his father had moved his heart. Judah pleaded — Joseph now reacts.

From the beginning until the end this is a very emotional chapter with tears being shed, kisses being shared, deep joy being expressed, and finally with Jacob's heart fainting and then reviving. For those of us who know it so well it is once again a tremendous challenge to step back and take a fresh look at this story of forgiveness and reconciliation.

Where, humanly speaking, we would expect to read about a grudge, we see grace; where fury would be a normal response, we find forgiveness; where there was opportunity for revenge, we find reconciliation; and, where bitterness could have appeared, we find blessings abounding. Let us re-learn the lovely lessons we find in this chapter and live them out from day to day, thus becoming more like our Lord Jesus.

These eleven men had not seen Joseph for twenty-two years, and now they were about to receive the surprise of their life, momentarily causing fear to arise in their hearts.

The Revelation (vv 1-8)

The Cry

Joseph was not concerned about hiding his emotions at this point! He "could not refrain himself", but at the same time was not going to carry on this conversation in front of all his household staff, and he thus caused them all to leave.

Here at the very beginning of the chapter we find an important practical principle: there is no need to deal publicly with private issues. Remember the words of the Lord Jesus: "Moreover if thy brother shall trespass against thee, go and tell him his fault between thee and him alone" (Matt 18:15). This is the right place to begin the process of reconciliation, although the Lord Jesus does speak of the need for others to be involved when there is a refusal on the part of the offending party to recognize their fault. Joseph, however, was not going to say anything in front of his servants that would harm the reputation of his own brothers.

Consider also the fact that God made us emotional, as well as rational, beings. Although Joseph was not able to "refrain himself", it is very obvious that he was in control of his thoughts and words as he revealed himself to his brothers. A weeping Joseph reminds us of a weeping Jesus, "Who in the days of his flesh, when he had offered up prayers and supplications with strong crying and tears unto him that was able to save him from death, and was heard in that he feared" (Heb 5:7). The occasion of His weeping in the garden was not the only time He wept, for we recall Him doing so over the city of Jerusalem as He considered the manner in which His own people were soon to reject Him (Matt 23:37). But He also wept as He drew near to Lazarus' tomb, and observed the ravages of sin in the lives of those whom He loved (John 11:35). We truly do have a Great High Priest who can "be touched with the feeling of our infirmities" (Heb 4:15).

His Character

Not only do we learn something about the character of Joseph in all of his tenderness, we also read a very simple statement: "I am Joseph" (v 3), and then again, "I am Joseph your brother" (v 4). They were "troubled", or terrified, when they heard his words, and could not answer him. Who was this very powerful and important man weeping in their presence? How did he know their brother's name? If it really was Joseph, what would become of them? Had this all been some sort of setup? Would this man now destroy them? As the conversation continued, they would learn more about this man's character, and, although not perfect, it certainly is imitable.

His Concern

Joseph also expressed his renewed concern for his father, perhaps brought to the fore in his mind due to Judah's constant repetition of "father" in the previous chapter. How this favoured son had missed his father! We can almost hear the pathos in his voice: "Doth my father yet live?" (v 3). Was it possible that his aged father was still alive? The last time he had seen him, Jacob was already an aged man well over one hundred years old. Could it be that Joseph would soon have the great joy of seeing him again after twenty-two long years?

His Compassion

Hear the compassion in Joseph's voice as he says to his brothers, "Come near to me, I pray you", and, although perhaps still concerned about their future, "they came near" (v 4). He noticed the apprehension and anxiety in his brothers and was now going to reassure them. Do these words not remind us of our Saviour saying, "Come unto me, all ye that labour and are heavy laden, and I will give you rest" (Matt 11:28)? In both cases, God was providing for the need of many by means of one man — Joseph in Genesis, and the Lord Jesus in the Gospel. We, as Gentiles, "sometimes were far off", but now "are made nigh by the blood of Christ" (Eph 2:13). What a position! What a privilege! What compassion and care shown to us!

The Charge

But before he gives them words of comfort, he does bring up the charge against them: "whom ye sold into Egypt" (v 4). We will come to the issue of reconciliation shortly, but let's remember that there is no reconciliation without confession. Sweeping true offenses under the rug is not what the Lord Jesus taught. These men, however, had already acknowledged to one another their sin before travelling back to their home (42:21), but as Joseph is going to express his full forgiveness, he does speak openly to them of their selling him into Egypt. However, he puts the charge against them, their culpability, into the context of God's preserving care over them rather than focusing on their evil behaviour when they traded him for silver.

His Cognizance

In the next five verses (vv 5-9) Joseph expresses his complete consciousness of God, using His name four times. "God did send me ... God sent me ... it was not you that sent me hither, but God ... God hath made me lord" (vv 5, 7, 8, 9). Joseph is able to look not only at the current picture, but also at the big picture, and take the long view of life. Too often we get completely wrapped up in our very present pressures, and don't remember that God is working in our lives to make us into what He wants us to be, and that often happens by means of difficult circumstances being brought into our experience. Joseph, long before the Bible was written, was cognizant of God's plans and His power to bring them about. Our responsibility is even greater, having God's Word in our homes, our hands, and our hearts — there is no excuse for ignorance.

We have discussed the truth of providence already, but it reappears again for us to consider. The fact that God is working behind the scenes in His providence does not remove the responsibility that man has for his decisions and his sin. But at the same time we recognize that God is at work and has the ability and the authority to use whatever instruments He chooses to employ. Thus God used Joseph's brothers to preserve "a posterity in the earth" and to save their own lives (v 7).

Understanding God's providence produces additional confidence in Him. We occasionally may begin to wonder if things are out of control but our God notices every sparrow, "not one of them is forgotten before God" (Luke 12:6). Remember the Lord Jesus said, "Fear not therefore: ye are of more value than many sparrows" (Luke 12:7). He is in control, He cares for us, and He comforts us.

The Comfort

As Joseph comforts them, he tells them to be neither grieved within nor angry with themselves (v 5). Left to their own thinking, this may have happened. Perhaps there is another indication of this later on when he exhorts them: "See that ye fall not out by the way" (v 24). Not only could they be hard on themselves, but they could begin to criticize each other. A truth that we sometimes fail to grasp is that once we are forgiven there is no need to be constantly bringing up our past failures and mulling them over in our minds and lamenting what "could have been". We can often be too hard on ourselves as we look back over life and consider certain events that we wish we had handled differently, perhaps unwilling to forgive ourselves for failures, and unable to move on. Although the context is different, Paul's words are wise: "forgetting those things which are behind, and reaching forth unto those things which are before" (Phil 3:13). We cannot advance in our Christian experience if we are constantly looking in the rear view mirror.

The Christ

We can observe wondrous truths in all of this that relate again to our Lord Jesus. Consider, first of all, a coming day when He will manifest Himself to His own. "They shall look upon me whom they have pierced, and they shall mourn for him, as one mourneth for his only son" (Zech 12:10). They will be confounded, and then assured — this Jesus truly is our Messiah. We observe, too, that Joseph speaks of his exaltation: he is "lord of all his house, and a ruler throughout all the land of Egypt" (v 8). As wonderful as that may have been, remember Paul's words to the Philippians: "Wherefore God also hath highly exalted him, and given him a name which is above every name: That at the name of Jesus every knee should bow, of things in heaven, and things in earth, and things under the earth; And that every tongue should confess that Jesus Christ is Lord, to the glory of God the Father" (Phil 2:9-11). Joseph was over the all the land of Egypt; our Lord is over all things in every sphere. May we know what it is to bow the knee and worship Him.

Remember, finally, that in the posterity that Joseph was going to able to preserve through the years of famine because of God's providence and power, there was the seed from which the Messiah would spring: "The sceptre shall not depart from Judah, nor a lawgiver from between his feet, until Shiloh come; and unto him shall the gathering of the people be" (49:10). The providence of God leaves no room for Joseph's brothers to boast about their part in causing all these events, but we can appreciate God's wisdom in working all things out for His purposes and glory.

The Invitation (vv 9-13)

Joseph, having mentioned his position as "a ruler throughout all the land of Egypt", now sends a personal invitation to his father. He urges *promptness*: "Haste ye, and go up ... come down unto me, tarry not" (v 9). This was no time for delay! The hope of seeing his father was increasing, and he wants to impress on his brothers the priority of haste and the peril of delay. There are times when we as believers need to take things slowly, as we seek the will of God, for example. But there are other times when we need to move forward deliberately — the work of the Kingdom requires diligence.

Joseph reminds them of their future *proximity* to him: "And thou shalt dwell in the land of Goshen, and thou shalt be near unto me ..." (v 10). Twenty-two years before this his brothers had done all they could to send him as far away from them as they could possibly imagine. With no sense of rancour or antipathy, without recalling their animosity, he invites them to live near. What goodness and grace! It was an invitation for all that they had, possessions and people — no restrictions or limitations.

Joseph was confident that what God had revealed to Pharaoh was going to be fulfilled: "for yet there are five years of famine" (v 11). The **possibility** was that they would perish, or "come to poverty" were they not to heed the invitation. We could consider the "gospel invitation" extended to one and all, but just think for a moment about the Lord's invitation to His own — an invitation to be near to Him, to come away from the busyness of this world for a few moments each day in order to enjoy fellowship with Him. How much do we appreciate and take advantage of these times when we are near to Him? In this dry and thirsty world our souls can wither without these experiences of sweet communion.

Joseph provides full **proof** — "your eyes see, and the eyes of my brother Benjamin, that it is my mouth that speaketh unto you" (v 12). The brothers, as they listen to him, become convinced that this thirty-nine year old man, dressed as an Egyptian, truly is their brother. The Lord Jesus, in His grace, gave proof to His disciples in the upper room: "he shewed unto them his hands and his side. Then were the disciples glad, when they saw the Lord" (John 20:20). We, too, look forward to a day when we will have this great joy: "when he shall appear, we shall be like him; for we shall see him as he is" (1 John 3:2).

As they journeyed back home, surely this scene would be played again and again in their minds. They had seen his glory, and they were now filled with hope! They had heard His voice — soon they would be with him, near him, and he would nourish them! Is it not true that a glimpse of the Lord Jesus, hearing His voice, the hope of being with Him, gives us a different perspective on life as we journey through this wilderness scene? "And every man that hath this hope in him purifieth himself, even as he is pure" (1 John 3:3) — the **prospect** of being with Him ought to have a wonderful and decisive effect upon our lives.

Joseph, however, has another message to send to his father. "And ye shall tell my father of all my glory in Egypt, and of all that ye have seen" (v 13). Their response to this request to speak well of Joseph would be another indication that God had done a work in their hearts. ***Praising*** the one that they had despised? Ah, does this not remind us of our privilege to praise One who is far more worthy than Joseph? We can offer the sacrifice of praise continually, the fruit of our lips, as we give thanks to His name (Heb 13:15). Once afar off, now brought near, with confident and complete access to the very presence of God! How are we doing in speaking well of our Lord to His Father? Can you imagine the delight in Jacob's soul as he heard of the worth and wonders of his son Joseph? We will soon see that, but let's remember that our Father delights to hear us speak well of His Son!

The Reconciliation (vv 14-15)

We have considered truths related to forgiveness before, but here we see full reconciliation, a result of gracious forgiveness. Joseph had been made aware of their acceptance of guilt and responsibility on their previous journey: "They said one to another, We are verily guilty concerning our brother ... therefore is this distress come upon us" (42:21).

Back at the beginning of this one-sided conversation "he wept aloud" (v 2). Again we are reminded that a display of emotion is not necessarily a bad thing, as these brothers weep together. Remember the psalmist's words: "weeping may endure for a night, but joy cometh in the morning" (Ps 30:5). There are moments when we weep for joy, and that surely was part of the reason Joseph and his brothers wept. But there must have been some regret and remorse in his brothers' hearts as memories of their cruelty to him flooded their minds. But now there would be joy — the joy of forgiveness and reconciliation.

As believers we should always have a forgiving spirit. "And be ye kind one to another, tenderhearted, forgiving one another, even as God for Christ's sake hath forgiven you" (Eph 4:32). Forgiveness can be difficult when we have truly been wounded. Reminding ourselves of the forgiveness we have in Christ Jesus helps us to be willing forgivers. W. E. Vine notes that this word means "to bestow a favour unconditionally", and that may seem difficult to us in certain circumstances. Ought we to forgive if the offender is not accepting his responsibility? There certainly ought to be a willingness to forgive, but full forgiveness does require the repentance of the offender. Holding a grudge or, worse yet, seeking revenge is not an evidence of Christian grace! Other words for "forgiveness" mean "to free", or "to cancel a debt", or "to send away". Forgiveness may be costly, but it frees the forgiver first, saving him from bitterness and wrath.

But having said that we do need to realize that there is a difference between forgiveness offered and reconciliation obtained. A believer should always be willing and able to forgive, but reconciliation requires a change of heart on the part of the offender. There is the possibility of not reaching full reconciliation, but rather stopping at the stage of pacification — this could be described as a truce or an act of disarmament! Whenever possible (and in very few cases will it truly not be possible) we should strive to arrive at the next stage.

This will not only require a change of heart in the offender, but also means one needs to confront the fault straight on. Joseph had done this, reminding them of their actions from long ago, saying, "... whom ye sold into Egypt" (v 4). Remember once more the words of the Lord Jesus, "go and tell him his fault between thee and him alone" (Matt 18:15). We are not speaking here about petty little details, but what would be considered true faults or offences. Too often believers attempt to sweep everything under the carpet, and do their best to pretend all is well, but from time to time lift up the corner of the carpet and find that the problem is still lurking in the darkness. It is an onerous task to constantly pretend that all is well whilst there is a grudge being held in the heart. Let us be willing not only to forgive, but also to seek full reconciliation.

Forgiveness is enjoyed, and reconciliation takes place when there is a true confession of the fault committed by the offender. As long as there is no honest admission of guilt, the process will be at a standstill. Forgiveness is not complete until it is received by the offender, and this cannot happen if there is not a proper and full confession. Confession comes on the heels of true repentance, a deep recognition of the wrong committed. It is more than remorse that one was caught in the act, or regret that things didn't turn out differently. Repentance includes a genuine desire to confess the sin, turn away from the evil, and make things right with the offended party. We find a beautiful example of this in the well-known parable in Luke 15. The younger son left home with his inheritance and squandered it all, finding himself in squalid conditions. When he "came to himself", understanding the heinous character of sin, he arose and went directly to his father, confessing the wrong done. He did, as we know, understand it was first of all a sin against God, but he did confess to his father, against whom he had sinned as well. He found a father willing not only to freely forgive but also to fully reconcile and then to restore him to the position he had enjoyed before.

Forgiveness is the answer to bitterness, wrath, anger, clamour, evil speaking and malice — these can not be put away if I am not willing to forgive (Eph 4:31-32). One more time we need to stress that personal offences are dealt with between the offender and the one offended when at all possible, with no need to spread the news any further. Remember, too, that forgiveness will not necessarily take away the consequences of the offence that was committed.

Finally we see the fellowship that the brothers enjoyed with Joseph: "after that his brethren talked with him" (v 15). Have you ever had that experience? Perhaps at home, or in the assembly, there has been a conflict, a disagreement, then forgiveness and reconciliation takes place. What joy fills the heart, or the home, when peace reigns again. Paul wrote of such truths to the Colossians, "Forbearing one another, and forgiving one another, if any man have a quarrel against any: even as Christ forgave you, so also do ye. And above all these things put on charity, which is the bond of perfectness. And let the peace of God rule in your hearts, to the which also ye are called in one body; and be ye thankful" (Col 3:13-15).

The Consideration (vv 16-20)

When we consider this brief section we learn that Pharaoh will show kindness to these men due to their connection with Joseph.

The news of all of that was taking place in Joseph's home reached Pharaoh's house — good news must be shared. One can imagine what the servants were thinking all the time they were outside while Joseph was conversing with his brothers, as they heard the weeping (v 2) and perhaps heard some words as well, but since it was in the Hebrew language it was unintelligible to them.

It is obvious that Pharaoh was altogether content with Joseph and his service to the country. Thus his heart was moved with compassion as he considered the situation and the deep need of Joseph's family. Pharaoh was willing to give them "the good of the land", and the "fat of the land" would be for their food (v 18).

This promise was wonderful, but he left absolutely no doubt in their minds as to his intentions, giving this command: "this do ye, take you wagons out of the land of Egypt for your little ones, and for your wives, and bring your father, and come" (v 19). It is wonderful to read of such tender care in the heart of a world leader, taking into account the fact that this would be a long journey for the many children and for the women — "take you wagons"; Pharaoh was not a believer in the true God, but he is a good example of the compassion we find in John's writings: "But whoso hath this world's good, and seeth his brother have need, and shutteth up his bowels of compassion from him, how dwelleth the love of God in him?" (1 John 3:17). How sacrificial are we willing to be when we see people in need? The human heart tends more towards selfishness when it comes to "our" possessions, but Christ has taught us another way to live.

In the phrase "regard not your stuff" we see yet another level to Pharaoh's willingness to help Joseph's family. While it is true that people lived far more simply back then than we do today, nonetheless moving a group of seventy people would be a challenge. Pharaoh makes it somewhat simpler with this exhortation regarding "stuff". Our pilgrim character, of which we formerly heard much from public platforms, is more difficult when we are surrounded by an ever-increasing availability of "stuff".

We're a pilgrim band
in a stranger land
Who are marching from Calvary,
Where the wondrous Cross,
with its gain and loss,
Is the sum of our history:
There we lost our stand
in a death-doomed land,
As children of wrath by the fall;
There we gained a place
as heirs of grace,
At the feast in the heavenly hall.
(A. B. Mackay)

There would be something better awaiting them upon their return: "for the good of all the land of Egypt is yours" (v 20). God's plan did include His people spending about four hundred years in this land, as difficult as that would become for the nation during that time. But let us remember the lesson: we as believers have something far better awaiting us than anything we can possibly accumulate and enjoy in this world.

The family back in Canaan would soon know the good of blessings because of their link to Joseph, a man many had never even seen. The blessings we have are due to our connection with Christ, a truth so frequently expressed by Paul in the simple words "in Christ", especially in the Ephesian epistle.

Consider briefly two portions from Paul's pen. "Blessed be the God and Father of our Lord Jesus Christ, who hath blessed us with all spiritual blessings in heavenly places in Christ" (Eph 1:3). We see that our blessings have more to do with the spiritual, heavenly and eternal sphere than with that which is tangible, earthly and temporary. Obviously God can, and does, bless His people here on earth, but the best is yet to come! Do we live in the good of that?

"The Spirit itself beareth witness with our spirit, that we are the children of God: And if children, then heirs; heirs of God, and joint-heirs with Christ; if so be that we suffer with him, that we may be also glorified together" (Rom 8:16-17). Amazing truth! We are joint-heirs with Christ and He has been "appointed heir of all things" (Heb 1:2). The day is coming when we will be glorified with Him, and we look forward to that day. But Paul reminds us that in the present we will suffer with Him. A time of difficulty will be followed by a time of delight. Joseph had suffered for many years and was now in a position of exaltation; in like manner our heavenly Joseph suffered and has been exalted. This truth ought to help us as we move through the challenges and trials of life — we shall be glorified one day because of our link with the Christ of Calvary.

The Preparation (vv 21-24)

The eleven brothers are now preparing to go back to Canaan, pack up their belongings, and return to Egypt. This would be a much slower journey than the previous ones as they would travel as a larger group of people, including women and children. Therefore we notice the repetition in this short section that "Joseph gave them ... gave them ... gave each man ... he gave" (vv 21-22). What grace and kindness! Wagons for transportation and food for their physical sustenance, all they would need for travelling such a distance in the desert came from his bountiful hand. The wagons were Pharaoh's kind suggestion, but the "provision for the way" was surely abundant, a token of Joseph's goodness.

Then we read about clothing and coins — each brother received a "change of raiment", but Benjamin received five! Benjamin received three hundred pieces of silver, and the other brothers received none! This type of preferential treatment, had it occurred years before, would have caused an eruption of jealousy and envy amongst the rest, but now their hearts had been changed. Is it possible that jealousy and envy can exist amongst believers today? Or have we learned to rejoice when others are blessed? "Rejoice with them that do rejoice" (Rom 12:15).

Joseph, with joyful anticipation, sends more than plenty for his father. There are ten donkeys who carried "the good things of Egypt", and ten more that were laden with "corn and bread and meat for his father by the way" (v 23). The importance of this we will see in the next section, but before we get there consider the contrast to what had happened with Joseph's brothers twenty-two years before.

They had taken away his raiment — Joseph gives them all a change of raiment. They had sold Joseph for twenty pieces of silver — Joseph now hands out three hundred pieces. They had wanted to send him so far away that they would never see him again — Joseph's deepest desire is to bring them all close to him. Again we marvel at the forgiveness given and the reconciliation accomplished.

But as well as the fullness of provision for the journey we read these words: "See that ye fall not out by the way" (v 24). Falling out was a possibility that Joseph foresaw. True, his brothers had been changed, but this did not mean they were perfect! Would it be possible that they would restart the "blame game" that we noticed back in chapter 42 when Reuben said: "Spake I not unto you, saying, Do not sin against the child; and ye would not hear?" (42:22). It would be a long and difficult trip for them all, both to Canaan and then back to Egypt. Paul again helps us see that conflict during our journey homeward is possible, although not desirable. Believers are prone to use their tongues in ways that are not edifying, so we read: "Do all things without murmurings and disputings" (Phil 2:14) — murmurings are the expression of displeasure or complaint, and can lead to disputings, or arguments. "But if ye bite and devour one another, take heed that ye be not consumed one of another" (Gal 5:15) — attacks within the body of Christ will end up destroying believers. What is one antidote? Joseph had forgiven his brothers, wept over them and kissed them. Paul tells the Romans to "Salute one another with an holy kiss" (Rom 16:16). Perhaps our culture does not express affection and acceptance with a holy kiss, but we ought to be able to warmly greet all of our brethren in the faith.

The Declaration (vv 25-28)

This last section brings us much joy as we consider this man Jacob, one hundred and thirty years old. The caravan finally arrives in Canaan where the rest of the family, as well as their father, awaits them. Even though only gone a few months, one can still imagine the happiness in the hearts of the children and the wives as they see these weary men coming with wagons this time. But this section focuses on Jacob.

"Joseph is yet alive ...". This proclamation of good news was too much for dear old Jacob. "... he is governor over all the land of Egypt." Jacob was stunned, so much so that he fainted in his heart. He had given up any hope of seeing Joseph again many years ago — right from the beginning he had been convinced Joseph was dead. "He believed them not", and we cannot fault him for this unbelief. Not only alive, but administering rule in Egypt? Impossible!

But Joseph had sent along full proof that would convince his father. He hears about the words of Joseph, sees the wagons sent to carry him to Egypt, and is persuaded. His spirit is revived when he hears tell of all Joseph's glory in Egypt just as Joseph had instructed his brothers to do (v 13).

Jacob, at his advanced age, was about to undertake another journey, all with the hope of seeing his son once more. "It is enough: Joseph is yet alive; I will go and see him before I die" (v 28). He had not thought of more travel at his age but the possibility of seeing his son wrought a tremendous change in him. In the same way, the anticipation of seeing the Son of God ought to produce an effect in our lives. Obviously Jacob had no way of knowing that God would grant him another seventeen years with Joseph before he died — all that he wanted was to lay his eyes upon his beloved son.

All this reminds us of Christ's resurrection. Thomas is one who would not believe until he saw the proof, saying, "I will not believe" (John 20:25). But eight days later, when he saw the Lord and heard His words, he believed, and confessed: "My Lord and my God" (John 20:28).

CHAPTER 11

The Clan Arrives in Egypt

Genesis 46-47

Jacob has heard from his sons that Joseph was yet alive and has seen the evidence in the wagons Joseph had sent along with his brothers. He said, "It is enough ... I will go and see him before I die" (45:28) but as we begin Genesis 46 we can presume that dear Jacob was still concerned about this journey. Both Abraham and Isaac had had difficulties during their forays into Egypt — was this truly what God wanted him to do? God had promised the land of Canaan to his forefathers — was he forsaking what God had promised to them? Surely these, and other questions, were swirling through his mind while preparations were being made to travel.

The Confirmation from God (46:1-7)

It is a tremendous thing to observe Israel packing up all of his family and commencing this new stage of his life, and at such an advanced age. But more marvellous yet is seeing him take the time to stop in Beersheba to offer "sacrifices unto the God of his father Isaac" (46:1). One could hardly have blamed Jacob for trying to make record time! His stopping to sacrifice to God shows us the spiritual growth and strength in this aged man. Is it not possible in our day and age to become so taken up with the speed at which everything seemingly has to be done, with deadlines and pressures on every hand, that we let slip our time alone with God? The world may consider it to be an utter waste of time to stop in our tracks and spend moments in God's presence, but we notice here that this time of sacrifice became a time when God spoke directly to Israel's heart. We have no recorded instance of God having spoken to Jacob since Joseph was a young lad, more than twenty years before. How sad when we, too, can allow time to pass without being conscious of God speaking to our hearts through His infallible Word.

Certainly these words of surety from God Himself would have provided the peace in Jacob's heart that he longed for. Consider for a moment this conversation with God. God calls him: "Jacob, Jacob" (46:2), a double-call such as we find in the experience of Abraham on the mount (22:11); Moses at the burning bush (Ex 3:4); Samuel as he slept in the tabernacle (1 Sam 3:10), among others. God was looking for his complete attention, and Jacob quickly responded: "Here am I". We are certainly not suggesting that there will be an audible voice from heaven calling your name twice over, but could we suggest that our Father in heaven does long to have our attention as He speaks to us through His Word? Are we oftentimes hurrying through our daily reading, hardly pausing long enough to allow God, through His Holy Spirit, to speak into our lives? Worse yet, do we allow our Bible to be neatly stowed away and used only when meeting with His people? Jacob, although wanting to see Joseph as soon as possible, stopped in his tracks to hear the voice from heaven.

God gives his words of confirmation and comfort. There was no need to fear as, not only would God go with him, but He also would make him into great nation (46:3). Then God graciously refers to Joseph, saying, "Joseph shall put his hand upon thine eyes" (46:4). More than twenty years of silence, and now God confirms to Jacob that his beloved son is still alive, and not only that, he would be with his father when the time came to pass into eternity.

Jacob then rises up with all of his seed, the cattle and their goods, and leaves the "Promised Land". This truly was an act of faith — God had revealed His Word to Jacob, and Jacob responded in obedience, just as God expects us to do today.

The Enumeration of the Family (46:8-27)

Since we are looking at the life of Joseph we will not stop here to consider this list of all the seed of Israel in any detail. The decision that Jacob had made with regard to a move to Egypt affected many people, not just him. There is a practical lesson here for fathers in a family as well — Jacob was doing not only what was best for his family from a pragmatic standpoint, but he was definitively obeying the will of God for him.

We do get a brief reference to Joseph in this section: "And the sons of Joseph, which were born him in Egypt, were two souls" (46:27). This is yet another reminder to us of the grace and goodness of God in Joseph's experience. Despite afflictions in the body and anguish in his soul, God had richly blessed Joseph with two sons who would form part of this great nation He was establishing.

The Reunion of Father and Son (46:28-34)

Judah, who had been instrumental in the process of reconciliation in the previous chapter, is the one that Israel selects to go "before him unto Joseph" (46:28). This forerunner had had his failings and struggles in life, but Jacob saw in him a responsible man in whom he could now place his trust. One can hardly imagine the excitement that arose in Joseph's heart when he saw Judah — his father must be nearby! So when the writer simply states that "Joseph made ready his chariot, and went up to meet Israel his father" (46:29), we can rightly assume that there was much eagerness in his heart and lightness in his step as he headed towards Goshen.

Imagine the solace, the true consolation, the profound joy in the heart of both father and son when Joseph "presented himself unto him" (46:29). Twenty-two years is a very long time to miss your father! Twenty-two years is a very long time to think that your son had died a violent death! Now at last they lay eyes upon each other, and although the years certainly would have brought many physical changes in both of them, there is no question whatsoever that there would have been instant recognition. Joseph fell on his father's neck and wept "a good while", meaning "a long time". A long time had passed with no communication, but now the separation was over and there was an abundance of joy. One can only wonder what the other brothers must have been thinking as they observed this scene, saw the tears, and heard the weeping — weeping, yes, for joy, but perhaps weeping for the years of companionship that they had missed out on. Although we have no intimation that Jacob ever found out the details of what had transpired that fateful day, he obviously was now completely aware of the fact that his sons had somehow deceived him for a very long time.

Not only the solace, we see that Jacob was fully satisfied, as he said to his son, "Now let me die, since I have seen thy face, because thou are yet alive" (46:30). There was nothing else in his heart that he desired more than this, and God had fulfilled that desire. Remember the scene twenty-two years before: "And all his sons and all his daughters rose up to comfort him; but he refused to be comforted; and he said, For I will go down into the grave unto my son mourning. Thus his father wept for him" (37:35). He was now comforted; he would not go down to the grave mourning, and his weeping had been turned into joy: "weeping may endure for a night, but joy cometh in the morning" (Ps 30:5). One day we, too, will see our heavenly Joseph, our blessed Saviour, and the weeping of this present wilderness scene will be turned into joy on that glad morning.

Joseph was not only the saviour of the nation of Egypt, and of his family, he also was wise in his dealings with Pharaoh. He was going to prepare Pharaoh for their arrival. Why is this important? We can see that Joseph understood the importance of keeping his family separate from the Egyptians, and he would do this in two ways. First of all he would emphasize their work: "the men are shepherds". He would then also cause them to dwell in the land of Goshen.

Not only were shepherds an abomination to the Egyptians, but that nation also considered themselves to be superior beings, descending from the gods. Other peoples had lesser and lower origins than they. It would be essential for a God-fearing man like Joseph to keep his family far from such heathen and pagan beliefs and practices, safe from any dangerous influences on their lives. In Genesis 47 we will see that Pharaoh is indeed polite, but at the same time is quite content to think that this people will live separately from the Egyptians.

Could we speak a word about separation? Paul wrote: "Wherefore come out from among them, and be ye separate, saith the Lord, and touch not the unclean thing; and I will receive you, And will be a Father unto you, and ye shall be my sons and daughters, saith the Lord Almighty" (2 Cor 6:17-18). Paul's context is that of an idolatrous, pagan system, but the principle is still certain in our lives: God wants us to be a separated, sanctified people, serving Him in the midst of a dark world. We need not look odd or act eccentrically, but there ought to be a marked distinction in our outlook on life in contrast to those who are simply earth-dwellers. The nation of Israel would have its challenges years later, but Joseph was wise enough to start them off correctly as they lived in a wicked world — keep them separate from the evil and debased society. May we learn a lesson from them!

Joseph gives them these clear instructions, precise words to repeat to Pharaoh when they meet him face to face, so that they could "dwell in the land of Goshen" (46:34). They are fairly warned that they would be considered as an abomination. We, too, have been fairly warned by the Saviour, who said, "If the world hate you, ye know that it hated me before it hated you" (John 15:18).

As we move into Genesis 47, we find first of all:

The Presentation to Pharaoh (47:1-10)

Joseph already had received previous authorisation from Pharaoh regarding the territory where his family would be able to live - Goshen. However, some months had passed since his brothers had left for Canaan with the provision and carts, and the correct and courteous thing to do now was to make a formal presentation to Pharaoh.

First we see that "he took some of his brethren, even five men, and presented them unto Pharaoh" (47:2). Which five they were and why he selected them we do not know, but we can surmise that these would be those whom Joseph assumed would make the proper impression on Pharaoh. Some have suggested they would be the "most presentable" but is it not possible, even likely, that Joseph would have chosen the least-threatening, the most humble of them all, in order to show Pharaoh the reality of their base condition as shepherds?

It is obvious that the main concern Pharaoh had in his mind was regarding their occupation. They responded: "Thy servants are shepherds, both we, and also our fathers" (47:3). They had heeded Joseph's instructions very carefully. Not only were they shepherds, but they also expressed their desire to "sojourn in the land" (47:4). They were indicating their desire to return to their homeland, expecting that their time in Egypt would be brief. We know that the people of Israel ended up spending more than four hundred years here, becoming slaves for much of that time, but none of this was in their minds — this was a temporary solution to their current problem: "thy servants have no pasture for their flocks; for the famine is sore in the land of Canaan" (47:4). Three times over they call themselves "thy servants" (47:4-5), showing a sense of humility before such a great leader. Surely they, as shepherds from a far-off country, had never thought that someday they would be presented to one of the world's great rulers of the time. Who would have thought that this group of men would develop into a people that would become a perceived threat to Egypt's national security! But that is precisely what we see when we move into Exodus and "there arose up a new king over Egypt, which knew not Joseph" (Ex 1:8).

Pharaoh's verdict is that Joseph's family should indeed dwell in Goshen. He was being generous, giving them "the best of the land" (47:6), but at the same time maintaining the proper distance between the Egyptians and these Canaanites. At the same time he recognized an opportunity to utilize their experience and knowledge: "if thou knowest any men of activity among them, then make them rulers over my cattle". Knowing Joseph was a man of great capabilities, Pharaoh assumed there would be some of his brothers who would be sufficiently competent to become the chief herdsmen of his own cattle.

Then Joseph presents his father, setting him "before Pharaoh". Here Jacob takes the lead, as we read: "Jacob blessed Pharaoh" (47:7). The deference here is perhaps due to the Jacob's apparent advanced age. But how did Jacob bless Pharaoh? Perhaps he entered the room with his hands raised, thankful for the opportunity that Pharaoh was affording him and his family to survive these years of famine. Jacob was not only fully aware of God's sovereign control in all of these circumstances, but also of God's promise to his grandfather Abraham: "I will bless them that bless thee, and curse him that curseth thee: and in thee shall all families of the earth be blessed" (12:3). Pharaoh was considered to be a direct descendant from the sun god Ra, but here was this old man, a Canaanite, blessing him in the name of the one true God, the One who is the fount of every blessing.

We, too, as believers can and should be a source of blessing to those around us just as Joseph had been in Egypt for some years already, and now his father was also blessing the king. The Lord Jesus taught that His followers are not only the salt of the earth but also the light of the world (Matt 5:13-16). We are to have a preserving effect in a decaying society as well as spreading light to those around us — light that not only reveals the evident sin in the world, but also points to the One who is the True Light.

But then Pharaoh does what is not considered to be acceptable in many cultures in the world, and asks, "How old art thou?" (47:8). The ideal life span for the Egyptian people was one hundred and ten years, and there was a deep respect for those who reached old age. One could rightly assume that Jacob was not able to hide his age, having spent his lifetime looking after livestock under the sun of the Middle East. A direct question received a direct answer, with no hint of embarrassment — "The days of the years of my pilgrimage are an hundred and thirty years: few and evil have the days of my life been" (47:9). As Joseph listened to this conversation, he would have been impressed with not only the brevity of life (no matter how long one spends on earth) but also with his father's description: "few and evil". What sadness Jacob had passed through in his life: the death of his beloved wife Rachel, and then the supposed death of their first son, Joseph. Not only these happenings, but also the actions of his sons on various occasions — acts of immorality and cruelty, for example. Joseph would surely have been filled with sadness as he considered all that had brought his father to this conclusion. At times this word "evil" is translated as "grievous", "sad", "trouble", or "adversity". Jacob did not know that God would graciously give him seventeen "good" years, years of gladness and joy, with plenty of provision.

Twice Jacob uses the word "pilgrimage" (47.9). He lived as his forefathers, moving through this world as a pilgrim. This world was only a temporary abode, as it is for us as well. Joseph would obviously be living in much greater luxury in a much more permanent dwelling than his father and brethren, but it was certainly a good reminder to him on this occasion.

Once more Joseph hears his father bless Pharaoh before departing from his presence. Those of us who are parents can take Joseph's experience with his father before Pharaoh as a challenge to us. Jacob commenced the encounter with a blessing, spoke about the brevity of life, the burdens he had borne, but nonetheless could conclude with yet another blessing. Do our children see that we are a blessing to others? Not in the sense of boasting of what we do for others, but in practical manners that are obvious to them. Recall that the Lord Jesus, as He taught that we are salt and light, told us the purpose He had in mind: "... that they may see your good works, and glorify your Father which is in heaven" (Matt 5:16). Would to God that we could live in this way as well — recognizing the reality of burdens in life, but at the same time seeing the needs of others to be blessed.

The Possession for the Family (47:11-12)

As we will notice in the next section of this chapter, the Egyptian people ended up losing much during this time of famine. At the very same time, God's people were being blessed in a special way, and instead of losing much they were gaining. We will not fall into the trap of the "health and wealth gospel" that is so prevalent in the religious world, but we do want to remember that God's people today do occupy a place of special blessings. It is true that many of God's people in the world do experience abundant material blessings, but let us never forget that many more believers enjoy very few, or perhaps none, of the things we take for granted — a roof over our heads and plenty of food for the week to come, for example. We do all, however, possess the same spiritual blessings in Christ Jesus.

Let us remember that these men who had been living in Canaan had at times acted like Canaanites. Reuben and Judah were involved in immorality (49:4; 38:18); Judah and Simeon had taken women from amongst the Canaanites (38:2; 46:10); and most of the brethren had been involved in human trafficking as they sold Joseph as a slave (37:28).

So allowing them to live in Ramses, the best of the land served two purposes: they would be at a distance from the Egyptian people, thus providing less opportunity for mixing with them and being influenced by them, and they would be close enough for Joseph to be constantly providing them with nourishment.

But the blessing involved much more than just nourishing them, as it says he "gave them a possession in the land of Egypt" (47:11), while in the next section we find Joseph buying the land from the Egyptians. We, as God's heavenly people are not so concerned about the land, but we have this promise: "Blessed be the God and Father of our Lord Jesus Christ, who hath blessed us with all spiritual blessings in heavenly places in Christ" (Eph 1:3). There was a very similar purpose in God's mind to that of Joseph's when God gave us these blessings: "that we should be holy and without blame before him in love" (Eph 1:4). Joseph was setting his family apart just as God has set us apart, calling us "holy". Joseph wanted his family to be different in their character and conduct, just as God wants us to be "without blame before him in love".

God's purpose, as He had explained to Jacob before the southerly journey commenced, was to make of him a great nation (46:3), obviously separate from the nation of Egypt. It is wonderful to see how God preserved His people during the more than four hundred years despite their being in the midst of the land of Egypt. Recall the words of the Lord Jesus: "I pray not that thou shouldest take them out of the world, but that thou shouldest keep them from the evil. They are not of the world, even as I am not of the world" (John 17:15-16). We, too, are **in** the world, but always need to have in our mind this truth: we are not **of** the world.

The believer can become comfortable, not only in the world, but also with the world's perspective, becoming "a friend of the world" (James 4:4). He then can become contaminated by the world, while James warns us that "Pure religion and undefiled before God and the Father is this ... to keep himself unspotted from the world" (James 1:27). An unhealthy attachment to the world can then begin, as one cherishes or loves what he sees around him, forgetting John's exhortation: "Love not the world, neither the things that are in the world" (1 John 2:15). How can we maintain the proper distance from the world, living in it, but not being of it? Although the word "world" is different from the mentions above, the truth remains the same, as Paul gives the Romans a simple answer: "And be not conformed to this world: but be ye transformed by the renewing of your mind, that ye may prove what is that good, and acceptable, and perfect, will of God" (Rom 12:2). Is there a desire in our heart to not be conformed to this world? Be careful what you cherish in your heart; don't allow the world to contaminate your thinking, and don't allow yourself to become comfortable with, or in, this world that will soon be judged.

But think again of Joseph's kindness: "Joseph nourished his father, and his brethren, and all his father's household, with bread, according to their families" (47:12). First of all we notice not only that he was aware of the varying needs amongst the different families, but that he was also willing and able to meet those particular needs. Obviously Joseph was not showing partiality, but rather was plenteous in his generosity. He brings to mind the work of our Great High Priest, who seeing our individual needs is more than able to meet them without ignoring the needs of others — abundant provision. He does long for us to depend upon Him even more, to find in Him our source of sustenance and strength. "Let us therefore come boldly unto the throne of grace, that we may obtain mercy, and find grace to help in time of need" (Heb 4:16).

The Provision for the Nation (47:13-26)

But now we turn to the Egyptians who also were struggling through this time of famine. "And there was no bread in the land ... the land of Egypt and all the land of Canaan fainted by reason of the famine" (47:13). While some have been critical of Joseph's actions in the following verses, we need to remember first of all that he was considered to be the saviour of the nation; it was he who had warned Pharaoh about this time of pressing need, and he had devised the plan to rescue the nation from utter destruction.

The first thing the people did once the famine was sore was to purchase corn with their money. All this money was brought to Pharaoh's house — there is absolutely no corruption. He had gathered up "all the money" (47:14), which must have been a considerable contribution to the government's coffers.

Once the people had run entirely out of money, they arrived at Joseph's office, saying, "Give us bread: for why should we die in thy presence?" (47:15). They understood that the only source of provision was Joseph. At this point he told them they could pay with their cattle, or livestock. So in exchange for horses, flocks, cattle and donkeys the people were able to survive. But this only lasted for one year (47:17).

The next step was to offer to Joseph both their bodies and their lands (47:18). It was their request to Joseph, not Joseph's instructions. They were willingly offering themselves to be "servants unto Pharaoh". The people were wise as they considered their own future, and that of the land. "Give us seed, that we may live, and not die, that the land be not desolate" (47:19). Thus all the land, with the exception of the priests' portion (47:22) became Pharaoh's.

It certainly is not our purpose here to speak about diverse forms of government, but we need to keep in mind that these were different times, and it was a tremendously difficult crisis that the nation was facing. At no point in the story do we see any hint of the abuses that are so prevalent in various societies and countries today. The people were more than willing to do all this; they actually suggested selling what they had in order to survive into the future, obviously believing what Joseph had said about the timeline of the famine.

Remember that, in that day, being a slave was preferred to death. Having willingly offered their lands and their own bodies meant that they were rightfully expecting that Joseph would provide for their daily needs. Do not take this in any way as condoning the slavery that afflicted so many societies later on in human history when there was tremendous abuse of human beings created in the image of God - such was not the case in this story.

By the time the famine came to its end after seven long years, Joseph now had their lucre, their livestock, their land, and their very lives. But he was very gracious and kind, and not only gave wise instruction but also provided seed. "Lo, here is seed for you, and ye shall sow the land" (47:23). It would take some measure of faith on the part of the Egyptians to take precious seed and plant it after seven years of famine. Was Joseph right? Was the time of the famine truly over? They obviously trusted his counsel. We have a "Wonderful Counsellor" available to us, longing for us to take full advantage of His wise words (Isa 9:6) and not to depend on our own understanding and wisdom.

Joseph continued to show his governmental ability in relation to the finances of the nation. The new law would be that the people could retain eighty percent of the increase each year, and give twenty percent to Pharaoh. The eighty percent would include the seed for the next crop, as well as food for the households. The short phrase "and for food for your little ones" (47:24) once more shows us the tender compassion of Joseph, and makes us ponder our Saviour when He said, "Suffer the little children to come unto me, and forbid them not: for of such is the kingdom of God" (Mark 10:14). Both Joseph and the Lord Jesus saw the tremendous value in the little ones, and the need to care for them. In a world that values life at both ends of the spectrum, let us always keep in mind the value of every human soul.

There is no bitterness nor anger in the hearts of the Egyptians but rather deep gratitude. "Thou hast saved our lives; let us find grace in the sight of my lord, and we will be Pharaoh's servants" (47:25). First of all, note their recognition of Joseph's goodness to them — he had saved their lives. Then we see their understanding of their need for grace — not just in saving their lives, but on an ongoing basis. Finally we see a willingness to be servants. We, too, look to the Lord Jesus and see One who not only has saved us, but richly bestows His grace upon us from day to day. Are we, like them, willing servants in the service of a far better Master?

The Promise to his Father (47:27-31)

God was prospering Joseph's family just as He had promised to Jacob before he descended to Egypt, and was beginning to make them into a great nation while they dwelt there. "They had possessions therein, and grew and multiplied exceedingly" (47:27). Surely it would have thrilled Joseph to see God not only preserving the family, but causing it to prosper.

"I will also surely bring thee up again" was another part of the promise God had given to Jacob seventeen years before (46:4). Now his life was coming to an end, but we can rightly assume that these seventeen years had been the most peaceful and happy times in his life. Remember how he had told Pharaoh upon his arrival that his days had been evil (47:9). He deeply appreciated the goodness of God in bringing Joseph again into his life, and as he prepares to die, he calls for him: "If now I have found grace in thy sight, put, I pray thee, thy hand under my thigh, and deal kindly and truly with me" (47:29). He had no reason to think that Joseph would not do this, but the custom of the time was an oath of this nature. Abraham had done this with his servant when he sent him to find a wife for his son Isaac (24:2). Now Jacob has some serious instructions for Joseph and elicits an oath from him.

"Bury me not, I pray thee, in Egypt: But I will lie with my fathers, and thou shalt carry me out of Egypt, and bury me in their buryingplace" (47:29-30). Jacob had faith in God's promise to him, but at the same time realized that human instruments would be involved in bringing this about. Since Joseph was not only the favoured son but also the man in charge of the nation, he chose to give him these instructions. We remember that faith is not only taking God at His word, but also acting upon what He has revealed. We see this time and time again as we read through Hebrews 11, for example.

This would also be a reminder to Joseph that the land of Egypt was not his final dwelling place either, but rather that God had promised to Abraham and his descendants the land of Canaan. So Joseph responded: "I will do as thou hast said", and then "he sware unto him" (47:30-31).

Joseph was now forty-seven years old. If these last seventeen years had been wonderful for his father, they surely had been for Joseph as well. Preparing for the departure of a loved one is never easy but it is necessary. Here we notice the absence of any bitterness on the part of either father or son. Undoubtedly Joseph's responsibilities during the first five years of his family's time in Goshen were considerably greater than the following twelve years, however the uncertainly about how long his aged father would yet live would assuredly have produced a desire within him to make the most of the time available. Let us take the lesson to heart, and look for God's direction for balance in our lives with our distinct responsibilities.

CHAPTER 12

The Contemplation and Affirmation

Genesis 48-49

At the end of chapter 47 Joseph's father spoke with him about the burial of his body, but now, as he continues to contemplate his departure from this world, he will bless each of the brothers, as well as Joseph's two sons, the only grandchildren that came into a special blessing like this.

Preparing for our death is wise, even though we as believers "look for the Saviour, the Lord Jesus Christ: Who shall change our vile body, that it may be fashioned like unto his glorious body" (Phil 3:20-21). It is possible that before the Lord comes for His own He will call us into His presence, and although there will be much joy as we enter into our eternal home, those left behind will not only mourn, but will also have the solemn responsibility of burying us. Thinking about these things, as Jacob did when he instructed Joseph, is not only wise but it is also kind, removing some of the burden in those difficult moments.

People still believe the lie of the devil: "Ye shall not surely die" (3:4). We do all we can to avoid that moment, trying to ignore our own mortality, but reminders do come into our lives. Perhaps the death of a loved one, or even watching a hearse drive slowly by, will remind us of the frailty of our frame. The onset of an illness, or the increasing difficulty in accomplishing what used to be a simple part of life, tells us that our life will soon come to its end.

Jacob specified where he was to be buried, not so much because of the geographical location, but more especially because of its spiritual connotations. He would teach his sons that they were not from Egypt, did not belong to Egypt, and that one day they would leave Egypt and return to the land that God had promised to them. He wanted them to remember that they were a "peculiar people", a phrase repeated in the New Testament about Christ's church (1 Peter 2:9). It refers not to being strange, but rather "a people for a possession" (JND). Peter then told his readers that they were "strangers and pilgrims" (1 Peter 2:11), and the same applies to us today. We need to recognize and remember that we are pilgrims quickly passing through earth's sad scene as strangers. We are not known, or understood, in this world, as the Lord Jesus taught His disciples in the Upper Room, speaking to them about the persecution they would face: "They shall put you out of the synagogues ... And these things will they do unto you, because they have not known the Father, nor me" (John 16:2-3). Later, as He prayed in John 17, He stated: "They are not of the world, even as I am not of the world" (v 16). Remembering these truths daily ought to affect life's decisions.

As he blesses his sons in Genesis 49, Jacob makes many honest references to their character, but we will only look at what he says to Joseph, affirming the special place he had in his father's heart. Today's society considers the distribution of wealth to be the most important issue to be dealt with in a will, but Jacob does little of that, being more concerned about the conduct of his sons. As he speaks to them, he is also telling them about God's plans and purposes for their descendants' lives.

The Report (48:1-2)

"Thy father is sick" are not words that any son wants to hear. This report perhaps did not come to him as a complete surprise for a couple of reasons: his father was now one hundred and forty-seven years old, and Joseph did not live so far away as to be unaware of his father's declining health, one of the effects of which is mentioned clearly further along: "Now the eyes of Israel were dim for age, so that he could not see" (48:10).

Surely with great speed Joseph gathered his two sons, Manasseh and Ephraim, and made his way to his father's bedside. These young men would now be into their early twenties, and this event in their life would be unforgettable. This would be the last time they would see their grandfather, and Joseph quite obviously expected there to be a blessing for them as well. We need to remember the importance not only of parents but of mature believers in the experience of our children. Their perspective on what is truly important in life can be of tremendous influence and impact on young people. Beyond the family setting, there is a wonderful advantage for the younger generation in assembly fellowship as they interact with older and mature believers.

When Jacob heard that Joseph was on his way, he "strengthened himself, and sat upon the bed" (48:2). He somehow knew that the time of his departure was very near, and this was the moment to give his final blessings to his offspring. His physical vision was cloudy, but his spiritual perspective became very clear. One who faces up to the frailty of life often has a sudden change in their thinking. Material possessions lose their attractiveness, while family relationships become far more important.

The Recollection (48:3-4, 7, 15-16)

Joseph listens to his father as he goes back in time, remembering certain instances in his life where God was very evidently at work. Although Joseph perhaps had heard these things before, the last words of his father would have stayed with him for the rest of his life. Perhaps many of us have vivid recollections of a father or mother's last words as their life ebbed away from them and they passed into the presence of their God.

Joseph heard his father call God the "Almighty" (48:3), the Omnipotent God who had blessed him at Bethel when he was leaving his parents and heading to Mesopotamia. God had given him several promises. He would be fruitful and would multiply into a multitude of people, and receive the land of Canaan for his seed (48:4). He had also said: "I am with thee ... and will bring thee again into this land" (28:15).

Joseph knew that God had fulfilled the promise of making his father into a multitude, albeit a small multitude at this point. In relation to a return to the land God had already brought him back from a foreign land once, when they all left his grandfather Laban's home to come back to Canaan. This surely would give Joseph additional confidence that God would make this happen again now, with his father's body being taken from Egypt to Canaan. This would be a token of what would eventually be the case for the entire family. This promise obviously affected Joseph's own burial plans years later.

After speaking about Joseph's sons in verses 5 and 6, Jacob goes back in his memory to the day he had to bury his favoured wife Rachel. "Rachel died by me in the land of Canaan in the way ... and I buried her there in the way of Ephrath" (48:7). Would this recollection not have moved Joseph as he considered his mother whom he had lost when only a young boy? Although Jacob was obviously saddened by his wife's departure, there is no note of bitterness now, another lesson his son would have noted.

Later he recalls God's faithfulness to him all along life's pathway. "The God before whom my fathers Abraham and Isaac walked, the God that shepherded me all my life long to this day, the Angel that redeemed me from all evil, bless the lads" (48:15-16, JND). Joseph now hears his father mention two more titles for his God, but also understands something of the responsibility in life of walking before God, that is, being continually and constantly conscious of His presence. This was the experience of Joseph's father, grandfather and great-grandfather, and obviously was that of Joseph, too. "The God that shepherded me all my life" — what a statement regarding God's faithful care, guiding and providing along the way. Some translations give God the title here of "my Shepherd", showing again the tender care of our God. But He is also "the Angel" that had rescued him from dangers along the way, of which there had been many. This is the God whom Jacob was invoking as he blessed Joseph and his sons. This is the same God we know today, and in whom we trust all along life's pathway.

The Replacement (48:5-6)

Israel had twelve sons, but we read in this chapter and then through the rest of the Old Testament that the two sons of Joseph each had a place amongst the twelve, even though they were not sons but grandsons. Twelve is the number of administrative completeness, but such was the esteem and love that Jacob had for Joseph that he found a way to bless him richly. Levi would not have a portion in the inheritance, thus leaving space for both of Joseph's sons. Both Ephraim and Manasseh would become independent tribes with their own portions in the land.

"Thy two sons, Ephraim and Manasseh ... are mine; as Reuben and Simeon, they shall be mine" (48:5). Reuben and Simeon were Leah's sons, and were Jacob's firstborns. But now Jacob is giving Joseph, his eleventh son, the privilege of having a double portion. We find later that the Levites also were not numbered: "Only thou shalt not number the tribe of Levi, neither take the sum of them among the children of Israel" (Num 1:49) as their portion was spiritual, not territorial. They would be dispersed throughout the nation in order to serve amongst the other tribes.

Thus we see that Ephraim and Manasseh took the place of Levi and Joseph at this stage in the nation's history. Jacob probably was also safeguarding the Hebrew identity of these two grandsons born, not only in Egypt, but also by means of an Egyptian mother. Although we do not read of any other of Joseph's children, Joseph was told that any other sons born to him would be his own; the first two sons were considered to be as though they were Jacob's own sons.

The Recognition (48:8-16)

Due to his advanced age, Israel's eyesight was failing significantly. He could make out the form of his two grandsons, but not their faces, and thus asked: "Who are these?" (48:8). Despite the fact that his father had just said "they shall be mine", Joseph kindly responded, "They are my sons, whom God hath given me in this place" (48:9). Notice the responsibility and accountability that Joseph felt with regard to his sons, "They are my sons." He felt responsible for them. Then he added: "whom God hath given me", so he understood they were his as a stewardship from God, for which one day he would be called to account. The psalmist wrote "Lo, children are an heritage of the LORD: and the fruit of the womb is his reward" (Ps 127:3).

In a society that has attempted, with far too much success, to blur or erase the distinction of roles, parents need to remember that they have a God-given responsibility for their children, and that one day there will be an accounting for the way they have been brought up in the nurture and admonition of the Lord. We cannot save our children but we can preserve and protect them from many of the dangers and errors that abound in the world today. Joseph had done just that in the idolatrous and immoral nation of Egypt. Such was his influence on them that the descendants of these two sons would not choose to remain in Egypt, although they were part Egyptian, but would one day leave for Canaan just like the other tribes.

Jacob said: "Bring them, I pray thee, unto me, and I will bless them", and then "he kissed them, and embraced them" (48:9-10). The emotion in that room must have been palpable, as Joseph observed his father's love towards these two young men. Israel then expresses the deep gratitude and joy in his heart: "I had not thought to see thy face: and, lo, God hath shewed me also thy seed" (48:11). Decades before, he had given up hope of ever seeing his beloved son again, and yet now God had given him the opportunity to see his son's sons. In a society that has become increasingly unthankful to God (and to one another) we find a good reminder here to encourage us to see how God graciously works in our lives and gives us far more blessings than we could ever deserve.

Jacob reaches the highest point of a believer's experience at this point. "By faith Jacob, when he was a dying, blessed both the sons of Joseph; and worshipped, leaning upon the top of his staff" (Heb 11:21). God seeks worshippers, and Jacob worshipped at the end of his life. Joseph observed his father, listened to his words, and learned the importance of worship. Jacob had shown some scheming and supplanting along the way, but it is wonderful to observe the triumphal finish to his life, worshipping God.

Joseph deeply respected his father, and as he moved his sons towards him, he, "bowed himself with his face to the earth" (48:12). Once again, as we consider modern society we can see a decreasing level of respect for the aged, a deeply concerning trend. The sanctity of life applies not only to the beginning, but also to the end of life. Abortion is accepted in today's society, with laws allowing it abounding, and any attempts to pass legislation to protect the life of the unborn child are met with fierce and vocal opposition. At the other end of the spectrum we see more and more countries allowing euthanasia, or "doctor-assisted suicide". It is not our intention to enter into any debate or detail about this subject, but we do need to be aware, as the people of God, about these disturbing trends, and not allow the world to influence our biblically-guided thinking. The psalmist cried out: "If the foundations be destroyed, what can the righteous do?" (Ps 11:3). The foundations of society are being attacked, but remember what he wrote next: "The LORD is in his holy temple, the LORD'S throne is in heaven: his eyes behold, his eyelids try, the children of men" (Ps 11:4). So, yes, we need to be aware and cry out to God that He will preserve some sense of moral boundaries in society, and at the same time remember that He indeed is still on His throne in heaven, observing all these things that grieve our hearts, and His heart too.

It is interesting to notice the position of the two sons: Joseph moved Ephraim towards his father's left hand, and Manasseh towards his right hand. Manasseh, we remember, was the firstborn, and the right hand was the place of special privilege and blessing. Thus Joseph expected, and desired, that Manasseh would receive the special blessing of "the firstborn" from Israel.

However, despite his blindness, Jacob guided his hands "wittingly", or "intelligently" (48:14, JND). We could say that Israel, guided by God Himself, made a change, taking his right hand and placing it on Ephraim's head, the younger of the two. After that he blessed Joseph.

Think of the source of the blessing: the God who had fed, or shepherded him all his life, and the Angel who had rescued him from all evil (48:15-16). Consider the scope of the blessing mentioned in these verses: the continuation of the family name, from Abraham and

Isaac to Israel himself, and then the fact that they would "grow into a multitude in the midst of the earth" (48:16). As we continue to read through the Old Testament, we see how this did come to pass.

The Reprimand (48:17-18)

When Joseph saw the how his father was positioning his hands on his sons, "it displeased him" (48:17). Such was his displeasure that he attempted to move his father's right hand from Ephraim's head to Manasseh's head. Then we hear him reprimanding his father, "Not so, my father: for this is the firstborn; put thy right hand upon his head" (48:18). Joseph seemed to be guided and governed by the natural and normal instead of the spiritual sense that his father possessed. We are not blaming Joseph for wanting his older son to have the preeminence; it was to be expected, and he had perhaps even been preparing him for this.

Joseph, who had shown deep respect for his father, bowing down before him moments before, was now expressing his disagreement both by his actions as well as by his words. Do we not need to exercise extreme caution when we speak to those who are older than us, those that have more experience along life's pathway, more spiritual discernment, and perhaps walking closer to God than we are? Joseph, for all the wisdom and insight he had, is outshone here by his father who had shown carnal tendencies so often in his life. By faith Jacob had been guided by the Lord and would not be moved.

The Reiteration (48:19-22)

The older man "refused, and said, I know it, my son, I know it" (48:19). There was still this determination in Israel at one hundred and forty-seven that had been seen earlier in his life, but here, in contrast with many other occasions, it was controlled by his spiritual vision.

Joseph now listens to what will become of his two sons. The older would become a people, and would be great, but his younger brother would be even greater, and his seed would become "a multitude of nations". What would have filled Joseph's mind as he considered the goodness and grace of God towards him? What wonder as he thought of what would become of his descendants! A people, and a multitude of nations! And this multitude from one who had been despised by his brothers and sold into slavery in a foreign land, thinking he would never again see his father and family. Now his progeny was being doubly blessed!

We then come to the fifth and sixth mentions of the word "bless" in this chapter. The first had to do with Jacob himself being blessed (v 3), but now we read these words: "And he blessed them that day, saying, In thee shall Israel bless" (v 20). The one who had been blessed by God himself was now speaking on behalf of God, invoking His blessing upon his grandsons.

Again, the source of the blessing is God: "God make thee as Ephraim and as Manasseh" (48:20). These sons were brought up in a remarkable way, with tremendous privileges that their cousins in nearby Goshen would not have enjoyed. The immoral and secular society in which they lived and the probable influence of Poti-pherah in their lives had not adversely affected them. Poti-pherah was their grandfather and the priest of On, surely not a God-fearing man. Is it not the case today for many believers bringing up their children in a very secular society that there are conflicting worldviews being brought to bear upon the family? Perhaps there are unsaved grandparents who may create some level of confusion in the minds of young children being brought up in a Christian home, but we are thankful for the example of men like Joseph who impressed lasting spiritual truths on the minds of their children.

This phrase "make thee as Ephraim and Manasseh" is a Sabbath blessing still used by Jewish parents as they bless their sons. (For daughters the phrase is "… as Sarah, Rebecca, Rachel and Leah".) They understand that it is difficult enough to be a good person when all the circumstances are favourable, but even more difficult when they are completely unfavourable. These two young men were showing the godly character that obviously impressed their grandfather Jacob, and this is the desire of God-fearing parents today.

Then "he set Ephraim before Manasseh" (48:20). The firstborn would normally have the first place in regards to blessings, but Joseph well knew that his own father had received the blessing instead of his brother Esau, the firstborn in the family. This had been prophesied to Rebekah (25:23), but later both she and Jacob had connived together in order to ensure God's promise would be fulfilled. Before that we find that Isaac, although the second son of Abraham, had been the one to receive the blessing of the firstborn (25:5). Even Joseph, in a certain sense, had been designated by his father as the preferred son by the time he was seventeen years old, clearly indicated by the special robe he received.

Remember, too, the meanings of their names: Manasseh means "forgetful" while Ephraim signifies "fruitful". Manasseh had made Joseph forget the difficulties of the past, but Ephraim made him look to the future. So as Jacob places Ephraim ahead of Manasseh, he is looking towards the coming years when there would be fruit from this particular tribe.

Finally, as we come to the end of Genesis 48, Jacob not only reiterates the blessing upon Joseph's sons, but now also repeats the certainty he felt about his impending death: "Behold, I die" (48:21). Sorrow is mixed with promise, however, as Joseph hears his father say, "God shall be with you, and bring you again to the land of your fathers". It makes us recall words the writer penned to the Hebrews centuries later: "I will never leave thee, nor forsake thee" (Heb 13:5). While we tread this desert scene, let us remember He is always with us, and at the end of the journey, however He may allow that to happen, we will be with those who have gone on before.

He didn't only give the promise that God's presence would be with Joseph but said: "Moreover I have given to thee one portion above thy brethren" (48:22). This was land he had taken from the hand of the Amorite years before in an unrecorded battle. When the children of Israel finally left Egypt and made their way to the Promised Land, they brought Joseph's bones. "And the bones of Joseph, which the children of Israel brought up out of Egypt, buried they in Shechem, in a parcel of ground which Jacob bought of the sons of Hamor the father of Shechem for an hundred pieces of silver: and it became the inheritance of the children of Joseph" (Josh 24:32). Jacob had rights to this property both by conquest and by purchase. Hundreds of years later we read about this same portion of land again: "Then cometh he to a city of Samaria, which is called Sychar, near to the parcel of ground that Jacob gave to his son Joseph" (John 4:5). The Lord Jesus richly blessed the Samaritan woman with salvation at this very place.

The Richness (49:22-26)

As we move into Genesis 49, we observe Jacob sharing his final thoughts with his twelve sons. "Gather yourselves together, that I may tell you that which shall befall you in the last days" (49:1). Some of what Jacob says is actually quite sad; consider, for example, his words to Reuben, "thou shalt not excel" (49:4); but this was because of his character and conduct. Both he and his brothers Simeon and Levi had not learned to control their fleshly urges. Self-control is essential in life, especially in a believer. But there are also some lovely prophetic truths concerning the Lord Jesus in the chapter. We will focus, however, on the words to Joseph, remembering that he presents to us a lovely, although not complete, picture of Christ.

The Scope (49:22)

Joseph, said Jacob, was "a fruitful bough" (49:22). Jacob himself had been the beneficiary of the fruit of Joseph's love and labours, especially during the last seventeen years of his life. Part of fruit-bearing in the natural world has to do with having a constant source of water, and Jacob saw this spiritually in his son's life, as he was a "fruitful bough by a well". Psalm 1 comes to mind as we consider Joseph, as he was a blessed man. He did not walk in the counsel of the ungodly, although surrounded by them; he did not stand in the way of sinners, although he had to work with them; he did not sit in the seat of the scornful, although he lived in a nation full of them. Rather his delight was in the law of the Lord — although we recognize there were not any written Scriptures when he was alive, he had learned much about the character of the God who was with him. We have noticed before that Scriptural principles guided him in his decisions and preserved him from bitterness. What else helped him? Like the blessed man of Psalm 1 he no doubt knew how to meditate on the law of God constantly, day and night.

The idea of being fruitful is not that of being self-centered or even only family-centered, but to have branches that "run over the wall". Jacob had been aware while still living in Canaan that the provision coming from the hand of Joseph had gone beyond his own immediate and extended family, and indeed, beyond Egypt. Nations were coming to him for years, receiving sustenance from his hand. His fruitfulness blessed others.

Jacob would have been thinking as well of the fact that the tribe of Joseph would become two tribes, extremely fruitful and abundant in numbers. "So the children of Joseph, Manasseh and Ephraim, took their inheritance" (Josh 16:4), but then in the next chapter they come to Joshua, and say: "Why hast thou given me but one lot and one portion to inherit, seeing I am a great people, forasmuch as the Lord hath blessed me hitherto?" Joshua's response indicates that Jacob's prophetic utterance hundreds of years before was correct: "Thou art a great people, and hast great power: thou shalt not have one lot only" (Josh 17:14, 17).

Thinking practically for a moment, what does God expect from us? Fruit. Fruit is the outward expression of the condition of our heart and is dependent upon the Holy Spirit. We read in Galatians 5:22 that "The fruit of the Spirit is ...", followed by a nine-fold list of characteristics that will be manifested in and through us. It does not come by human effort, although this is not excluded. Although we hear of this list being divided into three parts, God-ward, man-ward and self-ward, we ought not to think that we can pick and choose at our whim. They all go together. Very simply we could reduce the description of fruit to a few words: Christ's character seen in the believer. This is God's desire for us.

The Lord Jesus also taught us that fruit is dependent upon Him. "As the branch cannot bear fruit of itself, except it abide in the vine; no more can ye, except ye abide in me". In the context of fruit-bearing, He also said: "Without me ye can do nothing" (John 15:4-5). Do we know what it is to abide in Him, to enjoy intimate fellowship with our Lord and Saviour? We can draw our sustenance and strength from Him, the True Vine, the never-ending source. Let us not reach a level at which we are satisfied with ourselves. The Lord Jesus spoke of fruit, more fruit and much fruit (John 15:2, 5).

The Spite (49:23)

Despite being such an exemplary young man, Jacob recalled some sad stages in Joseph's life: "The archers have sorely grieved him, and shot at him, and hated him". Because of envy, when only seventeen years old, he had been hated by his brothers. Sold into slavery in Egypt, he was "sorely grieved". Later, when Potiphar's wife tempted him, he was again attacked as she sought revenge for his spurning her advances. Joseph, as a result of this calumny, was in prison for a number of years, the final two of which were after he had interpreted the butler's dream and asked him to remember him once he was restored to his employment.

So we see at least four challenges that Joseph faced in his youth: envy that led to his being stripped and sold; temptation that led him to losing his cloak and his employment; slander that led to his losing his liberty, and finally being forgotten by one he had helped, leading to two more years in prison. When we go back to earlier chapters we remember that "the LORD was with Joseph" (39:2, 21), and thus we, too, can take courage when the circumstances in our lives are challenging and difficult. The enemy today is active, and we ought not be ignorant of his devices, but always be alert, ready to resist the devil so that he may flee from us. We are not suggesting that every attack is from the devil, but he does hate those whom God loves, and actively seeks their downfall.

All these attempts to destroy Joseph had not worked. Why not?

The Strength (49:24-25a)

Jacob was aware that Joseph depended upon God in order to make progress. "But his bow abode in strength, and the arms of his hands were made strong by the hands of the mighty God of Jacob". Jacob here is not only pointing to the fact that Joseph had found strength in God, but that he, Jacob, knew God as a personal God, He is "the mighty God of Jacob". What words to be able to share with your son — this God that has helped you is the same God I know, I call Him my own. In this figurative language, we can picture God's hands taking hold of Joseph's hands so that "his bow abode in strength" — God tenderly taking control in Joseph's life, preserving and helping him along the way.

But this mighty God of Jacob is described now by two additional names: "The Shepherd, the Stone of Israel", and then "the God of thy father". The One who had guided and provided along the way for Jacob was the same Shepherd who would continue to guide Joseph.

Remember the words of the hymn writer:

I have a Shepherd, One I love so well;
How He has blessed me tongue can never tell;
On the cross He suffered, shed His blood and died,
That I might ever in His love confide.

Following Jesus, ever day by day,
Nothing can harm me when He leads the way;
Darkness or sunshine, whate'er befall,
Jesus, the Shepherd, is my All in All.

(Leonard Weaver)

The Stone would remind us of the words of the psalmist: "The stone which the builders refused is become the head stone of the corner". The Lord Jesus applied this directly to Himself in the Gospels, as well as the following words, "This is the LORD'S doing; it is marvellous in our eyes" (118:22, 23). It is indeed marvellous to us to consider how the Lord's rejection by His own nation became the means of the Gentile nations coming into tremendous blessing. This very Stone was referred to by Israel in this prophetic statement.

Jacob once more reminds Joseph about the fount of his strength: "the God of thy father who shall help thee" (49:25). Despite the sadness of the moment, we have to consider what consolation this old man was giving to his son. Joseph had many responsibilities but had this certainty: God would help him. Do we need more? Perhaps at times life's events may seem overwhelming, but let's remember this truth: It is God who can help us throughout life's pathway, no matter how dark and difficult it may be.

The Source (49:25b)

Jacob was about to speak of more blessings, but, first of all he mentions the Divine Source. "Every good gift and every perfect gift is from above, and cometh down from the Father of lights" (James 1:17). Jacob is not going to boast about how hard he worked to obtain all that he had, but instead recognizes that the Almighty was the source of the blessings he was about to bestow upon Joseph. There is nothing wrong with hard work, indeed it is commendable, but let us never forget that any blessing we have, material or otherwise, is because of God's goodness and kindness to us.

"Blessings of heaven above, blessings of the deep that lieth under, blessings of the breasts, and of the womb." What abundance! What variety! Natural blessings, spiritual blessings, material blessings, and family blessings were all included. From heaven above he would receive the rain and the sunshine; from the deep there would be rivers and springs. The breasts would speak to us of provision and the womb of fruitfulness. Whenever you look at Joseph's descendants, all these blessings are clearly seen in their lives.

What Jacob was blessing his son with was really just what God had promised to Abraham and his descendants. Remember these words, "By faith Jacob, when he was a dying, blessed ..." (Heb 11:21).

Jacob, although living far from the land God had promised first to his grandfather Abraham, believed the promise would be fulfilled, and thus with confidence spoke all these words to Joseph.

The Separation (49:26)

All these blessings were to come upon the "head of Joseph, and on the crown of the head of him that was separate from his brethren". Jacob realized that God had blessed him even more than his forefathers, "unto the utmost bound of the everlasting hills". He was not thinking so much about a geography lesson here, but the tremendous height to which he had risen, and all due to God.

Joseph was not receiving this special blessing because of the separation that he had endured for thirteen years, having been violently taken from his father. Israel was speaking as the mouthpiece of God. This was something he had thought of before, not just some spur of the moment decision, but at the same time we recall once more the position of favour in which Jacob had always held Joseph. So he is receiving the special, the double, portion of the inheritance.

The Rest (49:33)

Imagine the scene for a moment. Jacob has now spoken clearly and plainly to his twelve sons, in complete control of his faculties, but now his life has come to an end. Once more he tells them where he is to be buried, and then "he gathered up his feet into the bed, and yielded up the ghost, and was gathered unto his people" (49:33). He had gone to a place of rest.

Sadness followed, as we read that "Joseph fell upon his father's face, and wept upon him, and kissed him" (50:1). But we "sorrow not, even as others which have no hope" (1 Thess 4:13). There is sorrow when a loved one who is a believer is called home, but not the same sorrow that tears at the soul when unbelievers bury their loved ones.

CHAPTER 13

The Concern and the Appeal

Genesis 50:1-21

This is a chapter about grief and guilt, but also about grace, goodness and gentleness. There was grief when Jacob died, but after he was buried his sons again felt the burden of guilt for the sin they had committed against Joseph decades before. They feared that Joseph would perhaps still hold a grudge against them and now, with his father gone, would exact justice. However, Joseph's reaction to his brothers' renewed confession was gracious; he spoke to them gently and promised to continue to show them the same goodness that they had now experienced for close to twenty years.

The Preparation and Sorrow (vv 1-3)

Back in Genesis 46:4 God had made this promise to Jacob as he commenced the journey to Egypt: "Joseph shall put his hands upon thine eyes", a reference to Joseph being the one to close his father's eyes upon dying. So, having done this, sadness obviously filled his heart, as should be expected when a loved one comes to the end of their life's experience here on earth. We read that "Joseph fell upon his father's face, and wept upon him, and kissed him" (v 1). We will return to this thought, but as you read through chapter 50, ponder the fact that we do not see any mention of the brothers reacting in the same way. We are certainly not suggesting they did not mourn, but it does indicate that there was a special bond and relationship between Joseph and his father, and we will see, too, at the end of this chapter another possible reason - that of concern over their welfare now that their father was gone. They would be left alone with Joseph, and they well remembered wronging him.

When one of our loved ones passes into eternity, knowing Christ as Saviour, we "sorrow not, even as others which have no hope" (1 Thess 4:13). Paul is not denying that there is sorrow, but emphasizes that it is not the same sorrow which is so obvious in many cultures when unbelievers bury their loved ones. No knowledge of sins forgiven leads to no hope. We have observed the weeping and wailing at the graveside of unsaved people and it grips the heart to hear their pain expressed in such a visible and audible way. Joseph wept upon his father, and he kissed him, but we don't get any notion that there was a feeling of hopelessness as Jacob was not uncertain about his death.

As was the custom at that time, Jacob was embalmed. Notice that it was "his [Joseph's] servants the physicians" that were charged with this solemn responsibility (v 2). Egypt had professional embalmers, but these physicians were obviously capable of doing it properly, and they were in Joseph's direct employ. Beyond that, it is quite possible that Joseph was avoiding the professional embalmers deliberately in order to prevent the involvement of his father's body in any ritualistic or pagan practice during the embalming. This preparation of the body was needed due to the long period of mourning, as well as the upcoming expedition to Canaan for the burial. This process was very detailed and lasted a full forty days (v 3).

A pharaoh would normally be mourned for seventy-two days, and here we see Jacob almost reaching that same level: "and the Egyptians mourned for him threescore and ten days" (v 3). This was probably due, at least in part, to the tremendous esteem and respect in which Joseph was held in Egypt, he being considered to be the saviour of the nation.

The Promised Sepulchre (vv 4-14)

There are many details given in this section, which is the longest burial narrative recorded in the Bible. Joseph was a man of his word; what he promised, he had every intention of fulfilling. Someone of lesser character might have considered the reasons why such a carrying out of this vow would be illogical or maybe even impossible.

His approach is both cautious and wise. He speaks humbly to Pharaoh's servants, saying, "If now I have found grace in your eyes, speak, I pray you, in the ears of Pharaoh" (v 4). Surely these were servants of high standing and position, who obviously would appreciate what Joseph had done for the nation in past years, and yet at the same time we find no sense of entitlement in Joseph; he does not bring up his past successes to insinuate that he "deserved" this, but rather humbly asks. It is quite probable that Joseph himself did not come personally before Pharaoh at this time because during the mourning period he may not have shaven, and to appear in this manner before Pharaoh would not have been acceptable.

These intermediaries would bear this message to Pharaoh: "My father made me swear, saying, Lo, I die: in my grave which I have digged for me in the land of Canaan, there shalt thou bury me" (v 5). Remembering that Jacob had blessed Pharaoh upon his arrival in Egypt seventeen years before, surely Pharaoh himself would not turn down this man's dying request. But Joseph continues with these words, "Now therefore let me go up, I pray thee, and bury my father, and I will come again" (v 5). This was not a way to take his family out of Egypt forever; it was not an expression of his desire to leave his important position in the government of Pharaoh; it also was not meant to be offensive to the Egyptians, that is, not wanting to bury Jacob with full honours in the land where he had died; it was simply a desire to honour his father, fulfill his request to be buried in his own land, and then Joseph would return to his daily responsibilities. In a prudent manner, he asks for permission, makes a promise, and then awaits the answer. Permission is granted, with Pharaoh understanding Joseph's need to discharge his vow to his father: "Go up, and bury thy father, according as he made thee swear" (v 6).

The focus in this next section seems to be on Joseph again, as we mentioned earlier. "And Joseph went up to bury his father" (v 7), and then there is a list of the whole delegation: "all the servants of Pharaoh, the elders of his house, and all the elders of the land of Egypt, And all the house of Joseph, and his brethren, and his father's house" (vv 7-8). Joseph, the favoured son, was obviously in charge of all the burial plans, and his brothers seemed to have just followed along. Besides the representation from the government, we read about the transportation and protection afforded to this large group: "both chariots and horsemen" (v 9). This was going to be no usual ceremony, as "it was a very great company" (v 9). Such had likely never been seen before — such pomp for a herdsman, and a foreigner at that!

Consider the distance this delegation had to travel in order to obey Jacob's last wishes. Nobility and military accompanied the family some three hundred miles to reach the "threshingfloor of Atad, which is beyond Jordan" (v 10). This was just on the border between Egypt and Canaan. The route they took was similar to one a much larger group would take more than four hundred years later when all the descendants of Israel would leave Egypt. On this occasion they had to leave behind "their little ones, and their flocks, and their herds" in the land of Goshen (v 8). The journey would be too dangerous to their well-being. Three hundred miles may not seem too daunting to us in today's era of quick and easy transportation, but it was certainly a long and difficult one for them, with the sorrowful thought hanging over them of having to bury their father and then return to Egypt.

Such was the depth of their sorrow that the Canaanites were deeply impressed: "This is a grievous mourning to the Egyptians" (v 11). They were mourning with a "great and very sore lamentation" (v 10). It wasn't only the depth of their sadness, but the duration of the mourning that made an impact: "he made a mourning for his father seven days" (v 10). Thus they designated the place Abel-Mizraim. The meaning of this is generally understood to be "the mourning of Egypt".

At this point there appears to be a dividing of the company, with Joseph and his family leaving the main part of the group behind. Their duty to Jacob was to do "unto him according as he commanded them" (v 12), so they took the body of their beloved father, "carried him into the land of Canaan, and buried him in the cave of the field of Machpelah" (v 13). During this time the Egyptian contingent remained at the border while the family took on the solemn and sad responsibility of placing the remains in the cave.

This section concludes with Joseph returning to Egypt, as he had assured Pharaoh, along with his family. Although God had promised the land of Canaan to Jacob's descendants, it was not yet God's time for them to return. Joseph had spent the first seventeen years of his life in a special relationship with his father, and now this latter period of another seventeen years of happiness and joy had come to its end. As they travelled back to Egypt surely Joseph had time to reflect upon God's kindness to him in restoring his father to him. But he was not the only one reflecting along these three hundred miles.

The Preoccupation and Scepticism (vv 15-17a)

It seems rather obvious that the foremost thought on the mind of Joseph's brethren during this time was not grief at having lost their father (although surely they did grieve as well), but rather a preoccupation: now that their father was gone, was it possible that Joseph would still bear a grudge and would now seek vengeance upon them? They seemed to be sceptical about all they had observed during the last seventeen years: "Joseph will peradventure hate us, and will certainly requite us all the evil which we did unto him" (v 15).

Doubts are a terrible affliction, and sadly at times can affect true believers too. These men wondered whether they were truly forgiven, their consciences were again active, and their minds filled with dread as they wondered about possible consequences for wrongs that had already been freely forgiven. They perhaps thought that there were conditions placed on the forgiveness that Joseph had kindly extended to them back in Genesis 45; as long as their father was alive, they were safe, but now that he was gone, Joseph would take action against them. After having seen the evidence of Joseph's kind heart during the previous seventeen years, they still were unable to discern the true motives behind Joseph's forgiveness, disbelieving not only his words but also the abundant proof of his gentle character.

The moment of crisis revealed the truth: they did not know Joseph well, and were not enjoying the full forgiveness he had already extended. Is this perhaps in part because they could not imagine their own selves being in Joseph's position and acting so benevolently? Perhaps they had not been able to spend sufficient time with him due to their work in Goshen and Joseph's high position in the Egyptian government. Is it not sometimes true that a believer can come to doubt the goodness of God and the forgiveness in Christ when they do not make the time to enjoy fellowship on a regular or daily basis?

Their words indicate that they were condemning themselves: "Forgive, I pray thee now, the trespass of thy brethren, and their sin; for they have done unto thee evil" (v 17). We notice again their recognition of the ill done to Joseph, and although this is not entirely negative (since confession is a positive step), it had been dealt with already, and so there really was no need to bring it up again.

As believers, we have the Word of God to fully instruct us on these matters, so think with me about the Apostle John's teaching in his first epistle, where he tells us we are "called the sons of God" (3.1). Being in the family, we are far more than servants, which is what Joseph's brothers called themselves on this occasion. John also writes. "If we confess our sins, he is faithful and just to forgive us our sins, and to cleanse us from all unrighteousness" (1 John 1:9). Once we have confessed our sin, we need to rest upon His Word that all is well — the sin has been dealt with, fellowship has been restored, and there is nothing pending between us and God. (Obviously, we are not here dealing with sins or offenses between believers, or of crimes committed, which need to be handled in a more complete manner.) Unfortunately it is possible for us to live not enjoying this truth, and then we feel condemned in our own conscience, or heart. Remember more of John's teaching: "For if our heart condemn us, God is greater than our heart, and knoweth all things" (1 John 3:20). Our conscience can be so tender that we are always doubting God's forgiveness, but John is encouraging his readers with this fact: God, in His great wisdom, knows us better than we know ourselves, and knows our failures. We can live in the good of His love, grace and mercy, enjoying His forgiveness, and leaving the past in the past. Remember that what God says is far greater than what we feel.

Finally we have to notice their devices: "Thy father did command before he died, saying, So shall ye say unto Joseph ..." (vv 16-17). While it is not impossible that Jacob had said this to his other sons before he died, it is rather doubtful. Jacob had not lived doubting Joseph's goodness and grace, and there is no reason to think that he would have feared Joseph's mistreatment of the rest of his sons once he died. They would have assumed that appealing to their father's "command" would move Joseph's heart, thus attempting to manipulate him.

Perceiving the Sovereign Control (vv 17b-21)

Joseph had not been manipulated as he listened to his brothers' pleas, which quite likely was their intention when they mentioned their father's supposed wishes, but rather he was sincerely and strangely moved by what he heard.

To what did his tears give testimony? He was truly saddened to observe that his own flesh and blood could think so poorly of him. We read this, "And Joseph wept when they spake unto him" (v 17b). The conversation had not been long, but it had a real impact on Joseph. Basically, they were calling into question all of Joseph's goodness and grace during the previous years. You will notice that Joseph's response, once again, was kind and gentle, yet another proof of his true character - so very Christ-like. There was no anger, nor did he attack them for their wrong perception of him.

Then we read about the brothers coming and falling "down before his face" — this was yet another fulfillment of Joseph's dreams when he was seventeen years old, but quite likely he had not seen this happen during these seventeen years that his brothers had lived in Goshen. They purposefully recognized his greatness. "They said, Behold, we be thy servants" (v 18). They were gladly willing to give to Joseph the service they felt he deserved. As they looked to the future, without their father but in Joseph's domain, there was much apprehension, so they were attempting to do all they could to allay any possible challenges they feared they would face.

Joseph makes a tremendous statement in the next verse, manifesting very evidently the humility of heart that had characterized him during his life. He has them all bowing before him, but his first words are, "Fear not" (v 19). He does not take advantage of the moment to explain to them his greatness, his power, or his control over their very lives, but rather speaks grace into their hearts. This is a very common phrase throughout both Testaments, sometimes attributed to God, sometimes to Christ Jesus, and other times to a mere mortal. In any instance, "Fear not" is always meant to alleviate any sense of alarm in the hearer. "Am I in the place of God?" (v 19). Obviously both he and they knew full well that he was not. But Joseph is both calming them and challenging them at the same time. Remember, he says, that God is in control — this would calm them, giving them some tranquility of mind. But it was also a word of challenge — he is telling them that they need to adjust their thinking as their perception was weak and erroneous; they saw only the human element in all of life.

We have looked at this next thought before, back in Chapter 45: God was in control of all life's events. Joseph wants his brothers to really perceive this marvellous truth that he had understood long before. Listen in to his wise words: "But as for you, ye thought evil against me; but God meant it unto good, to bring to pass, as it is this day, to save much people alive" (v 20). Think of their intention, "ye thought evil"; but consider God's intervention, He "meant it unto good". This does not mean that God was the author of the evil done to Joseph, but it does mean that God can take the difficult circumstances of our lives (indeed He may well permit them to come into our lives), and use them for His purposes. He is in sovereign control. All of what had happened to Joseph had resulted in the saving of "much people alive". Therefore, Joseph did not bear a grudge, was not seeking revenge, nor was he going to continue to bring this up to his brothers. At the same time we need to bear in mind the fact that the brothers did confess their "trespass", "sin" and "evil", and Joseph does not deny that they had "thought evil" against him — this was no cover-up, but the sin had rather been confronted square on.

We should also reflect on Joseph's care and comfort seen in verse 21, repeating first of all what he had said back in verse 19: "Now therefore fear ye not". Everything was going to be fine; he was not going to change his manner of treating them, his own brothers, just because his father was gone. It goes without saying, but we will say it anyway: sadly some families become very conflictive once the parents are gone; perhaps a dispute erupts over the family fortune, a treasured family heirloom, or a large library, causing much harm to all, and hard feelings that may persist for years. These things ought not to be!

He would continue to care for them, saying, "I will nourish you, and your little ones". This was a substantial undertaking, as they were surely a larger group of people now than seventeen years before when they arrived in Egypt, a band of seventy persons. What a lovely promise that would surely have touched their hearts. They were working men, yet obviously Joseph felt a need to continue to provide some sustenance for his extended family.

Many times, many years before, his brethren had spoken roughly to Joseph. But Joseph did not retaliate now that he had yet another opportunity, but rather we read: "And he comforted them, and spake kindly unto them". We don't want to read things into the passage, but one can almost imagine that tears were shed on this occasion as they were when Joseph had revealed himself to them years before. Tears of relief and tears of happiness. Joseph could likely scarcely believe that these fears of his having hard thoughts towards them had been going through their minds for who knows how long! Thus, he comforts them, showing them his heart, and his words were kind.

Suffer the word of exhortation from Paul: "And be ye kind one to another, tenderhearted, forgiving one another, even as God for Christ's sake hath forgiven you" (Eph 4:32). Joseph personified the truth in this verse, his tears evidencing the reality of his grace and goodness towards his brothers.

CHAPTER 14

The Conclusion and Affirmation

Genesis 50:22-26

We have finally come to the end of Joseph's long life. Amazingly, the impact of this fruitful life lived in the fear of God continues until this day. It should cause us to ponder the faithfulness of God to His people in times long ago, and thus rest on His unchanging promises for His people today.

We would do well to consider again some lessons in dying from this godly man. Joseph, decades before, had been with his father when he had died, and much of what he observed then is seen now at the end of his own life. Joseph, as Jacob before him, was mainly concerned about his family, and made very little mention of himself. "I die: and God will surely visit you, and bring you out of this land" (v 24). His focus was on the future. As with his father, too, his burial place was not to be Egypt as we will see in more detail. There would be a significant delay in burying Joseph instead of taking his bones immediately to Canaan.

Remember, too, what the writer to the Hebrews penned about this man: "By faith Joseph, when he died, made mention of the departing of the children of Israel; and gave commandment concerning his bones" (Heb 11:22). Faith is based upon what God has revealed to His people, and although Joseph did not have a Bible he would have known what God had promised to his grandfather Abraham years before, and he believed what God had said: "... afterward shall they come out with great substance" (15:14).

The Danger of Dwelling (v 22a)

"And Joseph dwelt in Egypt, he, and his father's house" (v 22). Let's go back to the beginning of the story for a moment and recall why it is that this had happened. Joseph, so very much loved by his father, had been despised by his own brothers to such a degree that they sold him as a slave. Sadly, human trafficking exists even in our more enlightened age, with current estimates suggesting that twenty to forty million people have been sold into modern-day slavery. There is obviously tremendous financial profit for those who exploit other human beings in this way.

Joseph certainly is not the only slave we find in the Bible, and his case, an exception to the usual experience, does have the proverbial "happy ending".

But what about his father's house and their reason for dwelling in Egypt? They were not slaves, but rather somewhat wealthy farmers with herds and flocks. God, in His sovereign will, and in a providential way that shows His wisdom, caused a famine to arise in the land of Canaan so that they would become, in today's terms, "economic refugees". An economic migrant freely moves from his or her home to seek a better life and greater opportunity, away from their current situation. However, an economic refugee is forced from his or her home due to the impossibility of economic survival. We as believers need to love mercy and show kindness to those that suffer in this way, thus following Joseph's example. The Lord Jesus spoke of the danger of loving only those who love us; there is no reward for that, He says, because even the "publicans" did so (Matt 5:46). God allows His rain to fall on the just and the unjust, His sun to shine on the evil and the good (Matt 5:45).

When Joseph's brothers arrived in Egypt, he met their every need. It is true that we cannot meet the need of all who cross our path, but perhaps we could do more to help those with whom God has brought us into contact. In this way we would be imitating Joseph, and even more importantly, imitating our heavenly Father. It is the right thing to do.

The danger was that, in dwelling in Egypt, these refugees would put down roots. This certainly was not part of God's long-term plan for this people, and therefore was of deep concern to Joseph. He "dwelt in

Egypt" with an Egyptian wife and was in Egyptian employment, but he was well aware that he was not Egyptian, much like Moses' position four hundred years later.

There is silence about the first seventeen years of Joseph's life and then again we read nothing about what happened during the last five decades of his life, between his father's death and his own departure from this world. This does not mean that he wasn't active during this time. Although we look at younger ones and consider that the future awaits them, let us remember that "retirement years" are times when mature believers can impart words of wisdom to younger ones. Life's experiences shared with youth can help them make wise decisions. A word of warning - there is danger in segregating older and younger believers such that there is little or no contact between them. Time spent "at the feet" of older believers can be tremendously beneficial. Joseph, in his piety and perhaps the calm routine of older age, would have had ample time to be with his descendants, instructing them.

The time of prosperity and tranquility in Joseph's life was far longer than the time of persecution and trial. God had richly blessed him. This does not mean that the same will always be the case for every believer, as some reach the end of their lives still being persecuted, or still passing through a deep trial. Remember, though, the words of the Psalmist: "weeping may endure for a night, but joy cometh in the morning" (Ps 30:5).

The Duration and Delight of Joseph's Life (vv 22b-23)

"Joseph lived an hundred and ten years" (v 22b). This life span was considered both long and ideal by the Egyptian people, a true blessing. He had lived seventeen of his one hundred and ten years in Canaan, and ninety-three in Egypt. Eighty years before, he had met Pharaoh for the first time, interpreting his dreams. Jacob, his father, had died fifty-six years before, when Joseph was fifty-four, having spent the last seventeen years of his father's life with him. It had been a prosperous and productive life, a good example of faithfulness until the very end.

Consider a few verses that cause us to ponder our own frailty, much as we try to avoid these topics. Moses wrote: "The days of our years are threescore years and ten; and if by reason of strength they be fourscore years, yet is their strength labour and sorrow; for it is soon cut off, and we fly away" (Ps 90:10). Lifespan may be increasing in some parts of the world, but seventy is still well-nigh unattainable in many other areas. Nonetheless, seventy years, in relation to eternity, is not a very great amount of time, so Moses continues: "So teach us to number our days, that we may apply our hearts unto wisdom" (Ps 90:12). Perhaps we have heard these words applied in the preaching of the gospel, but as believers we need to take them to heart as well. How many days do we have left upon earth? How many days do we have to serve the Lord with the health and strength He gives us? We have little idea of what time we have left, and thus ought to be deeply impressed with the need to apply our hearts unto wisdom, in order to make best use of the remaining time we have.

We know little about the duration of our life but we know there are many possible distractions that can keep us from what ought to be the priorities. This obviously was Paul's thought as he wrote to the Ephesians, "Redeeming the time, because the days are evil" (5:16), and to the Colossians, "Walk in wisdom toward them that are without; redeeming the time" (Col 4:5). Buying up each moment as it comes along in order to use it for God's glory and purposes requires both diligence and wisdom. Joseph lived this way, with no complaints, using his time for God as well as for the good of others.

The writer remembers hearing a message in his youth that made a significant impression. The text was, "For what is your life? It is even a vapour, that appeareth for a little time, and then vanisheth away" (James 4:14). What is your life? It is not difficult for us to determine what it has been up to this point if we take the time to examine our use of the time, energy, earnings and possessions that God has graciously given us. Perhaps the question should be framed this way, "What will be the aim and result of the rest of my life?" For this we need wisdom and help from above.

Then we read something delightful: "And Joseph saw Ephraim's children of the third generation: the children also of Machir the son of Manasseh were brought up upon Joseph's knees" (v 23). This would indicate to us that Joseph had the wonderful joy of seeing his great-grandchildren before he died. Machir was one of the prominent men in the tribe of Manasseh, and known as "a man of war" (Josh 17:1). He was not only given the area known as Gilead, but also had a son by this name (Num 32:40; Josh 17:1). We see something of the grace of God here in mentioning the descendants of Manasseh, not those of Ephraim. Ephraim had received the special blessing from Jacob, but there was blessing for the tribe of Manasseh as well. We also recall that Joseph had been unhappy with his father's choice of Ephraim, and perhaps there was still some favour shown by him towards the firstborn's descendants. The phrase "brought up upon Joseph's knees" could possibly indicate that Joseph had in a certain sense adopted these children, as we read back in Genesis 30 the story of how Rachel, unable to bear children, gave her maidservant Bilhah to Jacob, saying: "Go in unto her; and she shall bear upon my knees, that I may also have children by her" (30:3).

Besides considering the possibility of some kind of adoption, the phrase tells us something of the affection of Joseph's heart. There is a tender picture seen when we consider a grandparent holding their grandchild upon their knees, perhaps comforting them, or instructing them. The Bible has much to say about grandparents; their rejoicing, responsibility and role. Grandchildren are a source of great rejoicing: "Children's children are the crown of old men" (Prov 17:6). In the Old Testament, the people of God had the responsibility of reminding their children and grandchildren of God's goodness and government: "Only take heed to thyself, and keep thy soul diligently, lest thou forget the things which thine eyes have seen, and lest they depart from thy heart all the days of thy life: but teach them thy sons, and thy sons' sons" (Deut 4:9). In the New Testament Paul writes about a grandmother who influenced a young man for good: "When I call to remembrance the unfeigned faith that is in thee, which dwelt first in thy grandmother Lois, and thy mother Eunice; and I am persuaded that in thee also" (2 Tim 1:5). Faith is not contagious or hereditary, but it certainly can be exemplified in the lives of grandparents as they live before their grandchildren in an evil world. The prime role of bringing up children is that of the parents, but it is a wonderful blessing also to have godly grandparents as role models in the Christian life. This perhaps is increasingly necessary in the ever more secular and digital age in which we live. We are not suggesting that grandparents should only be functioning as "Sunday School teachers" in the home, but rather that the spiritual side of things should not be ignored and overlooked.

Joseph's Declaration and Death (vv 24-26)

As we come to the end of Joseph's life, he faces death without fear, and simply says, "I die" (v 24). The writer to the Hebrews wrote, "These all died in faith, not having received the promises, but having seen them afar off, and were persuaded of them, and embraced them, and confessed that they were strangers and pilgrims on the earth" (11:13). So Joseph encouraged his family, saying, "God will surely visit you, and bring you out of this land unto the land which he sware to Abraham, to Isaac and to Jacob" (v 24). What a tremendous declaration of faith made by this man who was faithful to the very end of life.

Having considered the frailty of life, here we have the certainty of death, an inescapable moment for all, unless the Lord comes for us beforehand. Notice the simple courage in Joseph's words, "I die"; no fear as he faces death, no complaint or bitterness expressed, no second-guessing decisions that he had made, no regrets conveyed. What a marvellous way to come to the end of life. He does not bring up wrongs done to him ninety-three years ago, but rather expresses his main concern - that for others: "God will surely visit *you*, and bring *you* out of this land". We can easily become self-centered as we move through life, thinking of our own needs and desires, or we can be like Joseph, concerned about others. Paul, too, wrote about this mindset that ought to exist in us as well: "Look not every man on his own things, but every man also on the things of others" (Phil 2:4) and then gave the supreme example of the Lord Jesus, always taking others into account. It is wonderful to talk to older believers who, when asked about their own welfare, immediately turn the conversation around to ask about the work of God or share something from the Word of God.

Joseph expressed his confidence in God's promises, too, as he twice says, "God will surely visit you" (vv 24, 25). God's promise to give the land of Canaan was given first to Abraham: "Unto thy seed will I give this land" (12:7). Then it was repeated to Isaac: "For unto thee, and unto thy seed, I will give all these countries" (26:3). Jacob, as he returned from Mesopotamia with his family, heard God say along the way, "And the land which I gave Abraham and Isaac, to thee I will give it, and to thy seed after thee will I give the land" (35:12). Surely this was a promise ofttimes repeated in the family, from generation to generation, even when it seemed that all hope was lost. Joseph, despite living longer than the rest of his family in Egypt, remained completely convinced that God would fulfill His promise. He had not been "conformed to this world" (Rom 12:2), but rather was moulded and guided by God's Word, a tremendous example for us today as well.

Joseph wanted a confirmation from his family. He had affirmed his belief, but now "took an oath of the children of Israel ...". His charge to them was direct and expressed the hope he had: "... ye shall carry up my bones from hence" (v 25). His people would not be left forever in Egypt, but God would surely look upon them and visit them to help them. He was following the good example of his father in insisting on not being buried in Egypt.

Part of what God had revealed prophetically to Abraham was not at all positive, and perhaps was almost unbelievable even during Joseph's time, when all was going well; peace and prosperity reigned in the life of the small Israelite nation. "Know of a surety that thy seed shall be a stranger in a land that is not theirs, and shall serve them; and they shall afflict them four hundred years; And also that nation, whom they shall serve, will I judge: and afterward shall they come out with great substance" (15:13-14). They were already strangers and had always been that. One could argue that already they were in a certain sense serving, but this prophecy was something different.

This would be enforced service; they would become slaves. The span of time would be long, a total of four hundred years! But finally God, as Sovereign, would act, judging the enslaving nation, and the descendants of Jacob would leave, taking great substance with them. For now, however, Joseph merely insists that when that happens, his bones were to leave too.

"So Joseph died, being an hundred and ten years old: and they embalmed him, and he was put in a coffin in Egypt" (v 26). Just as his father had been embalmed, so also was Joseph. Perhaps there was more pomp and ceremony involved in Joseph's embalming, but the end effect was the same. He was placed in a coffin. It is hard to tell if the family understood the significance at the time of not burying Joseph. Where the coffin was stored is something else we do not know, but it was obviously going to be accessible for a very long time. Egypt is not short of examples of the long preservation of those embalmed and in stone coffins. The coffin would be a constant reminder during the next four hundred years of a few truths: God had made a promise regarding His people, and Joseph believed the promise, right to his dying day. Remembering Joseph would help the people remember God's provision for them in time past, and thus encourage them that God could still provide; and, finally, that there was a marvellous prospect for them — God would visit them, and would bring them out of the land of Egypt into the Promised Land. If you will allow a practical application, think of the promise of God to His people today, expressing the prospect that we have: "And if I go and prepare a place for you, I will come again, and receive you unto myself" (John 14:3). Consider God's faithful care in providing for His own, "Let your conversation be without covetousness; and be content with such things as ye have: for he hath said, I will never leave thee, nor forsake thee" (Heb 13:5). When we meet together to remember the Lord we have no coffin to consider, but we recall that there is an empty cave. We also have been given the Lord's words, "... this do in remembrance of me" (1 Cor 11:24-25). So as we participate in the bread and the cup we are reminded of His promise, His provision, and the prospect we have, as we do it "till he come" (1 Cor 11:26).

The Delay and Discharge of Duty (Ex 13:19; Josh 24:32)

"God will surely visit you" were Joseph's words, but far too soon "there arose up a new king over Egypt, which knew not Joseph" (Ex 1:8). Political leaders quickly pass from favour, even when they are decent men like Joseph; the good done is promptly forgotten. God's chosen people were soon afflicted with burdens as the taskmasters mistreated them. Strangely, at least in the eyes of the Egyptian people, "the more they afflicted them, the more they multiplied and grew" (Ex 1:12). Things grew increasingly hard for the Hebrews, and the Egyptians "made their lives bitter with hard bondage" (Ex 1:14). A plan was hatched to kill all the sons, but there, too, we see God's providential care of His chosen people as the "midwives feared God" and did not follow the king's command (Ex 1:17).

Years passed before God raised up Moses, who, although brought up in the Egyptian palace, knew of God's promises and plans with regard to His people. What Joseph had said to his family, that God would visit them, was now going to take place. He said to Moses, "I am come down to deliver them out of the hand of the Egyptians, and to bring them up out of that land unto a good land and a large, unto a land flowing with milk and honey" (Ex 3:8). The four hundred years were coming towards their end, and, although it would be difficult, God was going to redeem His people.

Look at Exodus 13.18-19 and consider how God rewarded Joseph's faith: "But God led the people about, through the way of the wilderness of the Red Sea: and the children of Israel went up harnessed out of the land of Egypt. And Moses took the bones of Joseph with him: for he had straightly sworn the children of Israel, saying, "God will surely visit you; and ye shall carry up my bones away hence with you". For all these intervening years the Hebrews had had Joseph's coffin with them, but the time of fulfillment had come.

The duty would be discharged, not by Moses, since he never entered the Promised Land, but rather by Joshua. Joshua, who also died at the age of one hundred and ten, had the solemn responsibility for the burial. "And the bones of Joseph, which the children of Israel brought up out of Egypt, buried they in Shechem, in a parcel of ground which Jacob bought of the sons of Hamor the father of Shechem for an hundred pieces of silver: and it became the inheritance of the children of Joseph" (Josh 24:32).

The interval had been long, but Joseph is now awaiting another day, not that of his burial, but rather that of his resurrection. Times of patient waiting come to an end. The Hebrews had waited for their deliverance, but it had come. Simeon was waiting for "the consolation of Israel" and He came (Luke 2:25). At the same time many in Jerusalem were waiting for "redemption in Israel" and it came (Luke 2:38).

What about today? "And not only they, but ourselves also, which have the firstfruits of the Spirit, even we ourselves groan within ourselves, waiting for the adoption, to wit, the redemption of our body" (Rom 8:23). Our Saviour is coming, one of those of whom Joseph reminds us in so many ways but yet imperfectly. He will come to complete the redemption that was provided at Calvary's cross, and is now enjoyed by us in some measure since the day of conversion. In the meanwhile we enjoy glimpses of Him, even as we consider Joseph in the myriad of ways he causes us to think on Christ. Joseph experienced the truth that Peter wrote about centuries later: sufferings precede glory. Glimpses of men like Joseph cause us to bow in wonder and worship as we consider the Christ of God, of whom the Spirit had testified beforehand: "the sufferings of Christ, and the glory that should follow" (1 Peter 1:11).

This has been a story of grace, goodness and generosity; a story of faith, faithfulness and forgiveness; a story of providence, promise and perseverance. It is a beautiful portrait of a life lived for God, fulfilling His purposes even in the midst of tremendous trials.

APPENDIX

Glimpses of Christ in the Life of Joseph

Joseph is not someone who would formally be thought of as a type of the Lord Jesus, yet as we have considered his life throughout this book we have seen many occasions which make us marvel at the similarities which exist between the two men. Very obviously this is not just chance. Rather we see God providing us with a lovely glimpse of the Lord Jesus in the character and experiences of a man of God in the Old Testament. There are many other men in the Scriptures who foreshadow the Lord Jesus, but Joseph is the most complete picture we have. Some have suggested there are close to 130 ways in which Joseph corresponds to Christ. We certainly won't be looking at them all! However, there is much profit for us as believers to take the time to find Christ pictured in Joseph.

Remember the words of the Lord Jesus: "Search the scriptures; for in them ye think ye have eternal life: and they are they which testify of me" (John 5:39). The apostle Paul wrote: "For whatsoever things were written aforetime were written for our learning" (Rom 15:4). So we do rightly when we read the Old Testament searching for Christ, and thus learn something for ourselves today.

The following is a limited list to which other aspects can be added by the reader.

1.   Both Joseph and Jesus Christ were born miraculously. Rachel's womb "was opened" by the Lord (Gen 30:22), and Mary was still a virgin when she conceived by the power of the Holy Spirit (Luke 1:27ff).

2.   Both were the beloved sons of a wealthy father (Gen 37:3; Matt 3:17).

3. The Lord Jesus and Joseph were both taken into Egypt, resulting in their preservation (Gen 37:28; Matt 2:13).

4. Both were misunderstood and disbelieved by their immediate families (Gen 37:8; John 7:5).

5. Both men became shepherds; Joseph in the natural sense (Gen 37:2), and the Lord Jesus in a spiritual sense (John 10:11).

6. Both were sent by their father to their brethren (Gen 37:13-14; John 5:23), but were rejected (Gen 37:19-20; John 1:11).

7. Both Joseph and the Lord knew what the future would hold (Gen 37:6-11; Matt 24:3ff).

8. Both men were envied by others (Gen 37:11; Matt 27:18), and hated for their claims (Gen 37:8; John 7:7).

9. The Lord Jesus and Joseph both confronted temptation and were victorious over it (Gen 39:8-9; Heb 4:15).

10. Joseph's brothers, Israelites, conspired to kill him, just as "his own" did not receive the Saviour but attempted more than once to do away with Him (Gen 37:18; Luke 4:29).

11. Both were sold for the price of a slave and delivered into the hands of Gentiles (Gen 37:28; Matt 26:15; Luke 23:1).

12. Special robes had been given to them both, but were unceremoniously stripped from them (Gen 37:23; Matt 27:31).

13. Both men were falsely accused (Gen 39:14; Mark 14:56), yet remained silent before their accusers (Gen 39:20-23; Mark 15:4-5).

14. Joseph and the Lord Jesus were with two prisoners, conversed with them, and showed care for them. They both saw one saved while the other was lost (Gen 40:2-3, 7-23; Luke 23:32, 42-43).

15. Both men became a servant to others (Gen 39:4; Phil 2:7). Although Joseph had no choice in the matter, we see a willingness to serve. The Lord Jesus came to serve, willingly choosing this pathway.

16.   After a period of suffering, both were exalted to high positions (Gen 41:41-43; Phil 2:9-11).

17.   Both were humble men, unspoiled by their position (Gen 45:7-8; John 13:12).

18.   The Spirit of God was deeply involved in the lives of both men (Gen 41:38; Luke 4:1).

19.   Their public service began at the age of thirty (Gen 41:46; Luke 3:23).

20.   Both men were able to supply bread to the hungry who came to them, albeit there is a great distinction here as well: Joseph fulfilled his duty in selling grain to those who came to him, while the Lord Jesus freely gave to those in need (Gen 41:57; John 6:11).

21.   Other men came before Joseph and the Lord Jesus and had to bow before them (Gen 41:43, 42:6; John 18:6)

22.   Both men accepted difficult circumstances as part of God's will and plan (Gen 45:5-7; Matt 26:39).

23.   Their authority and power were only used for good (Gen 45:7; Matt 28:18).

24.   Joseph was made "lord", while Christ is described as "Lord of Lords" (Gen 45:8; Rev 19:16).

25.   Joseph was given a Gentile bride, and part of the Lord's bride is made up of Gentile believers (Gen 41:45; 2 Cor 11:2).

26.   Joseph became the saviour of his family, of Egypt and surrounding peoples physically, while, spiritually speaking, the Lord Jesus became the Saviour of the entire world (Gen 50:20; 1 John 4:14).

27.   Both men returned good for evil (Gen 45; 1 Peter 2:21-23).

Although there is much more we could write, we finish with this comment. In both the Lord Jesus' life as well as in Joseph's experience, we see God's sovereign control, moving providentially to accomplish His purposes - "But as for you, ye thought evil against me; but God meant it unto good, to bring to pass, as it is this day, to save much people alive" (Gen 50:20); "Him, being delivered by the determinate counsel and foreknowledge of God, ye have taken, and by wicked hands have crucified and slain" (Acts 2:23). God used human instruments to accomplish His perfect will, and the same God is in control of the circumstances in our lives today.